THOSE 30 SECONDS

PARUL MATHUR

ISBN
Paperback 979-8-89777-654-2
Hardcase 979-8-89929-345-0

Preface

As I sit with these words, a quiet tide of gratitude rises within me—not just for the path I've walked, but for the pauses, the stumbles, the detours, and the quiet whispers of grace that carried me forward. This journey wasn't planned. I never set out to become an author. I never dreamt of holding a book in my hands that bore my name. And yet—here it is. And here I am.

Somewhere between lived experiences and unspoken thoughts, between sleepless nights and moments of sudden clarity, the words found me. They began as a whisper—uncertain, hesitant. But with time, and the unwavering belief of those I love, they grew louder, clearer, more insistent. Every chapter I wrote felt like peeling back another layer of my soul—revealing not just stories, but truths I had long carried within me.

This was never about titles or recognition. It was about purpose. About legacy. About answering a quiet call I could no longer ignore. It was about trusting that even in the fog of doubt, something bigger was guiding me—asking me to share, to serve, to speak.

Over the years, I've come to believe that life doesn't change in years—it changes in moments. Not the grand, public moments—but the quiet, internal ones. A flicker of doubt. A rush of conviction. A pause before a leap. And it is in these fleeting, breathless seconds—where the heart races and the mind hesitates—that we shape the future.

My love for stories began in the warmth of my father's voice, through tales whispered at bedtime—myth, magic, history, and truth interwoven with wisdom. Those stories didn't just entertain me; they awakened something inside. A curiosity. A hunger to understand the world not just as it is, but as it could be.

As I grew, so did that hunger. I found myself drawn to ancient texts—the Valmiki Ramayana, the Bhagavad Gita, the Garud Purana, the Shiv Purana—sacred words that felt timeless, and yet, so intimate. They didn't just teach me. They spoke to me. Especially the Bhagavad Gita, which became a quiet anchor in turbulent times. No matter how many times I returned to it, it met me where I was—offering new wisdom, deeper meaning, and silent strength.

Life has taken me across cities, cultures, and classrooms—nine schools, four institutions, and one unending journey of learning. From Delhi University to IMT Ghaziabad, from XLRI Jamshedpur to my ongoing Ph.D. at Golden Gate University, I've carried one thing consistently: a deep-rooted desire to understand, connect, and contribute.

Across all these experiences—amid the diplomas, designations, and demands—storytelling has remained my truest calling. My way of making sense of the chaos. My way of healing, of giving back, of saying, "You are not alone."

My journey and purpose extend far beyond boardrooms. I have had the privilege of mentoring emerging leaders and guiding individuals as a life coach—those who seek clarity in chaos, courage in doubt, and growth in both the personal and professional corners of their lives.

And through it all, I remain profoundly grateful to the divine. For the opportunities. For the obstacles. For the moments when I questioned everything, and for the silent reassurances that carried me through. Each setback came wrapped in a lesson. Each victory came laced with humility. And all of it, I now see, was part of a plan more intricate than I could have ever imagined.

This book is not just a reflection of my story—it is a tapestry woven from the stories that shaped me. Stories of resilience, of doubt, of breakthroughs and breakdowns. And it is my hope, with all my heart, that as you turn these pages, you find something of yourself. A thought. A question. A flicker of hope. A quiet reminder that your story, too, matters. That the moments you think are small may, in truth, be the turning points.

Because within each of us lies the power to pause. To choose. To change everything.

And sometimes... that power lives in just thirty seconds.

About 'Those 30 Seconds'

In our fast-paced world, where the urgency of each passing moment drives us forward, we often make decisions without a second thought. Reflexes, instincts, and pressures from society or our own minds dictate our actions in ways we might not fully realize. We judge, we react, and we do so in the blink of an eye. It's easy to be swept away by the tide of life, to choose the path of least resistance, to act without reflecting—because, after all, the world keeps moving and demands we keep pace. But what if the most powerful tool at our disposal is not speed or reflex, but the art of stillness, the strength to pause before we act? What if just 30 seconds—thirty fleeting, transformative seconds—could change the course of our lives?

These 30 seconds may seem trivial. How much can happen in half a minute? A few deep breaths, a moment of reflection before reacting, or the courage to choose the more difficult path over the easy one. And yet, those seconds are the ones that often define us, that give us the clarity to make choices that align with who we truly are, rather than who we are expected to be. A breath before speaking a harsh word, a pause before acting on anger, or a fraction of time to reconsider a life-altering decision. These simple acts of reflection carry weight that far exceeds their fleeting nature.

Those 30 Seconds is a journey through those moments. It is not just a book; it is a reminder that within us lies the power to change, to course-correct, to build a life of purpose rather than impulse. This collection of stories, rich with history, mythology, and everyday wisdom, invites you to reflect on the transformative moments that are all too often overlooked in the rush of life. What if you could harness the power of these brief pauses to unlock your truest potential?

Each chapter begins with a verse from the Bhagavad Gita, not as a sermon or directive, but as a source of guidance and contemplation. The teachings from this ancient text serve as a lens through which to view the dilemmas we face in our own lives. Through these stories, you won't find answers handed to you—what you will find is a reflection of the internal battles we all face. These are the moments when we stand at a crossroads, torn between our immediate desires and the voice of reason, when we are confronted by fear, doubt, and uncertainty. In those 30 seconds, we can choose to listen, to reflect, or to let the moment slip by.

This book is not a call to action but an invitation to pause, to be present in the moment, and to question the decisions we make. What if, in those

30 seconds, we were able to shift our perspective, challenge our automatic responses, and step into a more conscious way of living? What if we could see that the choices we make, no matter how small they seem, are the threads that weave the fabric of our future?

Those 30 Seconds invites you to explore the dilemmas, inner conflicts, and moral quandaries that shape our lives. Whether it is the mythological tale of a hero torn between his duty and his heart, a historical figure wrestling with the consequences of his actions, or a modern-day individual standing at the precipice of a life-altering decision—each story invites you to reflect on your own moments of hesitation. These are the moments when the world around us fades away, and we are left with nothing but the raw honesty of our thoughts. These are the moments that can change everything. This book delves into those defining moments, where hesitation, conviction, or a single shift in perspective can alter the course of a life, a legacy, or even history itself.

But this book doesn't promise easy answers. It doesn't give you a blueprint for a perfect life. What it does offer is an opportunity—a chance to step outside the whirlwind of daily life and to engage in the practice of reflection. It challenges you to slow down, to examine the stories of others, and in doing so, uncover truths about yourself. It reminds you that sometimes, the answers we seek aren't found in grand gestures or sweeping changes. Sometimes, the most profound revelations emerge in the stillness, in the space between one breath and the next, in the pause before we act.

The central theme of *Those 30 Seconds* is simple yet profound: the mind, that ever-present force, can be our greatest friend or our fiercest adversary. When we are caught in the throes of impulse, our decisions often reflect the chaos of our minds. But when we take the time to pause, to reflect, we can shift the balance—our mind becomes a guide, a source of wisdom, and a partner in our journey. The stories within these pages reflect the struggle between impulse and wisdom, fear and courage, desire and discipline. It is in the moments of pause that we find our power—the power to choose our path, to create a legacy, and to step into the life we are meant to live.

This book is more than a collection of stories—it is a mirror, reflecting back at you the choices that shape your destiny. It asks you to step into the lives of its characters and consider: What would I do in their place? How would I navigate these crossroads? It challenges you to find the courage to pause, the strength to reflect, and the wisdom to choose wisely.

And perhaps, in doing so, you will recognize your own 30-second moments—the fleeting instances that hold the potential for transformation, the moments where clarity emerges from chaos, where hesitation gives way to understanding, and where a single decision can alter the course of everything.

Those 30 Seconds is not just a book; it's a journey into the moments that have the power to change everything. In a world where we often rush through decisions, this book invites you to slow down and discover the life-altering potential hidden in the simplest of pauses. Each chapter uncovers the power of those fleeting moments when we hesitate, reflect, and choose with intention.

What if the next 30 seconds could shift your perspective and shape your future? What if the next 30 seconds could change everything for you? Are you ready to embrace the transformative power of these brief yet profound moments? Will you take the pause that could change your life forever? Will you take a moment that could unlock your truest potential?

With Deepest Gratitude

This book's existence would not have been possible without my husband, Ravi, and my son, Vedaant—the two guiding stars of my life. They are my greatest inspiration, my unwavering support, and the reason I have given words to the stories and reflections that have shaped my understanding of the world.

Ravi, my friend, my mirror image, my soul, and the very essence of my being, has always stood by me with boundless encouragement, lifting me up in moments of doubt and celebrating every triumph as if it were his own. His love is my anchor, his belief in me my strength, and his presence my greatest comfort. He is the steady hand that holds me firm in storms, the silent reassurance in my moments of uncertainty, and the unwavering light that brightens my darkest days. His patience, kindness, and deep understanding make him not just my husband but the very foundation of my dreams. With him, I feel invincible, as if no challenge is too great and no dream too far. More than that, he has also been my most honest critic, my sounding board, and officially the editor of this book. His keen insights and thoughtful feedback have shaped these words into their best form, ensuring that this book remains true to its intent.

And Vedaant, my heartbeat, my universe, and the twinkle in my eye, reminds me every day of the magic in storytelling. Now on the cusp of adulthood, nearing 18, he stands at the threshold of a new chapter in life, yet his innocent curiosity, his endless questions, and his ability to find joy in the simplest of moments remain untouched by time. He is my little philosopher, my guiding light, and the purest reflection of love and wonder. His laughter is the sweetest melody, his dreams the most precious treasures, and his presence the greatest blessing in my life. I always tell him that whenever I look at him, I feel as if I have won a billion-dollar lottery—he is my greatest treasure, my purest happiness, and the reason I believe in the beauty of life. Though he is growing into a remarkable young man, his boundless enthusiasm and innate kindness remind me daily of what truly matters. Watching him evolve into the person he is becoming is like witnessing a miracle unfold, and I am endlessly grateful for the privilege of being his mother.

If love and gratitude could be measured, mine for them would surpass all limits. They are not just my family; they are my greatest blessings, my most cherished dreams, and the very soul of my existence.

Beyond them, I am grateful to my friends, who have been my quiet pillars of support. Their encouragement, belief, and patience through this journey have meant more than words can express. They have listened to my scattered thoughts, debated ideas with me, and lent their unwavering support when I needed it the most.

Finally, to you—the reader—thank you for picking up this book. If even one story resonates with you, if even one moment of reflection emerges from these pages, then this endeavour has been worth every effort.

A Journey of Reflection

As a first-time author, this book is not just my debut—it is an extension of my belief system. I believe that every individual, at some point, stands at the threshold of a defining moment. Some seize it, some let it slip away, and some remain forever haunted by *what could have been*.

Through these stories, I hope to ignite that self-reflection in you. I want you to pause, to introspect, and to ask yourself:

- Have I ever let hesitation stop me from making a life-changing decision?

- Have I trusted my mind, or have I let it betray me with doubt?

- In my moments of uncertainty, have I chosen fear or courage?

We may not control every event in our lives, but we do control how we respond. And sometimes, all it takes is **those 30 seconds** to redefine who we are.

I invite you to embark on this journey with me—to experience, reflect, and perhaps, find your own *30 seconds* of transformation. Perhaps, somewhere in these pages, you will find your own defining moment—one that shifts your perspective, strengthens your resolve, or reminds you that the power to change your story has always been within you.

From my heart to yours

– Parull Mathhur

Contents

The Power of Equanimity

Bhagavad Gita, Chapter 2, Verse 38

सुखदुःखे समे कृत्वा लाभालाभौ जयाजयौ।

(Treating happiness and sorrow, gain and loss, victory
and defeat as equal)

Equanimity in the Face of Destiny

Life is a constant interplay of opposites—joy and sorrow, success and failure, gain and loss. Often, we find ourselves caught in the highs of triumph or the depths of despair, defining our worth by fleeting victories or temporary defeats. Yet, the Bhagavad Gita reminds us of a higher truth: true strength lies in equanimity—the ability to remain steady, undisturbed by life's changing tides.

The greatest leaders, visionaries, and warriors have all faced moments of overwhelming adversity. Some were met with loss when they expected victory. Others stood at the brink of despair before discovering their greatest breakthroughs. But what set them apart was not just their talent or ambition—it was their ability to maintain balance, to treat both success and failure as mere waypoints in a larger journey.

This chapter delves into three powerful stories—of a hero who refused to let defeat define him, a scientific genius who embraced failures as stepping stones, and a cunning warrior who found wisdom in loss. Through their experiences, we explore the strength of resilience, the wisdom of detachment, and the power of maintaining an unwavering mind in the face of life's uncertainties.

Gandhari & Krishna: The Curse That Shaped Destiny

After the great war of Kurukshetra, the battlefield was silent, but the echoes of loss still lingered. The war had raged for eighteen days, a brutal clash between the Kauravas and the Pandavas, leaving behind mountains of corpses and rivers of blood. In the end, the Pandavas emerged victorious, but at an unimaginable cost. The once-mighty Kuru dynasty was in ruins. All the Kauravs were killed.

Gandhari, the mother of the Kauravas, stood before Krishna, her heart heavy with sorrow. She had lost all her sons, her lineage wiped out in a single war. As the wife of the blind king Dhritarashtra, she had bound her own eyes for life, choosing to share in his darkness. Yet, despite her sacrifices, fate had been merciless.

Before her stood the very man she had once revered, the divine Krishna, the architect of dharma, the one whose wisdom had guided the Pandavas to victory. But now, in her grief, she could see nothing but betrayal. It was he who had encouraged the war, who had supported the Pandavas at every turn, who had stood by as her sons fell one by one. Was this justice? Was this righteousness?

With trembling hands, Gandhari clenched her fists, her nails digging into her palms as waves of anguish and fury surged through her. Her voice, once gentle and restrained, now cracked with raw emotion. "You speak of dharma, Krishna, but tell me—was this dharma? My sons, my children, slaughtered like animals! You, the so-called protector of righteousness, stood by and watched as my lineage was wiped out!"

Her breath came in shuddering gasps as grief turned to rage. "You guided the Pandavas to victory, but did you ever stop to think of the cost? Did you ever once think of a mother's pain? Of the nights I spent praying for their safety? The sacrifices I made? What justice is this, Krishna? What kind of god allows a mother to bury her own sons?"

Tears streamed down her blindfolded eyes as her voice broke into an anguished whisper. "I once revered you, trusted you... But now? Now, I curse the very day I believed in you!"

Krishna met her blind gaze with deep compassion, his voice laced with sorrow and reverence. "Mother, the war was not of my making. The seeds were sown long before, in the ambitions, the hatred, and the choices made by men. I merely played my role in the unfolding of destiny."

Gandhari's breath trembled with fury. "Destiny? Is that what you call this? The cries of a mother who has lost all her sons? The silence of a palace that was once filled with their laughter? Is it destiny, Krishna, or was it your will? You, who could have stopped this, who could have turned the tide, but chose to let my children perish!"

Krishna lowered his head, his voice steady yet heavy. "Mother, I did not choose their fate. I only guided dharma to its rightful course. Each of them walked their path, made their choices—choices that led them here."

Her body shook with the weight of her grief, her voice cracking as she spat her words. "Do not speak to me of dharma! If dharma is so righteous, why does it always favor one side? Why do the righteous suffer while the cunning thrive? Tell me, Krishna, was my devotion not enough? Were my sacrifices not worthy? Why did dharma not protect my sons?"

Krishna exhaled deeply, his voice tinged with sorrow. "Mother, dharma does not shield anyone from fate. It is not bound to any one family, nor does it take sides. Your sons… they chose their path, and destiny merely answered."

Gandhari let out a broken laugh, bitter and filled with anguish, her voice trembling with rage and sorrow. "Then hear me, Krishna! If destiny is so just, then let it come for you as well! As I stand alone today, bereft of my sons, my family reduced to ashes, so too shall you! As I watch the ruins of my lineage, you shall witness the fall of your Yadavas! You shall stand helpless as your own blood turns against itself, as your kingdom crumbles before your very eyes! You, who claim to be the protector of dharma, shall taste the very poison of fate that I now drink! You shall know the agony of watching your kin destroy themselves, the despair of being powerless to stop it! This is my curse, Krishna, and even you, with all your wisdom and might, shall not escape it!"

A hush fell over the space. The warriors, the sages, even the gods who stood as witnesses, held their breath. Would Krishna, the Supreme Being, the master of the universe, resist? Would he counter the curse?

Krishna closed his eyes for a moment, as if absorbing the weight of her words. Then, with a gentle nod, he whispered, "So be it, Mother. If this is the price I must bear, I shall accept it. But know this—never did I choose this destruction, nor did I desire this war. Fate has played its part, and I was but an instrument. Yet, if your sorrow demands this retribution, then let it be fulfilled."

Krishna exhaled softly, his voice carrying both sorrow and inevitability. "Because, Mother, life and death, victory and defeat—they are but passing waves in the great ocean of time. What is today's sorrow was yesterday's joy. What is today's loss was once a gain. None escape this cycle." There was no sorrow in his voice, no anger, only a deep understanding of the impermanence of all things. He bowed his head in acceptance.

Krishna smiled—a soft, knowing smiled and said, "If this is dharma's will, let it be fulfilled."

Years passed, and the Yaduvanshies, once the most powerful clan, began to crumble. The curse took root, not by divine intervention, but by their own arrogance and excess. One fateful night, during a grand feast filled with laughter and wine, a careless jest turned into a sharp insult. A drunken warrior, his pride wounded, hurled a goblet across the hall, sparking an argument that quickly spiraled out of control.

Voices rose, fists clenched, and weapons were drawn. Old rivalries resurfaced, wounds never healed reopened, and what began as a petty quarrel exploded into an all-out battle. The once-loyal brothers turned against each other, friends became foes, and blood painted the streets of Dwarka. The cries of war echoed through the palace, swords clashed, and the very foundations of the Yadava dynasty trembled under the weight of its own fury.

The mighty Yadava clan, which once stood invincible, destroyed itself, not by an enemy's sword, but by its own unchecked arrogance and wrath.

Krishna watched in silence. He did not stop them, nor did he grieve. For he understood—this was the cycle of time, the law of the universe. What is born must perish, what rises must fall.

Finally, as Gandhari had foretold, Dwarka itself was swallowed by the sea. The golden city, once a beacon of Krishna's rule, disappeared beneath the waves, leaving nothing but the endless ocean in its place.

With his task on Earth complete, Krishna walked alone into the forest, seeking solitude in the quiet embrace of nature. He sat beneath an ancient Peepal tree, his mind serene yet reflective, aware that the end of his mortal journey was near.

At that very moment, a hunter named Jara roamed the forest. A simple man, Jara was no ordinary hunter—he had once been a warrior, a soldier who had lost everything in the war, left to live a life of regret and obscurity. As he moved through the dense foliage, his sharp eyes caught sight of what he believed to be the glistening eye of a deer amidst the leaves. Without hesitation, he knocked an arrow, drew his bow, and let it fly.

The arrow struck true, piercing Krishna's foot. A sharp gasp escaped Krishna's lips, and a searing pain coursed through his body. Jara rushed forward, only to freeze in horror as he saw whom he had struck. His hands trembled, his heart pounded. "Oh, Lord! What have I done?" he cried, falling at Krishna's feet. "Forgive me! I did not see... I did not know!"

Krishna, ever compassionate, looked at the distraught hunter with kindness. His voice was soft, devoid of anger. "Rise, Jara. You have done nothing wrong. This was destined."

Tears streamed down Jara's face. "How can this be destiny? I have committed the greatest sin! I have wounded the divine!"

Krishna smiled, placing a gentle hand on the hunter's head. "In another life, long ago, I was Rama, and you were Vali. Then, I struck you down from the shadows, and today, you return the act. Such is the balance of time. Do not grieve, for you are merely an instrument of fate."

Jara wept, but Krishna's touch filled him with an unexplainable peace. As Krishna closed his eyes, a divine radiance enveloped him. His mortal form faded, merging into the infinite cosmos, his essence returning to the eternal.

Jara, still kneeling, felt the weight of his sorrow lift. He knew, then, that Krishna had not died—he had merely transcended. The forest was silent, the wind whispered through the trees, and the world stood witness to the departure of the divine.

Even in his final moments, there was no resistance, no despair—only acceptance. Because Krishna understood the greatest truth: Sukha and Dukha (happiness and sorrow), Labha and Alabha (gain and loss), Jaya and Ajaya (victory and defeat)—they are all the same in the grand play of existence.

As he lay there, the forest bathed in the golden hues of the setting sun, a deep calm settled over him. He had lived not for himself, but for dharma, for the world, and now, as his mortal body succumbed to fate, he felt no sorrow, no longing—only peace.

He looked at Jara, who still knelt before him, trembling with regret. "Do not mourn, my child," Krishna said softly. "For nothing is ever truly lost. The soul is eternal, untouched by birth or death. Today, my journey ends in this form, but the essence remains. Dharma remains. Love remains."

Jara, his eyes brimming with tears, pressed his forehead to Krishna's feet. "You are beyond death, my Lord," he whispered. "Forgive me."

Krishna smiled once more, his last gift to the world—a smile of reassurance, of eternal wisdom. And with that, he closed his eyes, merging into the cosmic expanse, leaving behind only the whispers of time, the echoes of his teachings, and a world forever changed by his presence.

His final moments mirrored the very essence of his teachings—acceptance in the face of fate. Even as his earthly body succumbed, Krishna left behind a legacy not of power or conquest, but of wisdom, love, and the ultimate surrender to dharma.

Because in those 30 seconds, when faced with destiny's harshest blow, the choice is never about fighting or fleeing—but about embracing one's fate with unwavering faith.

And so, with a peaceful smile, Krishna embraced his fate, becoming one with the eternal flow of time.

Stephen Hawking: The Universe Called, and He Answered

Stephen Hawking was born in Oxford, England, in 1942, into a family of intellectuals. His father was a respected biologist, and his mother had a keen interest in philosophy and politics. From an early age, Hawking exhibited a deep curiosity about the universe, though he was not an extraordinary student in his early school years. He later attended the University of Oxford, where he studied physics and quickly gained recognition for his sharp intellect, despite a lack of enthusiasm for rote learning. His IQ was believed to be exceptionally high, though he never officially took a test. After Oxford, he pursued a Ph.D. in cosmology at the University of Cambridge, where his brilliance truly began to shine.

During his time at Oxford, Hawking was known for his sharp wit and love for parties, despite his reputation for academic brilliance. He enjoyed rowing and had a mischievous streak, often finding creative ways to challenge the system. It was also during his time at Cambridge, while pursuing his Ph.D., that he met Jane Wilde, a literature student who would later become his wife.

At 21, just as he was stepping into his promising career, Stephen Hawking's world came crashing down. What started as occasional clumsiness—stumbling on stairs, dropping pens—soon spiralled into something far more sinister. His muscles weakened inexplicably, and simple tasks became herculean efforts. Jane, his beloved, noticed the changes first—his hands trembling as he held a book, the fatigue that overtook him after short walks.

Hawking fell into denial, refusing to acknowledge the slow betrayal of his body. He withdrew from friends, abandoned his usual haunts, and locked himself away in his room, trapped in a prison of his own making. The once-lively young man who thrived in debates and laughter now avoided conversation, his mind swirling in confusion and fear. He would sit for hours staring at the wall, lost in thoughts too heavy for his age. The weight of impending doom smothered him, making even the presence of loved ones unbearable.

Jane tried to reach him, knocking on his door, leaving notes, but he refused to answer. The world outside moved on, but for Hawking, time had stopped. He was drifting into an abyss of despair, questioning everything—his dreams, his existence, the cruel joke the universe had played on him.

Then came the doctor's words, like a death sentence wrapped in sterile indifference. "Stephen, you have Amyotrophic Lateral Sclerosis, or ALS. It's a neurodegenerative disease that attacks the nerve cells in your brain and spinal cord. Over time, your muscles will weaken, and eventually, you will lose the ability to move, speak, swallow, and even breathe on your own. There is no cure. You likely have two, maybe three years left."

The words felt like a hammer striking glass—shattering everything in an instant. Hawking gripped the arms of his chair, his knuckles white. "No... there must be a mistake," he murmured, shaking his head, his voice barely above a whisper. "I—I've been feeling tired, that's all. I trip sometimes, but I've always been clumsy. This can't be happening."

Jane's breath hitched, her hands trembling as she reached for him. "There has to be something you can do," she pleaded, her voice cracking. "Some treatment, some way to slow it down—anything."

The doctor's face remained impassive, hardened by years of delivering bad news. "I'm sorry," he said simply. "We can try to manage symptoms, but the disease will progress. The average life expectancy is three to five years, but in many cases, it's less."

The room spun. The air grew thick. Hawking's mind screamed in protest, but no words came. He saw Jane's tear-filled eyes, his father's tightened jaw, but all he could hear was the relentless echo in his own head: Two years. Three at most.

He was twenty-one. He was supposed to be solving the mysteries of the universe, not counting down the days to his own demise. His mind raced with protests, a silent storm of anguish crashing inside him. Why me? What did I do to deserve this?

A hundred dreams, once so vivid, now seemed like cruel illusions. I was supposed to marry Jane. I was supposed to have children. I was supposed to win the most prestigious awards, leave behind a legacy in physics. What will happen to all these plans?

His breath came in short, uneven bursts as his thoughts spiraled further. I fix everything—I always have. There must be a way to fix this. But there was no equation to solve, no hypothesis to test. Only an unforgiving fate, creeping closer with each passing moment.

He wanted to scream, to claw at the injustice of it all, but his body refused to cooperate. Instead, he clenched his fists, nails digging into his palms as despair pooled in his chest. The walls of the doctor's office seemed to close in, suffocating him. His entire future had collapsed in an instant, and there was nothing he could do to stop it.

The vibrant young physicist, who once rowed for his college team, now faced a stark reality: the slow erasure of his physical self. The thought was unbearable—his future, dreams, and ambitions reduced to a cruel joke. How could the universe he so loved betray him like this?

At first, despair consumed him. The future he had imagined—lecturing in grand halls, scribbling equations on blackboards, experiencing life without constraint—was slipping away. Each morning, he woke up weaker, his body betraying him, making even the simplest actions a challenge. He would reach for a pen, only to watch it slip through his fingers. He would attempt to stand, only to feel his legs give way beneath him. The cruelty of it all was unbearable.

One morning, as he tried to button his shirt, his hands refused to cooperate. Frustration bubbled into fury. He clenched his fists and slammed them against his desk, his breath ragged. "I am Stephen Hawking!" he whispered fiercely to himself, his voice shaking. "I am meant to unlock the secrets of the universe, not be trapped in this... this decaying body!"

The walls of his room, once filled with books and equations, now felt like the walls of a prison.

He buried his face in his hands, inhaling sharply, fighting back the sob that threatened to escape. He had spent his life chasing the answers to the universe's mysteries—yet now, the biggest question of all had no answer. Why had fate chosen him for this cruel, relentless suffering?

One evening, as he sat near his window, his eyes wandered to the vast, starlit sky. He had always been fascinated by the universe—its infinite mysteries, the way time bent around gravity, the silent dance of celestial bodies. For a brief moment, he detached from his suffering and simply observed.

"If the universe is infinite," he thought, "then so are the possibilities of the mind. The universe does not despair when stars collapse—it births new ones. It does not weep over the death of galaxies—it expands beyond them. If the cosmos can endure, then so can I."

He took a deep breath, his fingers twitching with newfound resolve. I must take inspiration from the universe. It is calling me, filling me with energy and wisdom. My body may fail, but my mind, my spirit, my energy—those remain untouched. I must rise. I must awaken. Maybe not physically, but mentally, emotionally, from the depths of my soul.

He clenched his fists, his heart pounding. If I embrace the good parts of life—the joy of learning, the beauty of discovery, the life of adulthood, the thrill of understanding the unknown—then why should I feel disheartened when life tests me? The way I embraced success, I will embrace this challenge the same way. It is not over till the time I will not stop believing in me.

"I will have a fulfilling life. I will get married, I will have children, I will study further, I will learn more and I will win the most reputed award too".

His lips curled into a small, determined smile. I will fix it.. I will fix this too.

In those moments of quiet reflection, something shattered inside him, but not in despair—in revelation. His breath hitched as he gripped the arms of his chair, his fingers trembling, not from weakness, but from the surge of something fierce and undeniable. He had spent weeks drowning in the abyss of grief, but in this single moment, a new realization broke through the darkness. If his body was failing him, then his mind—his greatest asset— would become his strongest weapon. If he could not change his fate, he would seize control of his destiny.

He whispered to himself, voice hoarse but firm, "I will not be a victim of this disease. I will not let it define me. I will not fade into nothingness. My body may betray me, but my mind will carry me beyond its limits."

Tears pricked his eyes, not from sorrow, but from the overwhelming weight of his decision. This was not resignation. This was a battle cry. The universe had tested him, and he had chosen to fight.

That moment of surrender was not weakness—it was a recognition of equanimity, the acceptance of both pain and possibility. He stopped resisting the inevitable and instead focused on what was still within his control. Loss and gain, success and failure, mobility and paralysis—he treated them as equal, choosing neither despair nor false hope, but quiet, unshakable resolve. It was not that life became any easier for him; in fact, it grew more challenging with every passing day. But he fought, and he fought fiercely, battling his destiny with the only weapons he had—his mind, his will, and his refusal to surrender to despair.

And so, Hawking redirected his life's work. He immersed himself in theoretical physics, using his mind as a tool to break the boundaries that his body could not. With time, he developed revolutionary theories on black holes and the origins of the universe. His voice, though synthesized through technology, became one of the most powerful in modern science.

Looking back, Hawking often spoke of how his disease, rather than destroying him, had given him clarity. He had lost everything the world deemed necessary—physical strength, mobility, even his natural voice—but he had gained something greater: the ability to think beyond limitations.

His story is not just one of resilience, but of a conscious choice to meet life's trials with balance—to not be swayed by sorrow, nor overpowered by joy, but to stay centred on his purpose. In his words:

"I may not control my body, but my mind is free to explore the cosmos."

And in those moments of surrender, he redefined not just his own possibilities, but the limitless potential of the human spirit. His journey was not just about overcoming adversity; it was about triumphing over it in a way that left an indelible mark on the world.

Over the years, he won numerous prestigious accolades, including the Albert Einstein Award, the Copley Medal, and the Fundamental Physics Prize, the Presidential Medal. His children, Robert, Lucy, and Timothy, carried forward his legacy in their own ways—Lucy becoming a writer and science communicator, ensuring that her father's love for knowledge reached young minds, while Robert and Timothy pursued careers in science and technology. Together, they honored his brilliance and resilience, proving that Hawking's impact was far greater than just his scientific contributions—it was a testament to the boundless strength of the human spirit.

Sita & Ram: The Burden of Dharma

The chariot moved steadily through the dense forest, its wheels cutting deep into the damp earth. The river Ganga glistened ahead, its tranquil surface betraying nothing of the storm raging within Lakshmana's heart. His breath was heavy, his chest tight with agony that no words could express. This was not just any journey—it was the bitterest task of his life, one that no warrior would ever wish upon himself.

Every turn of the chariot's wheels felt like chains tightening around his soul. His hands trembled as he gripped the reins, his knuckles white with the effort to suppress the storm within him. How could fate be this cruel? How could his brother Shri Ram, the man he revered as a god, ask this of him?

Anguish clawed at his insides. He wanted to scream, to refuse, to abandon duty and choose love. Sita was like a mother to him—pure, noble, kind. How could he be the one to shatter her world? His heart screamed for rebellion, but his feet followed the path of dharma, each step crushing his spirit further. The burden of loyalty, the weight of righteousness—it was suffocating.

And yet, he had no choice. His sorrow, his agony, his rage—it all had to be swallowed, buried beneath the cold steel of duty. Tears burned his eyes, but he refused to let them fall. He had to be strong. He had to be unwavering. But in his heart, Lakshmana knew—this would haunt him for the rest of his life.

The golden city of Ayodhya, once resounding with joyous celebrations of Rama's triumphant return, had now become a city of whispers—whispers that cut deeper than any sword. Rama, the embodiment of righteousness, had fought a devastating war to rescue Sita from Ravana's captivity, shattering the might of Lanka to uphold dharma. Yet, what he could not vanquish was the poison of doubt lurking in human hearts.

Ravana, the ten-headed king of Lanka, had been a formidable force—one who had abducted Sita, believing that fate itself had destined her to be his queen. But he had underestimated her unwavering faith and purity. Sita had endured captivity like a flame untouched by the storm, her spirit unbroken.

Yet, when Rama reclaimed her, the world was not silent. Even among his own people, whispers arose—doubts, insinuations, cruel murmurs that questioned the honour of a woman who had spent months in another man's house. It was not Rama who demanded proof—it was the world. The murmurs reached the ears of sages and commoners alike, and the weight of their doubt pressed upon the throne of Ayodhya.

One evening, at a gathering of nobles, an elder statesman sighed, shaking his head. "Rama is a righteous king, but does he not see? A queen should be above suspicion. The people talk, and talk will soon turn to unrest."

A merchant at the city gates whispered to a traveller, "If our king upholds dharma, how can he ignore this? Would any other husband tolerate such shame?"

A potter's wife, handing a clay vessel to a customer, scoffed, "No matter how many fires she walks through, can fire cleanse the minds of men? A king must think of his people before his heart."

The whispers had slithered into the grand halls of the palace, echoing in Rama's ears like an unrelenting curse.

For years, Shri Ram had ignored them, placing his faith in Sita above all else. But now, the voices grew darker & bitter. Shri Rama—who had always placed dharma above his own happiness—was faced with the cruellest decision of all.

A king is not just a husband; he is the protector of righteousness. And if righteousness demanded sacrifice, then he would bear that pain, even if it shattered his soul. But was this righteousness or cruelty? Was it justice or the tyranny of doubt? His heart raged, warring against his mind. He had fought demons, crossed oceans, waged wars for dharma—yet today, he was losing the greatest battle of all, the battle within.

The cries of Ayodhya drowned out the cries of his own soul. The people demanded, the throne commanded, but as a husband, as a man—was this truly his duty? Or was it the ultimate betrayal of love?

Shri Ram paced within the palace chambers, his mind torn asunder. He clenched his fists, trying to silence the turmoil within. "Am I not a husband first? Did I not vow to protect her, to stand by her through every storm?" But the murmurs of his people clawed at his conscience.

"A woman, even one as revered as Sita, must not carry the stain of suspicion!"

"A king must be above reproach, and his queen above all doubts."

Rama exhaled sharply, his voice a whisper of anguish. "Why does dharma demand this of me? Why must I choose between duty and love?"

But was he only a king? Was he not a husband as well? A man who had sworn to protect his wife, to be her shield in all adversities? And now, as a would-be father, was his duty not also to his unborn children? To ensure they grew up knowing love, not abandonment? His voice trembled as he whispered, "What kind of father allows his children to be raised without him? What kind of husband lets go of the one he vowed to stand beside?"

The walls of the palace offered no answers, only the silence of duty. "Ayodhya demands righteousness. But is this righteousness, or am I merely yielding to fear disguised as dharma?"

The room fell silent. The weight of destiny had spoken. And in that silence, the fate of the greatest love was sealed.

That evening, Shri Ram called Sita into their chambers. The glow of the oil lamps flickered as he took a deep breath, his heart weighed down by sorrow. "Sita," he began, his voice unsteady, "there is something I must tell you. The people... they whisper, they doubt... they refuse to see the truth even when it stands before them."

Sita looked at him, concern etching her delicate features. "What is it, my lord? Tell me what troubles you so."

Ram's eyes brimmed with anguish. He wanted to hold her close, to shield her from the pain he knew would come. Yet, he could not bring himself to tell her everything. He took a deep breath, his voice weighed down by sorrow. "I have to take a decision for my people, but my heart does not agree with it. I am torn, Sita. Should I choose dharma, or should I choose what feels right to me?"

Sita frowned, stepping closer. "But what do you believe, Ram? What does your heart say? Do you think if you chose Dharma then it is best for the people of Ayodhya?"

He looked away, his fists clenched. "My truth does not matter if the people refuse to see it. A king's duty is to uphold dharma, even when it breaks his heart."

Sita studied him for a long moment, her eyes filled with quiet understanding. She reached for his hand, her touch gentle yet firm. "My

Rajan, I do not know what burdens your heart, but I trust you. I am with you, always. You will choose dharma over everything, as you always have. And I will stand by you, no matter what path you walk."

Her words pierced through his soul. He wished she had protested, given him a reason to defy the impossible choice before him. But she was Sita—unwavering, resolute. And so, the burden of duty only grew heavier upon his shoulders.

A deep silence settled between them. Finally, Sita stepped closer, her gaze unwavering. "Then do what you must, my Rajan. If this is the path dharma demands, then I will walk it without hesitation. You are my Ram—whatever you decide, I am with you."

His breath hitched. He wanted her to resist, to give him a reason to fight against the impossible choice before him. But she stood before him, resolute, unwavering in her devotion to him and to dharma.

Thus, the unthinkable was decreed—Sita, the queen of Ayodhya, the woman for whom wars had been waged, would be sent away. Not for any crime of her own, but for the burden of a doubt she did not deserve.

That evening, Rama called Lakshmana to his chambers, his voice choked with sorrow. "I have made my decision, Lakshmana. The people demand a sacrifice, and I cannot refuse them. But I cannot face her. I cannot answer her questions. I do not have the strength to see her leave."

Lakshmana stood beside him, eyes brimming with pain. "Brother, is there no other way? Sita has already walked through fire. What more can she do?"

Rama turned away, his jaw set in grim determination. "Even fire has not cleansed their hearts. If I defy them, my rule will be questioned. And if the people lose faith in their king, what remains of Ayodhya?" His voice wavered, betraying his torment. "I cannot be a mere man, Lakshmana. I must be their king first."

Lakshmana's voice trembled with barely contained fury. "And Sita? Must she forever bear the burden of sins that are not her own?"

Rama closed his eyes. "She is strong. Stronger than me. Stronger than all of Ayodhya. If anyone can bear this, it is her. And I... I must bear the burden of sending her away. I will always carry the defame of sending her away. I will take the punishment of not being with her, with my children. I am to be blamed forever"

He turned to the window, gazing at the city that revered him as a god, yet chained him in the shackles of duty. "The people ask for a sacrifice. And a king does not have the luxury of ignoring his people."

Lakshmana's breath caught in his throat. "Brother, you are asking me to do the impossible."

Rama grasped his brother's hands, his own trembling. "Please, Lakshmana. I beg you. Take her away. Leave her in the forest without telling her the truth. If she asks, let her believe she is going to seek the blessings of the sages. I… I cannot bear it."

Tears welled in Lakshmana's eyes. The weight of this command crushed him, but he could not refuse. He could never refuse his brother. And so, the one chosen to carry out this painful task was Lakshmana, the ever-loyal brother, the warrior who had stood by Rama through every battle.

And so, Ayodhya, once a city of celebration, became a city of heartbreak.

Lakshmana, bound by unwavering loyalty to his brother, had been given the painful command—to take Sita deep into the wilderness and leave her there. It was an exile worse than death.

A few days later, she was told to take his blessings, and Lakshmana decided to take her there. She did not know. She did not yet see the weight crushing Lakshmana's soul. Beside him, Sita sat in quiet contentment, her eyes scanning the trees with wonder. She was enjoying the serene beauty of the forest, the rustling leaves whispering secrets of ancient times. She spoke of the sages she wished to meet, eager to seek the blessings of the great Sage Valmiki.

His grip tightened on the reins, his knuckles turning white. How could he tell her? How could he utter the words that would sever all ties between them forever?

She spoke of sage Valmiki she wished to meet, of her desire to seek the blessings of the forest hermits. Lakshmana clenched the reins tighter, his knuckles turning white. How could he tell her? How could he utter the words that would sever all ties between them forever?

The whispers of Ayodhya had grown into an uproar, their doubts poisoning the air. How can a queen, even one as pure as fire itself, stay in the kingdom after living in another man's house? The duty of a king was to uphold dharma, and to Rama, dharma came before personal ties. His heart may have shattered in giving the order, but he had done what was expected of him.

And Lakshmana? He had been given the cruellest duty of all—to leave Sita, alone and abandoned, in the wilderness.

The moment has come.

As they approached the riverbank, Lakshmana felt his heartbeat slow, his vision blurring. Every breath felt like a betrayal, every step like a wound that would never heal. The towering trees bore silent witness to his anguish, their rustling leaves whispering the secrets of fate. The river, once a source of solace, now seemed to mirror the turmoil raging within him.

He stepped down from the chariot, each movement weighed down by an invisible force. He turned to Sita, who looked at him with innocent curiosity.

His hands trembled as he helped Sita step down from the chariot.

She smiled at him, her eyes filled with trust, oblivious to the storm that threatened to consume him. "Lakshmana, is the Valmiki's ashram nearby? I wish to offer my prayers."

His throat tightened. He could not meet her gaze. How could he utter the words that would shatter her world?

Laxmana's mind was racing.

"Should I tell her the truth?"

"Would it change anything?"

"Should I defy the order, fight for justice?"

"Or should I surrender to dharma, treating pain and joy, duty and sorrow, as one?"

His heart screamed for rebellion, but his soul whispered of duty.

Finally, he took a deep breath, his voice barely above a whisper.

"Devi… I have brought you here… not for a pilgrimage, but because… I have been commanded to leave you."

The words sliced through the air like a blade. Sita's breath hitched, but she did not recoil. Her gaze, sharp as ever, searched his face, seeing past his trembling hands and tear-streaked cheeks. In that instant, she understood.

"Why, Lakshmana?" she asked softly, her voice steady but laced with sorrow.

Lakshmana swallowed hard. "The people… they question, they whisper… They doubt your purity. And my brother, my king… He must uphold dharma above all else. Even if it…" His voice broke. "Even if it shatters him."

Sita closed her eyes for a moment, as if absorbing the weight of his words. When she spoke, there was no anger, only quiet acceptance. "And you, Lakshmana? Does this duty not break you?"

A tear slipped down Lakshmana's cheek. "I would rather have died a thousand deaths than carry out this task. But my life is not mine. It is my brother's. My king's."

She sighed, the sound heavy with wisdom. "Lakshmana, my fate was sealed the day I stepped into the fire to prove my purity. What is one more trial?"

He fell to his knees. "Forgive me, Devi. This is my duty."

Sita placed a gentle hand on his head. "There is nothing to forgive. Go, Lakshmana. Do not let sorrow take root in your heart. This is not your burden to bear."

Lakshmana hesitated, his body torn between duty and devotion. "Devi, please… if you command me, I will take you back. I will fight for you."

She shook her head, her smile unwavering. "No, Lakshmana. A war fought for me has already burned a kingdom to the ground. I will not let another begin."

Lakshmana bowed low before her, his forehead touching the ground.

Then, without looking back, he rose and walked away.

His heart shattered, but his mind clear. He had abandoned not just Sita, but also his own attachment—to sorrow and joy, gain and loss, victory and defeat.

He had become, in that moment, the embodiment of true detachment.

As they approached the riverbank, Lakshmana felt his heartbeat slow, his vision blurring.

As Lakshman walked away, leaving Sita behind, his heart trembled under the weight of his actions. He had always seen himself as Ram's shadow, unwavering in his loyalty, yet today, he felt like the bearer of unbearable pain. To strip himself of feeling, to accept that duty and suffering were inseparable? But if dharma was meant to uphold righteousness, why did it feel like he was shattering it?

Sita stood amidst the towering trees, unaware of the cruel design woven around her fate. Yet, even in that moment of unknowing, her soul resonated with truth. She had always placed her faith in Ram, in dharma, and in the path destiny laid before her. She closed her eyes and smiled, trusting the unseen force that had guided her through fire once before. She had no reason to doubt it now. *If this was dharma's course, then so be it.*

And Ram—seated alone in his chamber—felt the weight of a world he could no longer hold. His love as a husband and his duty as a king had waged a war within him, and he had chosen dharma over himself. But in this moment of unbearable solitude, he asked himself—was this victory or defeat? Was this justice or sacrifice? His soul whispered that dharma was never meant to bring happiness, only righteousness. If his suffering was the price of duty, he would bear it.

Each of them—Ram, Sita, and Lakshman—stood at the crossroads of destiny, facing loss, sorrow, and sacrifice.

To treat joy and sorrow, gain and loss, victory and defeat as equal.

In those moments—when choices are made, when fate is sealed—the measure of dharma is not in happiness or pain. It is in surrender.

This is not a story of abandonment. It is a story of transcendence—the moment when Lakshmana lets go of all personal emotions and surrenders fully to dharma.

True mastery lies not in fighting fate, but in accepting it with unwavering equanimity.

Reflection: The Power of Acceptance

Life is an unending cycle of joy and sorrow, success and failure, gain and loss. At times, the weight of destiny feels unbearable, pushing individuals to the edge of their resolve. Yet, the ones who truly transcend are those who choose acceptance over resistance, seeing no difference between victory and defeat.

Gandhari, a mother consumed by grief, stood before Krishna, her heart heavy with the unbearable loss of her sons. She did not see destiny—only betrayal. Her words, laced with sorrow and rage, cursed the very man she had once revered. But Krishna did not resist. He did not deflect or deny. He accepted the curse, knowing that even the most righteous path is not free from suffering. And so, time played its course. The mighty Yadava clan, once indomitable, collapsed upon itself—not by the hands of enemies, but by the unchecked arrogance of its own people. Even as the ocean swallowed Dwarka, even as the end came upon him, Krishna remained unmoved. He had shaped the fate of the world, yet when his own time came, he embraced it with peace, knowing that nothing in this universe is permanent—not victory, not loss, not even life itself.

Stephen Hawking, a brilliant mind destined to unlock the universe's deepest mysteries, was confronted with a cruel reality. ALS threatened to take everything from him—his strength, his mobility, his future. At first, he despaired. He questioned the unfairness of it all, mourned the life he had imagined. But in the quiet of his suffering, he realized that though his body was failing, his mind remained limitless. And so, he surrendered—not in defeat, but in defiance. He chose to live not in bitterness, but in pursuit of knowledge, proving that even when control is lost, the ability to shape one's destiny remains. The universe did not conspire against him—it called him to rise above, and he answered.

Lakshmana, bound by unwavering loyalty, took the reins of a chariot, knowing that the journey ahead would shatter his heart. Sita, the queen of Ayodhya, was cast away—not for any fault of her own, but for the burden of suspicion that was never hers to bear. And Rama, the embodiment of dharma, made the ultimate sacrifice—not for himself, but for the people who placed their faith in him. The burden of duty is often the greatest test of all, demanding choices that wound the soul. But none of them resisted fate. Lakshmana did not defy his brother's command, Sita did not rage against the injustice, and Rama did not cling to personal happiness. They surrendered— not to weakness, but to the highest truth: that dharma is not about personal victory, but about unwavering commitment to what is right, even when it demands unbearable sacrifice.

Each of these stories reveals the essence of true mastery over life—not in the ability to control fate, but in the ability to remain unshaken by it. To treat success and failure, joy and sorrow, gain and loss as equal, and to walk forward, steady and unwavering. Because in the end, it is not resistance, but surrender to the grand design that leads to true transcendence.

Introspection: The Strength to Surrender

Life is a series of trials—some that demand action, others that demand patience, and the hardest of all, those that demand surrender. We are taught to fight for what we love, to stand our ground, to never give up. But what about the moments when holding on only deepens the suffering? When the battle is not against an enemy, but against fate itself?

True strength is not always found in resistance. Sometimes, it lies in acceptance. In the willingness to walk away when necessary, to let go of what cannot be changed, and to embrace what is beyond our control.

As you reflect on your own journey, ask yourself:

- Have there been times when you clung to something—an expectation, a relationship, a dream—despite knowing deep inside that it was slipping away?

- Do you associate surrender with weakness, or can you see it as an act of wisdom?

- When faced with loss, do you fight to reverse it, or do you seek peace within it?

- How much of your suffering comes from external circumstances, and how much comes from resisting what is?

- Have you ever had to make a choice between duty and desire? What guided your decision?

- If the past were unchangeable, would you still let it define your future?

- Can you embrace both joy and sorrow with the same steadiness, knowing that both are temporary?

The greatest battles are often fought within. But victory does not always mean conquering; sometimes, it means understanding when to let go. The weight of loss, the pain of sacrifice, and the burden of expectations can either shackle us to suffering or free us into wisdom.

So the next time you find yourself at the crossroads of resistance and acceptance, pause. Ask yourself: Am I holding on out of courage, or out of fear? And if I choose to surrender, does that make me weaker—or does it set me free?

Because sometimes, the greatest act of strength is not in fighting fate, but in rising above it.

Balancing Desire and Duty

Bhagavad Gita - Chapter 5, Verse 26

कामक्रोधवियुक्तानां यतीनां यतचेतसाम्।

(Those free from desire and anger, self-disciplined and
focused, attain lasting peace.)

The Fine Line Between What We Want and What We Owe

Life often presents us with crossroads where desire and duty stand in stark contrast. The Bhagavad Gita reminds us that peace lies in mastering the delicate balance between the two, by letting go of the extremes of longing and rage. While desires drive us forward, unchecked, they can disrupt our sense of duty and inner calm. On the other hand, blind adherence to duty without acknowledgment of our aspirations can lead to dissatisfaction. The key lies in thoughtful decision-making—pausing to evaluate and reflect before choosing our path.

At the heart of every decision lies the tension between what we want and what we owe—to ourselves, to others, and to the larger forces that shape our lives. History, mythology, and even our everyday experiences reveal how the struggle between desire and duty is not just a moral dilemma but a defining aspect of the human condition. Some choices demand sacrifice, while others call for courage to break free from expectations. Yet, in those crucial moments of hesitation, clarity can emerge—not from resisting either force entirely, but from understanding which path aligns with our deeper truth.

This chapter explores real-life scenarios of conflicting priorities, where choices made in "Those 30 Seconds" determined the course of relationships, careers, and personal happiness.

Cleopatra: A Throne Lost, A Legacy Defied

Cleopatra stood at the grand window of her palace, her gaze locked on the Nile, where the moonlight turned the waters into liquid silver. The scent of incense curled through the air, mingling with the salt of the distant sea breeze. From beyond the palace walls, the murmurs of her remaining loyalists carried the weight of despair. Rome was at her gates. The end of her reign, and possibly her life, was imminent.

The messenger's words still echoed in her mind: "Octavian demands your surrender. He will parade you through Rome as his prize."

Her hands clenched into fists. A queen of Egypt, a goddess to her people—reduced to a spectacle for the Roman masses? No. She could not— would not—allow that humiliation.

Cleopatra's downfall had been set in motion long before this moment. She had once ruled Egypt with cunning and intellect, forging powerful alliances to maintain her throne. Her most notable connection was with Julius Caesar, the great Roman general and statesman. When her father, Ptolemy XII, died, a civil war erupted between Cleopatra and her brother Ptolemy XIII. Seeking an ally, Cleopatra famously met Caesar, presenting herself wrapped in a carpet smuggled into his chambers. Captivated by her intelligence and charm, Caesar supported her claim to the throne, leading to her reinstatement as queen. Their alliance bore a son, Ptolemy XV, known as Caesarion, whom Cleopatra hoped would one day rule both Egypt and Rome.

However, Caesar's assassination in 44 BCE left her vulnerable. Rome plunged into chaos, and power struggles ensued. Mark Antony, one of Caesar's closest allies, rose as a dominant force in the Roman political sphere, opposing Octavian, Caesar's adopted heir. Cleopatra saw Antony as her next great protector, forming both a passionate romance and a military alliance with him. Together, they defied Rome's growing might, attempting to carve out their own dominion in the East.

But Rome, under Octavian's calculated leadership, sought total domination. Antony and Cleopatra had fought against Octavian's forces in the Battle of Actium, only to suffer a crushing defeat. With Antony's forces shattered, he had fled back to Alexandria, broken and hopeless. Now, with Octavian marching through Egypt, Antony had chosen death over capture, believing Cleopatra had already perished. The great Egyptian queen was alone, her empire crumbling, her fate all but sealed.

A sudden knock at the door snapped her out of her thoughts. Charmion, her most trusted confidante, entered, her eyes filled with silent understanding. "My Queen, we must decide quickly. The Romans will be here by dawn."

Cleopatra turned, her expression unreadable. "Is there any news of Antony?"

Charmion hesitated. "He... took his own life, believing you were already gone."

The words sliced through Cleopatra like a dagger. Antony, her love, her ally—gone, consumed by despair and deception. Her breath shuddered, but she would not weep. There was no time for sorrow. Yet, for a fleeting moment, she imagined another path—one where she surrendered, where she was led through the streets of Rome in chains, her children forced to watch as she was mocked, her legacy twisted into an amusement for the empire that sought to erase her. The vision burned her mind like a fever. She had lived as a queen. She would not die as a trophy.

She thought back to the days when Egypt was at its peak. Her father, Ptolemy XII, had struggled to maintain control, often relying on Roman support to keep his throne. Cleopatra had been different—bold, intelligent, and strategic. Fluent in multiple languages, she was the first Ptolemaic ruler to learn Egyptian, embracing the culture of the land she ruled. Her alliances with Julius Caesar and later Mark Antony had been more than romantic entanglements; they were political maneuvers designed to protect Egypt's sovereignty. Now, that empire was crumbling, and Rome was closing in.

Cleopatra paced the marble floors of her chamber, the scent of myrrh and burning oil thick in the air. The walls that had once echoed with laughter and strategy now felt like the walls of a tomb. News had arrived—Antony was dead, his forces crushed, and Rome's most ruthless leader, Octavian, stood at Egypt's gates.

She had faced powerful men before, outmanoeuvred them, seduced them, bent them to her will. But this time was different. Octavian was not like Julius Caesar, who had been enamoured by her wit, nor was he like Antony, who had been her equal in love and ambition. Octavian was cold, methodical—he saw her not as a queen, nor as a woman of influence, but as a problem to be eliminated.

The weight of defeat settled on her shoulders. Yet, there was one question that remained—one truth she needed to hear before she decided her next move.

She turned to Charmion, her most trusted handmaiden. "And my sons?"

Charmion hesitated, her voice barely above a whisper. "Taken captive. Octavian will raise them as Romans, stripping them of their birthright."

A cold, bitter rage settled in Cleopatra's chest. Everything she had fought for, every alliance she had forged, had crumbled in the face of Roman ambition. But she still had power over one thing—her own fate.

Charmion stepped closer, eyes pleading. "My Queen, there is still a way. We could flee. There are still those loyal to you who would take you beyond Rome's reach."

Cleopatra shook her head. "And live in exile? A queen without a throne? No, Charmion. I would rather choose my own end than have it dictated by Rome."

Charmion's hands trembled. "Then let us fight. Let us stand and meet them with steel, even if it means death in battle."

Cleopatra gave a sad smile. "A warrior's death is not mine to claim. I have ruled with wisdom, not the sword. My battle has been one of strategy, of alliances. And now, my last act must be my own choice."

She dismissed the servants, leaving only Charmion and Iras, her closest attendants. The candlelight flickered, casting long shadows as she retrieved the small woven basket that had been delivered earlier. Within it, coiled in ominous silence, was an asp—the symbol of divine royalty, a swift passage to the afterlife.

She knelt beside it, tracing the scales of the serpent with trembling fingers. The room seemed to shrink around her, every sound dulling except for the rhythmic pounding of her own heart. This was it—the moment. The world had stripped her of everything except her dignity, and she would not let Octavian take that too.

Her fingers tightened around the basket. Thirty seconds. That was all it would take. Thirty seconds to reject captivity. Thirty seconds to defy Rome.

The asp struck swiftly, its fangs piercing her skin with a bite as cold as death itself. Cleopatra gasped, her body stiffening as the venom burned through her veins, setting her soul aflame.

As her vision darkened, she heard Charmion's voice, choked with grief but steady: "A true Pharaoh to the end."

A final breath. The candlelight flickered. And then, darkness embraced her—not as an end, but as an ascension into legend.

Her final choice echoed the wisdom of the ancients—*Those free from desire and anger, self-disciplined and focused, attain lasting pace.* In those last thirty seconds, Cleopatra was not just a queen; she was the master of her own fate.

Elizabeth: The Weight of the Crown - Duty Over Desire

The dim candlelight flickered against the damp stone walls of the chamber, casting long shadows that whispered secrets of the past. The air with wax and parchment, silent witnesses to the weight of the moment. Outside, a distant bell tolled—a reminder that time pressed forward, indifferent to the turmoil within. The cold dawn seeped through the palace, its icy fingers creeping through the cracks, making the ancient stones feel even older, as if they carried the weight of history. Elizabeth sat motionless, her fingers tracing the worn edges of the letter in her lap. The cold seeped through her velvet gown, but she barely noticed. Her mind was elsewhere—entangled in the weight of the crown she both cherished and loathed.

She had once been a girl who longed for companionship, who had dreamed of love without consequence. But that girl had been buried beneath the crushing demands of queenship. Her father's legacy had left her with a kingdom divided, wary of female rule, fraught with schemers behind every smiling face. She had fought for her place, defied expectations, and ruled with a mind as sharp as any sword. Yet tonight, in the solitude of her chamber, she wondered—had she sacrificed too much?

The letter bore news she had anticipated yet dreaded. A choice loomed before her, one that would define England's future—and her own.

War threatened. The stability of her reign wavered. If she chose love over duty, it could shatter the alliances she had painstakingly built. Could she afford such a risk? Could she allow herself happiness when an entire nation looked to her for strength?

The parchment trembled in her grasp, a rare sign of her unrest. She clenched her fingers, willing herself to stillness.

The wind howled outside, rattling the windows of Whitehall Palace. She thought of her mother, Anne Boleyn, whose love had been her undoing. Of Mary, her sister, who had clung to duty but ruled unloved. What path would history carve for her?

She had learned early that love was dangerous, that trust invited ruin. The executioner's blade had not only ended her mother's life—it had carved a lesson into Elizabeth's soul. She had watched her father take wife after wife, each one discarded when she failed to meet his expectations. She had seen Mary alienate her people by choosing a foreign prince. Elizabeth had vowed to be different. To be strong. To be England's queen first, a woman second.

Robert Dudley stood beside her, his presence familiar yet distant. The warmth of his body, so close yet untouchable, sent a quiet ache through her. His voice, when it came, was gentle, tinged with sorrow. "You do not have to go through this alone, Elizabeth. There is still time to choose differently."

She turned to him, searching his face for an answer she already knew. His eyes, dark and earnest, held the weight of years—of unspoken promises and lingering hope. How many nights had she lain awake, wondering what life might have been if she were not a queen?

"And what path is that, Robert?" she asked quietly. "To trust blindly in men who see me as nothing more than a pawn?"

His jaw tightened. "You know I would never ask you to be anything less than what you are. But must you always bear it alone?"

She held his gaze. "A queen is always alone."

The chamber grew colder. He clenched his fists, his knuckles whitening. He had loved her for as long as he could remember, yet he had always known— she belonged to England first. It was a cruel irony, to stand so close yet know she would never truly be his.

Wriothesley cleared his throat from the doorway. "Your Majesty, the council is waiting. England is waiting."

Elizabeth let out a slow breath, her gaze drifting to the single window. The first light of dawn painted the sky in muted gold, a reminder that time would not wait. For a fleeting thirty seconds, she imagined a different life—one without the burden of rule. By Robert's side, far from the weight of expectation. The warmth of that dream brushed against her, sweet and fleeting.

A tear pricked her eye, but she willed it away. The Queen did not cry.

She turned back to Robert, as if committing him to memory. "If I choose love, England suffers. I will not be my mother. I will not be my sister."

His fists unclenched. He nodded. "Then England shall have its queen."

Straightening her shoulders, she met Wriothesley's gaze. "Tell them I will address the council shortly."

Robert hesitated, then reached for her hand. His fingers barely brushed hers before he stepped back.

She watched him go, her chest tightening. The crown was heavy, but she would bear it. Because she must.

As the first rays of morning light streamed through the window, illuminating the chamber in a golden glow, Elizabeth took a final breath and rose to her feet. In that moment, the finality of her choice settled deep within her bones. The silence of the room pressed in, stark and unforgiving. There was no turning back.

The moment had passed. The choice had been made.

England had its queen.

King Yayati: The Illusion of Eternal Youth

King Yayati, a name that resonated with power and grandeur, was once the embodiment of youthful vigor. Born to King Nahusha and Queen Viraja, he ascended the throne of his father's vast kingdom, inheriting not only riches but also a legacy of strength and beauty. His presence commanded attention—his sharp eyes brimmed with ambition, his chiseled frame radiated power, and poets sang of his unmatched charm. In his prime, Yayati was a figure of admiration, the jewel of his time.

He ruled wisely, guiding his people through years of prosperity, earning their love and admiration. Yet, beneath his kingly pride lurked a fear he could not ignore—aging. The mirror betrayed him; each passing day stole his youth. His golden skin lost its luster, his strong back stooped, his thick hair thinned, and the sharpness of his vision dimmed. Mortality, the one enemy no king could conquer, tormented him.

Alone in the grand halls of his palace, Yayati brooded. What use was power if time eroded everything? The thought consumed him. He had conquered lands and hearts, but he could not conquer age. If only I could turn back time, he mused. If only I could reclaim what I have lost.

Desperation took hold. The passing years felt like a cruel thief, robbing him of the vitality that once made him invincible. He observed younger courtiers with envy, feeling a deep chasm between himself and the world he once dominated. Every moment spent in the shadows of his former self became unbearable.

Summoning his sons, he stood before them, his once-mighty voice tinged with vulnerability. "My sons," he began, "I have lived a life of glory, but time is cruel. My youth is slipping away, and no wealth or power can restore it. If any of you are willing to exchange your youth for my old age, I will give you my kingdom, my treasures—everything."

A heavy silence followed. The princes, stunned, exchanged hesitant glances. They had never seen their father plead before. The weight of his desperation hung in the air.

Then, Puru, the youngest, stepped forward. His heart ached for his father, whose once-mighty form now trembled with longing. He had seen his father's growing restlessness, the nights spent in silent torment, the flicker of helplessness in his once-determined eyes. "Father," he said, his voice steady yet filled with emotion, "I will give you my youth. You gave me life. If this will bring you peace, I offer you what you desire."

Tears welled in Yayati's eyes. With profound gratitude, he embraced his son, and in an instant, the transfer was complete. Vitality surged through Yayati's veins—his back straightened, his skin glowed, and strength pulsed in his limbs once more. He stood tall, a man reborn.

At first, he rejoiced. He indulged in the pleasures of youth—grand feasts, exquisite wine, the company of beautiful courtiers. He surrounded himself with luxury, eager to reclaim the lost joys of his younger days. He rode his finest horses, danced at celebrations, and revelled in the adoration of the kingdom. He convinced himself that this was what he had longed for.

But something was different.

The feasts that once delighted him now felt excessive. The wine left a bitter aftertaste. The laughter of his courtiers rang hollow. No matter how much he indulged, a gnawing emptiness remained. Had these pleasures always been so fleeting? Had he truly lost his youth, or had he only ever chased illusions?

Doubt crept in. Nights turned restless. His chambers, once filled with music and mirth, now echoed with an unsettling silence. He sat by the window, watching the moon cast its silver glow over the kingdom, pondering the meaning of his restlessness. Was youth merely the absence of age, or was it something deeper? He looked at his reflection in the mirror, expecting to see a man content with his newfound vitality. Instead, he saw eyes that betrayed an unfulfilled longing.

His turmoil deepened. Had I always been a prisoner of my desires? He wondered if he had ever truly enjoyed youth, or if he had spent it constantly yearning for more. Perhaps I was never satisfied, even then. The realization unsettled him. He had thought youth was the answer to his fears, but it had given him nothing but a deeper void.

He sought answers in indulgence, pushing the limits of pleasure, yet each experience left him emptier than before. His heart, once filled with desire, now felt burdened with an unshakable sadness. He saw men of wisdom—sages who had renounced wealth and comfort—who seemed more at peace than he, despite their frail bodies and simple lives. Had they discovered something he had overlooked?

As the weeks passed, his joy turned into torment. He found himself growing irritable, snapping at his servants for the smallest mistakes. He longed for something, but he did not know what. The more he tried to lose himself in pleasure, the heavier the emptiness inside him grew. He envied the monks, the sages, the ordinary men who did not chase the fleeting joys of youth. Was I ever truly happy, even when I was young? Or was I always running, always reaching, never satisfied?

His thoughts became an unbearable storm. Why am I not happy? What have I done wrong? The questions tormented him. He had believed youth was the ultimate gift, but now, it felt like a prison. Was desire the disease, and not aging?

He looked around, and for the first time, he saw the cost of his desire. His beloved son, Puru, now weak and frail, bore the burden of old age without complaint. Once a strong and promising prince, Puru now struggled to walk without aid. Yet, his eyes held no bitterness, only an unshaken sense of duty.

Yayati observed his son closely, watching how he still carried himself with quiet dignity. Even as age weighed upon him, Puru never uttered a word of regret. Instead, he continued to serve his people, offering wisdom where strength once sufficed. This selflessness struck Yayati to his core. Had he, in his pursuit of youth, forsaken something far more valuable?

One evening, as he sat alone in his chambers, the weight of his choices became unbearable. The moonlight illuminated the room, casting shadows that seemed to whisper of his folly. He called for Puru. When his son entered, Yayati saw the toll his sacrifice had taken—his once-vibrant form now weary and bent. The sight shattered him.

Tears filled Yayati's eyes. "Puru," he whispered, "I have been blind. I thought youth was the key to happiness, but I was wrong. I have lived selfishly, clinging to desires that faded the moment I grasped them. And in doing so, I have wronged you. I seek your forgiveness."

Puru, though weak, met his father's gaze with quiet wisdom. "Father, true youth is not in the body but in the spirit. Desire can never be satisfied—it only demands more. But duty, honor, and wisdom—these endure."

Humbled beyond measure, Yayati returned Puru's youth, embracing the aging body he had once feared. But this time, he did not despair. A new realization dawned upon him—his true legacy was not in his youth, nor in indulgence, but in wisdom, in balance, in duty. Desire was a fire that could never be quenched, but responsibility was the path to peace.

As the weight of age returned to him, he felt something unexpected—a profound lightness. He had finally let go of his fear. The king, once consumed by the pursuit of pleasure, had found something far greater: the peace of a soul freed from endless longing. And though his body grew frail, his spirit was now stronger than ever.

Reflection: The Crossroads of Desire and Duty

Life constantly forces us to choose between what we want and what we must do. Desire pulls us toward dreams, ambitions, and personal fulfilment, while duty demands sacrifice, responsibility, and often, the strength to walk away from what the heart longs for. These stories reveal that the conflict between desire and duty is not just a momentary struggle—it is the defining challenge of human existence. The true test lies not in rejecting one for the other but in understanding which path aligns with something greater than fleeting wants or imposed expectations.

A queen who had wielded power with intelligence and strategy, Cleopatra had spent her life shaping Egypt's fate through alliances, diplomacy, and strength. Yet, when her empire crumbled, and Rome sought to reduce her to a mere trophy of conquest, she was faced with the ultimate choice: surrender and live in disgrace, or take control of her own fate. She could have accepted survival at the cost of her dignity, but she knew that to live without power, without autonomy, was no life at all. In her final act, she chose to define her own ending, proving that even in loss, there is power in choosing one's destiny. Her story reminds us that desire for control, for influence, and for one's own terms can sometimes take precedence over mere existence—and that true power lies in making decisions that uphold one's own truth.

In another time, another kingdom, a monarch faced a different struggle—not against a foreign empire, but against her own heart. A ruler first and a woman second, she had known from the beginning that love was a dangerous indulgence. Elizabeth's crown was not just a privilege but a burden, one that demanded her complete devotion. Love, trust, and companionship—things that most longed for—were luxuries she could not afford without risking her nation's stability. And so, when faced with the possibility of happiness, she made her choice—not as a woman, but as a queen. She sacrificed personal fulfillment for the greater good, understanding that duty sometimes demands a price that the heart is unwilling to pay. In choosing the throne over love, she did not abandon desire; rather, she transformed it into a commitment to something larger than herself.

And then, there was a king who, unlike Cleopatra and Elizabeth, was not torn between love and power but between youth and wisdom. Yayati, consumed by his fear of aging, believed that if he could hold on to youth, he could hold on to happiness. He sacrificed everything—his son's vitality, his own sense of balance—to chase the illusion of eternal pleasure. But in the end, indulgence gave him no satisfaction, and time, even borrowed time, left him feeling emptier than before. It was only when he let go of his relentless desire for youth that he finally understood—fulfilment does not come from endless enjoyment, but from accepting life's natural course. His story is a reminder that desires, no matter how powerful, are insatiable if left unchecked. True contentment comes not from possessing more, but from knowing when enough is enough.

Each of these stories is a testament to the delicate balance between duty and desire. Cleopatra refused to let Rome define her legacy, Elizabeth chose her people over love, and Yayati learned that the endless pursuit of pleasure leads to nothing but emptiness. Their struggles may have been different, but their lessons remain the same—there is no singular path to fulfillment. It does not lie solely in ambition or in sacrifice, in indulgence or in restraint. It is found in the moments of clarity, in the choices made when the weight of the world presses in. Because in the end, it is not about whether one follows duty or desire—it is about choosing the path that brings true peace, the path that, no matter the cost, feels right.

Balancing Desire and Duty: A Moment of Introspection

As you reach the end of this chapter, take a moment to reflect. Life constantly pulls us between what we long for and what we are responsible for. We chase desires that ignite our souls, yet we are bound by duties that shape our purpose. But what if fulfilment is not found in choosing one over the other, but in learning how to hold both—without letting either consume us?

- Have you ever sacrificed something you truly wanted, only to wonder if the cost was too high?

- Have you ever pursued a desire so relentlessly that you lost sight of the responsibilities tied to it?

- Have you ever felt torn between love and obligation, knowing that one would always come at the expense of the other?

- Have you ever mistaken sacrifice for strength, believing that denying yourself was the only way to do what was right?

- Have you ever clung to an idea of success, only to realize too late that it was never what you truly needed?

- Have you ever paused—just for a moment—to ask yourself: Am I living by choice, or simply fulfilling expectations?

Because sometimes, balance is not about resisting desire or obeying duty blindly—it's about understanding when to surrender and when to stand firm. True fulfilment lies not in abandoning one for the other, but in knowing which voice to listen to when the moment demands it. So, as you move forward, ask yourself—are you living a life of obligation, a life of longing, or a life of choice?

Facing Death and Mortality

Bhagavad Gita, Chapter 2, Verse 22 (2.22)

वासांसि जीर्णानि यथा विहाय।

(As a person sheds worn-out garments and wears new ones, so does the soul shed a worn-out body and enter a new one.)

The Inevitable Truth

Death is the one certainty in life, yet it remains the greatest unknown. We build, we accumulate, we attach ourselves to identities—only to be reminded, in the end, that none of it is truly ours to keep. The Bhagavad Gita offers a perspective that goes beyond fear—it tells us that death is not an end, but a transition, much like changing worn-out clothes for new ones. The soul remains, untouched by time, while the body is merely a vessel that must one day be left behind.

But what does this truly mean for those who stand at the edge of mortality? How do we reconcile the inevitability of death with the deep attachments we form in life? Is it possible to meet the end with peace rather than resistance? These are not just philosophical questions but deeply personal ones, faced by every individual at some point in life.

Throughout history, powerful figures have confronted death—not just as an event, but as a force that reshaped their perspectives, altered their choices, and, in some cases, set them free. Some clung to their empires, unable to accept that even kings must one day fall. Others, in their final moments, found a clarity they had never known in life. And then there were those who, upon witnessing death, saw their own illusions shatter—realizing that time does not wait, that control is fleeting, and that peace lies not in resistance but in surrender.

King Vikram: The Lesson of the Eternal Soul

King Vikram of Ujjain was renowned for his wisdom and bravery, yet an unease had settled in his heart. The weight of ruling a vast kingdom and the inevitability of death troubled him. Despite his victories and the prosperity of his land, he often found himself questioning—what is the purpose of it all if death claims everyone in the end?

From a young age, Vikram had been trained to be a warrior and a ruler. He had fought countless battles, expanded his kingdom, and ensured justice prevailed in his land. Yet, in the quiet moments of the night, he found himself haunted by a lingering emptiness. He had seen many perish—loyal soldiers, innocent villagers, even members of his own family. His father's passing, in particular, had left an unshakable mark on him. Though he had performed the final rites as duty demanded, he had never truly made peace with the loss.

One day, while riding through a dense forest, Vikram encountered a grief-stricken mother. She clutched the lifeless body of her young son, wailing in despair. "My son, my child, why did you leave me? What wrong did I do to be punished like this?"

Vikram, moved by her sorrow, dismounted his horse. He had comforted widows of fallen soldiers, reassured parents who had lost their children to illness, but no words seemed enough for this woman's anguish. "Mother, I grieve for your loss. But death is the way of the world. We all must part one day."

The woman, tears streaming down her face, looked up at him. "If that is so, tell me, great king, where has his soul gone? If he was meant to leave me, why was he given to me in the first place?"

Vikram had no answer. He had ruled with justice, upheld dharma, and lived by the code of a warrior, yet the mystery of life and death eluded him. A strange restlessness gripped him—was his role as king merely to rule over life, without ever understanding its essence?

At that moment, a saintly figure appeared—Rishi Narad, the celestial sage. His presence was luminous, as if wisdom itself had taken form. He was known to travel between realms, a messenger of the gods, and a seeker of truth. "O King Vikram," he called out, "you seek answers, but do you truly wish to know the truth?"

Vikram folded his hands in respect. "Rishi, my heart is burdened with questions. Why do we live if we must die? Why love if we must part? What is the meaning of this fleeting existence?"

Narad smiled, sensing Vikram's internal conflict. "King Vikram, death is not the end. Just as a person sheds worn-out garments to wear new ones, so does the soul shed the worn-out body and enter a new one. But only those who truly pause to reflect can grasp this wisdom."

Narad suddenly turned to the grieving mother. "What if I told you your son is not lost? What if I could show you where he is now?"

The woman's sobs halted. Hope flickered in her eyes. "Tell me, Rishi. Is he still here?"

Narad nodded and looked at Vikram. "You must help her find him."

Intrigued and skeptical, Vikram agreed. Narad led them to a small village nearby, where they came upon a humble home. Inside, a mother sat beside a wooden cradle, singing a soft lullaby to her new-born son. The gentle creak of the cradle filled the air as she nudged it rhythmically, her voice carrying the warmth of unconditional love. The baby stirred slightly, his tiny fingers curling as he drifted into sleep.

As the grieving mother stepped closer, her breath caught. Her eyes widened in disbelief, her heart pounding in her chest. The child, though swaddled in simple cloth, bore an uncanny resemblance to the son she had lost—his delicate features, the faint dimple on his tiny chin, the way his fingers curled in sleep. It was as if time had folded upon itself, offering her a glimpse of what she thought was gone forever.

She staggered back, her hands trembling. "This... this face," she whispered, barely able to find her voice. "He looks just like my son."

Narad's voice was steady, filled with quiet wisdom. "Because the soul never truly leaves, only the form changes. This child, sleeping peacefully in his mother's embrace, carries the same essence as the son you lost. His journey has continued, just as all souls move forward in new forms."

Vikram watched in stunned silence. The scene before him was achingly familiar, yet profoundly different. The mother before them was unaware of the past, unaware of the grieving woman who stood mere feet away, yearning for a connection that had already transformed.

"But how?" Vikram asked, his voice tinged with disbelief. "She mourns for her child, yet he now belongs to another mother. How do we reconcile this?"

Narad chuckled. "That is the nature of life, O King. The body is but a vessel, a temporary shell. The soul moves forward, unburdened by its past form. You see only what your eyes allow, but wisdom lies in looking beyond."

Narad then turned to Vikram and placed his hand upon the king's forehead. In an instant, Vikram's mind was flooded with visions—he saw himself in another life, a simple farmer, living and dying without the weight of a throne. He saw his father reborn as a poet in a distant land. He saw his soldiers returning in different forms, their essence unchanged, merely donning new identities.

The overwhelming nature of these visions left him breathless. He staggered back, his mind reeling. "This... this is the truth? That we never truly end? That we continue, again and again?"

Narad nodded. "Yes, but only the wise embrace it. The rest cling to what they have lost and suffer."

The mother, though still in pain, knelt before Narad. "I understand now, Rishi. My grief is for the form I lost, but his essence lives on. I must let go of my sorrow and accept the cycle of life."

Vikram, deeply moved, felt his heart lighten. But still, something troubled him. "Rishi, if what you say is true, then why do we fear death? Why do we suffer?"

Narad's eyes gleamed. "Because you cling. You hold onto what must pass, rather than embracing what must come. The wise do not resist change—they flow with it."

At that moment, a memory flashed through Vikram's mind—his father's deathbed, his own hands trembling as he performed the last rites. He had never let go of that pain, never accepted that life had moved forward. He had carried it with him, a burden that weighed upon his soul.

Narad placed a hand on Vikram's shoulder. "You have learned well, but let me reveal one last truth. I did not merely come here to teach—I came to test. If you had not stopped to listen, if you had not questioned, this wisdom would have eluded you. In life, the greatest moments of clarity come in the briefest of pauses. Those crucial seconds before we react, before we choose can change everything."

Vikram's eyes widened. "You mean, if I had simply ignored this grieving mother, I would have never understood this truth?"

Narad smiled. "Exactly. Wisdom does not come to those who rush past life's moments. It comes to those who stop and seek it."

Vikram bowed deeply, transformed. "I will remember this, Rishi. I will live with awareness, not fear."

Before parting, Vikram made one last stop—his father's final resting place. He stood before it, not with sorrow, but with understanding. He whispered, "You are not gone. None of us ever truly are."

As Narad disappeared, Vikram rode back to his kingdom, not just as a ruler but as a man who had glimpsed eternity in a single moment of pause.

Churchill: The Darkest Hour Before the Finest Hour

Winston Churchill, Britain's indomitable leader during World War II, bore the weight of an entire nation's survival on his shoulders. At 65, his health was failing, and the world around him seemed to crumble. The Nazi war machine had swept across Europe, and Britain stood alone against Hitler's tyranny. France had fallen, and invasion seemed imminent. The burden of leadership had never been heavier.

The Battle of Britain had begun—a desperate struggle in the skies where young British pilots fought relentlessly against the Luftwaffe. Every day, reports of bombings and casualties arrived, each one a reminder of how close they were to annihilation. The war cabinet was divided. Many, including Lord Halifax, urged Churchill to negotiate with Hitler, to consider peace at the cost of submission. But Churchill's soul revolted at the thought. How could he, after years of warning about Hitler's menace, now consider bending the knee?

One evening, as the echoes of sirens and distant explosions rattled London, Churchill found himself alone in his study at 10 Downing Street. He poured a glass of whiskey but barely touched it. Instead, he stood before the mirror, staring at his own reflection. The lines on his face, the exhaustion in his eyes—this was a man who had given everything to his nation. But had he given enough? Could he withstand the tide, or was Britain doomed to fall?

His mind whispered doubts. *Am I leading my people to destruction? Is it courage or sheer stubbornness that keeps me from negotiating?* He thought of the young pilots, mere boys, soaring into battle knowing they might never return. *Is my defiance worth their sacrifice?* The weight of history pressed upon him.

Suddenly, the room seemed to darken, and in the silence, he imagined the voices of the fallen. A young pilot, no older than 19, appeared before him—his uniform torn, his face smeared with soot. *"Did we fight in vain, sir?"* the boy asked. Behind him, others emerged—men from the trenches of the Great War, sailors lost at sea, soldiers buried in foreign lands. They stood watching him, waiting.

Churchill's breath caught in his throat. He had seen death before, in war and in life, but never had it felt so close, so expectant. He wanted to tell them that their sacrifice was not in vain, that their fight had meaning. But was he still certain of that?

Then, in the depths of his doubt, another vision overtook him—a nightmare of what could be. He saw a Britain that had surrendered. The Union Jack was torn down, replaced by the swastika. The people walked with their heads bowed, their spirits broken. The halls of Parliament were silent, its leaders mere puppets of a foreign power. The voices of resistance had been snuffed out, and history was rewritten by the victors.

A cold sweat formed on Churchill's brow. This was the price of surrender. Not just land lost, but an entire way of life—freedom, dignity, the soul of a nation. If he faltered now, this vision would become reality.

And then, a deeper realization struck him—his body was finite, but his duty was not. *What is my life in the grand scheme of time?* His physical form would fade, but the legacy of his actions would endure. Britain was not just a land—it was an idea, a spirit that transcended time and war. He could not let it falter.

The vision faded, and Churchill stood alone again. But now, his doubts had diminished. He turned to his desk and began drafting a speech. He hesitated, the weight of his choice still lingering. He could take the easier path—seek negotiation, accept defeat under the guise of survival. Or he could rally his people, knowing full well the cost in blood and suffering.

He clenched his fist. There was no choice. Britain would fight.

Yet even as he lifted his pen, the young pilot's voice echoed in his mind. *"What if we fall, sir?"* Churchill closed his eyes and exhaled slowly. *Then we fall with honor, knowing we never surrendered.* With renewed resolve, he let the words flow onto the page.

When he stood before Parliament the next day, the chamber was silent, waiting for his words. He inhaled deeply and spoke:

"Let us therefore brace ourselves to our duties, and so bear ourselves that if the British Empire and its Commonwealth last for a thousand years, men will still say, 'This was their finest hour.'"

The words electrified the room. A sense of purpose rippled through the hearts of those present. The time for hesitation had passed.

Days later, Churchill would deliver another defining speech to the House of Commons, one that would echo through history:

"We shall go on to the end. We shall fight in France, we shall fight on the seas and oceans, we shall fight with growing confidence and growing strength in the air, we shall defend our island, whatever the cost may be, we shall fight on the beaches, we hall fight on the landing grounds, we shall fight in the fields and in the streets, we shall fight in the hills; we shall never surrender."

Yudhishridhir: The Price of Righteousness

The battlefield of Kurukshetra lay silent, yet its silence was deafening. The war had ended, but the echoes of destruction still reverberated in the air. Yudhishthir, the eldest of the Pandavas, stood amidst the remains of an era— an era that had been shattered by war, ambition, and fate. The soil beneath his feet was stained with the blood of kin, friends, and foes alike. Victory had come, but at a price so steep that it felt like a hollow triumph.

Yudhishthir was the son of Kunti and the god of righteousness, Dharma. Born as a result of a divine boon granted to Kunti, he was destined to embody truth and justice. From a young age, he was taught the values of dharma, patience, and righteousness, setting him apart from his brothers. Unlike the impulsive Bhima or the valiant Arjuna, Yudhishthir was known for his wisdom and unwavering commitment to duty.

The battle of Kurukshetra, the great war of the Mahabharata, was not just a conflict over a throne but a culmination of generational enmity, pride, and betrayal. It began with a deep-seated rivalry between the Pandavas and their cousins, the Kauravas, led by the ambitious and arrogant Duryodhana. Despite numerous attempts at reconciliation, deceit and injustice forced the Pandavas into exile, and ultimately, war became inevitable. The battlefield witnessed the deaths of some of the greatest warriors of the age—Bhishma, the grandsire who had sworn allegiance to the throne; Dronacharya, the revered teacher who fought against his beloved students; Karna, the noble warrior cursed by fate and bound by loyalty to Duryodhana; and Abhimanyu, Arjuna's son, who fell to treachery in the Chakravyuha formation.

As Yudhishthir walked through the ruins of the battlefield, his heart felt heavier than the crown that awaited him. Every step he took brought memories of fallen warriors—Bhishma, Drona, Karna, Duryodhana, Abhimanyu, and countless others. His mind, weary from battle, yearned for peace, but his soul was restless. Was this the end he had sought? Was this the justice he had fought for?

Yudhishthir had always believed in dharma, righteousness above all else. And yet, as he stood amidst the wreckage of war, he found himself questioning everything. What was the purpose of war if it only led to grief? What was the meaning of justice if it left the world in ruins? What was life, and what was death? Had he truly upheld dharma, or had he merely been a pawn in a greater cycle of vengeance and destruction?

Lost in thought, he wandered into a secluded part of the forest, away from the cries of victory and the lamentations of the grieving. Here, under the vast canopy of the night sky, he encountered a radiant celestial being. The figure exuded an aura of wisdom and serenity, its very presence commanding reverence. As Yudhishthir approached, the being spoke in a voice that was both powerful and soothing.

"O King, you have won the war, yet you look defeated. Why does sorrow weigh you down even in victory?"

Yudhishthir recognized the voice—it was one he had heard in the depths of his soul. It was his father, Dharma himself, manifesting in a form beyond the physical realm. Overwhelmed, Yudhishthir fell to his knees and whispered, "Father, I seek answers. The war has ended, but my heart is restless. I do not know if what we have done was truly righteous."

Dharma smiled gently. "Tell me, my son, what do you seek to understand?"

Yudhishthir hesitated, then spoke the question that burned within him. "What is the ultimate truth of life and death? Why must we suffer, only to perish? And tell me, father, was this war truly righteous, or was it just another illusion?"

A deep silence followed. The air around him seemed to pause, and for a brief moment, time itself stilled. The weight of existence, the burden of choices, and the echoes of lost lives all condensed into this singular moment. It was his thirty seconds of reckoning—a moment where the mind wrestled with its deepest fears and sought enlightenment.

Before Dharma could respond, another voice pierced the silence. It was a voice that carried pain, accusation, and sorrow. "And what of me, Yudhishthir? Was my life merely a sacrifice for your dharma?"

Yudhishthir turned, his breath catching in his throat. Standing before him was Karna, his elder brother—his blood, whom he had refused to acknowledge until it was too late. Karna's eyes burned with the anguish of betrayal. "You call yourself the upholder of dharma, yet you denied your own brother his birthright. You speak of righteousness, yet you stood silent as I was mocked, humiliated, and abandoned by the very mother who bore us both. Was your dharma truly just, or was it only a justification for your victories?"

Yudhishthir's heart pounded. Karna's words were daggers, piercing through the moral certainties he had once held. Had dharma truly guided his actions, or had it merely been a veil to justify the suffering inflicted upon others? If dharma was absolute, why had it led to such immense loss? Why had noble men like Karna been condemned to tragic fates while others prospered in its name?

Dharma's voice broke through the storm raging within him. "O son, life and death are but two sides of the same river. Just as a man discards old garments and dons new ones, so does the soul shed the body and take another. Why grieve for that which is eternal? But know this—dharma is not without suffering. It is not an illusion, but neither is it absolute. It is shaped by the choices one makes, the sacrifices one endures. You have sought righteousness, and though your path was difficult, you must not let doubt consume you."

Just then, a gentle breeze swept through the battlefield, carrying the scent of earth and ashes. Yudhishthir looked up and saw a white lotus blooming in a pool of blood—a symbol of purity rising above carnage. The sight struck him deeply. Even in death, life emerged. Even in destruction, renewal began.

He closed his eyes, and in that moment, clarity dawned upon him. Life and death were but transitions. The soul was eternal, unbound by flesh and mortality. But dharma was not a rigid law—it was a path shaped by choices, by sacrifices, by the willingness to bear its weight.

His voice was steady as he spoke, "Father, I understand now. Life is not meant to be held onto with fear, nor is death something to mourn. We must live with honor, perform our duties, and accept that death is merely another passage—a doorway into something beyond."

That night, Yudhishthir did not mourn. He had walked through the fire of war, questioned the meaning of existence, and emerged with a truth that would guide him forever.

For in those moments of absolute introspection, he had understood the essence of life itself.

The soul does not perish. It merely moves on. And dharma—it is a path, not a destination.

Reflection: The Truth Beyond Mortality

Life is filled with moments that remind us of its impermanence—loss, war, change, and the inevitable passage of time. We strive for control, believing we can shape outcomes, but the greatest lesson comes in recognizing that some things are beyond our grasp. These stories reveal that death is not an end, but a transition, and that true wisdom lies in embracing the flow of life rather than resisting it.

King Vikram spent his life upholding dharma, ruling with wisdom and strength, yet he was troubled by the certainty of death. When faced with a grieving mother, he sought answers, only to realize that the soul never truly perishes—it simply moves forward, shedding one form for another. His moment of clarity did not come in battle or in power, but in pausing long enough to see beyond the illusion of finality. In that stillness, he understood that fear of death arises not from its reality, but from our attachment to the transient.

Winston Churchill, standing at the precipice of Britain's darkest hour, was not grappling with death itself, but with the survival of an entire nation. The weight of history bore down on him as he questioned whether he had the strength to resist Hitler's march across Europe. His vision of a conquered Britain, of a legacy lost to tyranny, was his moment of reckoning. In choosing to fight against overwhelming odds, he saw that while the body is mortal, ideals can be eternal. His decision to stand firm, to defy the illusion of inevitable defeat, became the foundation of a legacy that would outlive him.

Yudhishthir, the righteous king, won the greatest war of his time, only to find himself questioning its worth. Victory had come, but at the cost of family, honor, and countless lives. His encounter with Dharma, his celestial father, and the painful words of his fallen brother Karna, forced him to confront the deeper truth: righteousness does not always come without suffering, and justice does not erase grief. Through his thirty seconds of introspection, he realized that dharma is not a rigid law—it is a path shaped by choice, by sacrifice, and by the willingness to bear its burden without expectation of reward.

In each of these stories, the protagonists were confronted with mortality—not just their own, but the mortality of power, of control, of certainty. They each stood at the edge of despair, of doubt, of grief, and in that crucial pause, they found wisdom. Death, defeat, and loss were not the true enemies. It was the clinging to what must pass, the refusal to accept the cycle of life, that caused suffering.

The greatest truths often reveal themselves in silence, in surrender, in the brief moments before we react. When we release the illusion of control, we do not fall into chaos—we rise into clarity. For in letting go of what we cannot hold forever, we find the one thing that is truly eternal: peace.

Embracing Mortality: A Moment of Reflection Introspection

As you reach the end of this chapter, take a moment to reflect. Death is the one certainty in life, yet we spend much of our time fearing it, resisting it, or avoiding its reality. But what if mortality is not something to be feared, but something to be understood? What if the awareness of death is not a burden, but a guide—urging us to live more fully, love more deeply, and let go of what no longer serves us?

- Have you ever been so consumed by achievements that you forgot the fleeting nature of time itself?

- Have you ever witnessed loss and struggled to make peace with the absence it left behind?

- Have you ever held onto grief, unable to move forward because the past felt too sacred to release?

- Have you ever feared death—not for yourself, but for the ones you love—wondering how life could ever go on without them?

- Have you ever resisted change, forgetting that just as life is impermanent, so too are pain and suffering?

- Have you ever paused—just for a moment—to ask yourself: If today were my last day, have I truly lived?

Because sometimes, the true lesson of death is not about its finality, but about what it teaches us in life. It reminds us that control is an illusion, that time is our most precious gift, and that love, wisdom, and the choices we make are the only things that truly endure. So, as you step forward, ask yourself— are you living each day with the awareness that it is not forever?

The Strength in Letting Go

Bhagavad Gita, Chapter 12, Verse 12:

त्यागाच्छान्तिरनन्तरम्।

(From renunciation comes peace.)

Unburdening the Past, Embracing the Present

In life, we often find ourselves clinging to things that no longer serve us—whether it's emotional baggage, past regrets, or grief. The Bhagavad Gita teaches us that true peace arises when we let go of these attachments. Renunciation, or *tyag*, is not about giving up everything we hold dear but about releasing what weighs us down emotionally. The process of detachment offers the freedom to heal, to forgive, and to find inner peace.

But letting go is not easy. It requires strength, self-awareness, and a willingness to embrace the unknown. Often, it's in the most painful moments of our lives that we are called to practice the art of letting go. In these moments, it is the small pause, a 30-second reflection, that can shift our perspective and help us release the past to find peace in the present.

Amira: A Mother's Journey from Pain to Peace

Amira stared at the photograph in her trembling hands. It was of her son, Aarav, taken on his third birthday. His wide grin and sparkling eyes were frozen in time, a stark contrast to the void that had consumed her life since his death. It had been two years, but the pain remained a constant shadow, unyielding and oppressive. Her heart ached with questions she couldn't answer: Why him? Why her?

The accident had been sudden. One moment, Aarav was laughing as he ran across the park; the next, a reckless driver ended his short, vibrant life.

The loss had shattered Amira and her husband, Rohan. While he found solace in their shared grief and eventually resumed life's rhythm, Amira's world remained suspended in that singular moment of devastation.

Every corner of their house carried Aarav's presence. His toys still sat untouched in the living room. His room, preserved exactly as he had left it, was a shrine to a life too brief. Amira often found herself sitting there, holding his favourite teddy bear, letting waves of sorrow crash over her. The world outside moved on, but she was trapped in an endless loop of memories and guilt.

The guilt was the worst part. It gnawed at her, whispering accusations in the dead of night. What if she had held his hand tighter? What if she had called out to him a second earlier? What if she had just kept him at home that day? She replayed the accident over and over in her mind, dissecting every moment, searching for something—anything—that could have changed the outcome. The weight of self-blame crushed her, leaving her gasping for air in the silence of their empty home.

One evening, Rohan approached her with hesitant steps. "Amira," he began softly, "I think it's time we let go. Holding on to this pain is… it's tearing you apart."

Her eyes flared with anger. "Let go? How can you even say that? He was our son, Rohan! I can't just… move on."

"I'm not asking you to forget him," he replied gently. "But carrying this burden, refusing to live… it's not what Aarav would have wanted. Don't you think he'd want us to find peace?"

Amira turned away, tears streaming down her face. She knew he was right, but the idea of letting go felt like betraying Aarav's memory. How could she detach herself from the pain when it was all she had left of him?

She became a ghost of the woman she once was. She stopped meeting friends, ignored phone calls, and found solace only in the suffocating embrace of her grief. She would sit for hours in Aarav's room, whispering apologies to his picture, hoping that somehow, he would hear her. Rohan tried everything—suggesting therapy, encouraging her to step outside, even just sitting beside her in silence—but nothing reached her. She was drowning, and she refused to be saved.

Then came the day she hit rock bottom.

It was a cold, grey afternoon when Amira found herself standing on the balcony, staring down at the busy street below. The thought crept in, unbidden but persistent: What if she just… let go? Would the pain finally stop? Would she be able to see Aarav again? The wind howled around her, and for the first time in two years, she felt something other than numbness—a terrifying pull toward the abyss.

But then, she heard a voice. Soft, hesitant, yet filled with love.

"Amira."

She turned to find Rohan standing in the doorway, his face etched with worry. He didn't say anything more. He simply walked forward and wrapped his arms around her, holding her as if he was afraid she would disappear.

And in that moment, something inside her cracked. She broke down, sobbing uncontrollably into his chest. "I don't know how to live without him, Rohan. I don't know how to be happy again."

"You don't have to forget him to live," he whispered. "You just have to stop punishing yourself for surviving."

His words haunted her for days. She wasn't just grieving Aarav—she was punishing herself for being alive when he wasn't. She needed to find a way to let go of the pain without letting go of him.

Weeks later, with Rohan's encouragement, she decided to attend a local grief support group. The first session was terrifying. The group met in a small, cozy room at the community center. People of all ages sat in a circle, sharing stories of loss and resilience. Amira listened in silence, her heart heavy with her own pain. When her turn came, she hesitated before speaking.

"My name is Amira," she began, her voice barely above a whisper, "and… I am Aarav's mother." She paused, her throat tightening as tears welled up in her eyes. "I lost him two years ago, and… I don't know how to move on. I don't think I can."

A woman named Meera, who appeared to be in her sixties, reached out and placed a hand on Amira's. "I lost my daughter to cancer ten years ago," she said. "I understand your pain. But you must remember, detachment doesn't mean forgetting. It means finding a way to honour their memory without letting the grief consume you."

Amira's eyes filled with tears. She had never thought of detachment in that way. Could she really let go of the pain without losing the essence of Aarav?

Over the following weeks, Amira continued attending the support group. She heard stories of unimaginable loss and extraordinary resilience. Slowly, she began to see that letting go didn't mean erasing Aarav from her life. It meant cherishing the joy he had brought her while releasing the guilt and despair.

One morning, Amira stood in Aarav's room, the familiar ache gripping her chest. She looked around, her gaze lingering on his toys, his books, his drawings. Taking a deep breath, she picked up a box and began carefully packing away his belongings. Each item she touched brought back a flood of memories, but instead of breaking her, they brought a bittersweet smile to her lips.

When Rohan came home that evening, he found Amira sitting on the living room floor, the box by her side. She looked up at him, her eyes red but determined.

"I'm ready," she said. "I'm ready to let go of the pain. Not of Aarav, but of this weight I've been carrying."

Rohan knelt beside her, pulling her into a tight embrace. For the first time in two years, Amira felt a glimmer of peace.

To honour Aarav's memory, they decided to start a foundation in his name, dedicated to supporting children in need. Through this act of giving, Amira found a renewed sense of purpose. She learned that detachment wasn't about forgetting but about transforming pain into something meaningful.

The journey wasn't easy, and there were days when grief threatened to overwhelm her. But each time, she reminded herself of Meera's words and the wisdom of the Gita. Slowly, Amira began to live again, carrying Aarav's love in her heart without letting sorrow define her.

In those moments of quiet reflection, she realized that the act of letting go wasn't an end but a beginning—a way to honour the past while embracing the present.

Nelson Mandela: Beyond Vengeance: The Leadership of Letting Go

The waves crashed rhythmically against the jagged rocks of Robben Island, their ceaseless motion a stark contrast to the unchanging walls that enclosed Nelson Mandela. Located in the frigid Atlantic Ocean, 7 kilometres off the coast of Cape Town, South Africa, Robben Island had long been a place of exile, imprisonment, and despair. It was a fortress meant to break men, to crush their spirits, to make them disappear.

For 27 years, Nelson Mandela lived behind bars, his world confined to the barren, wind-swept Robben Island. Each day, they were forced into back-breaking labour, breaking rocks under the blinding sun, the white guards watching over them with contempt. Every insult, every beating, every moment of injustice carved itself into their souls.

Yet, the real punishment was not just the physical suffering. It was watching their people outside the prison walls continue to suffer, knowing that their fight for justice had led them here—trapped, powerless, unable to strike back.

And revenge became a fire that burned in many hearts.

Among the prisoners, whispers of the future were laced with anger.

"The day we are free, we will take back what they stole."

"They will pay for the years of humiliation, for every lash of the whip, for every drop of blood."

"They built this system to oppress us. It's only fair that we break it down when our time comes."

Even the most patient, the ones who once believed in peace, could feel the rage simmering beneath the surface.

When Mandela was finally freed in 1990, the world rejoiced. But South Africa still teetered on the edge of chaos. Violence had erupted between factions, and many believed that his return would mark the beginning of a reckoning. On May 10, 1994, Nelson Mandela stood before the people of South Africa—not as a prisoner, not as a revolutionary, but as their first Black President.

The streets of Pretoria were filled with celebration, the air electric with anticipation. Nelson Mandela, the man who had spent 27 years behind bars, the man whose very name had once been a threat to the apartheid regime, was about to walk into the presidential office—not as a prisoner, not as an activist, but as the first Black President of South Africa.

For millions of Black South Africans, this was the moment they had waited for their entire lives. The oppressors were gone, their voices no longer the law. This was the dawn of justice, of long-awaited freedom, of reckoning.

But for the white minority, the architects and beneficiaries of apartheid, this was their greatest fear realized.

Inside the grand offices of the Union Buildings, whispers filled the hallways. White government officials, bureaucrats, secretaries, security officers—many of whom had served under the apartheid regime—were packing their belongings. Stacks of files were being hurriedly shoved into boxes, personal effects removed from desks, chairs left vacant.

"Mandela will remove all of us. We'll be thrown out like we threw them out. This is the end."

It was not paranoia—it was expectation. After decades of brutality, segregation, and oppression, it was only natural that the man who had suffered at their hands would now seek revenge.

And yet, as Mandela walked into the corridors of power, taking in the sight of staff members preparing to flee before they could be dismissed, he did something that no one expected.

Mandela stopped in his tracks, watching as some of the longest-serving staff—most of them white—hurriedly packed up. There was fear in their eyes, fear that was a reflection of history itself, a cycle of oppression that had always dictated that when power changed hands, so did who suffered next.

He could have let them go. No one would have blamed him.

But instead, he made a choice that would define the future of South Africa.

Gathering all the existing staff, both Black and white, he called them into his office. They stood there in uneasy silence, waiting. Some clenched their hands, preparing for the dismissal they believed was inevitable. Others refused to meet his gaze, ashamed of the years they had spent serving a government that had brutalized millions.

Mandela looked at them, the very people who had once served the machinery that imprisoned him, and spoke not with vengeance, but with purpose:

"If you want to leave, that is your right. If you feel you cannot work for a government led by a Black man, that is your choice. But if you are willing to stay, if you are willing to serve not a party, not a race, but a country, then I will not only keep you—I will welcome you."

The words stung the air like a thunderclap.

Eyes widened. Whispers spread. The very thing that had seemed impossible had just happened: Mandela had chosen unity over retribution.

And then, he delivered the speech that changed South Africa forever.

Mandela had every reason to hate, to punish, to exile, to destroy. But instead, he chose something greater—a vision of South Africa that was not trapped in the past, but one that could move forward, together.

He knew that letting go did not mean forgetting. It did not mean absolving the crimes of apartheid. But it did mean choosing the future over hatred.

He once said: "As I walked out the door toward my freedom, I knew that if I did not leave my bitterness and hatred behind, I would still be in prison."

Mandela's freedom was not just the act of leaving Robben Island—it was the act of choosing hope over vengeance, reconciliation over resentment.

And in that defining moment, as he stood before a nation that had expected revenge, Nelson Mandela didn't just change South Africa.

He changed the world.

Margaret Thatcher: Leading with Strength, Choosing with Conscience

Margaret Thatcher's decision during the Falklands War became a defining moment in her career, embodying the themes of detachment and letting go. To understand her pivotal 30-second decision, we must first delve into her background and the context of the war.

Margaret Thatcher, known as the "Iron Lady," was the first woman to serve as the Prime Minister of the United Kingdom. Born in 1925 in Grantham, England, she rose from modest beginnings as the daughter of a grocer to become one of the most powerful leaders of the 20th century. Her tenure as Prime Minister from 1979 to 1990 was marked by her strong will, economic reforms, and an unwavering stance on issues of sovereignty and national pride.

The Falklands War in 1982 tested her resolve like no other event. The Falkland Islands, a British Overseas Territory located in the South Atlantic, had long been a point of contention between the United Kingdom and

Argentina. The islands were sparsely populated but strategically important. Argentina, led by a military junta seeking to bolster its waning domestic support, invaded the Falklands on April 2, 1982, claiming sovereignty over the territory. This act challenged British authority and Thatcher's leadership.

Thatcher's initial response was swift and decisive. She ordered a naval task force to sail 8,000 miles to the South Atlantic to reclaim the islands. This move was met with scepticism both domestically and internationally. Critics questioned the necessity of going to war over a remote archipelago with little economic value. However, for Thatcher, the invasion was a matter of principle—defending British sovereignty and deterring future acts of aggression.

The conflict escalated quickly, resulting in intense naval and aerial combat. As the British forces advanced, they faced significant losses, including the sinking of HMS Sheffield. The emotional toll on Thatcher was immense. Despite her steely exterior, she was acutely aware of the human cost of war. Each casualty report weighed heavily on her conscience, and she often spent sleepless nights reading letters from grieving families.

The pivotal moment came during a war cabinet meeting. Intelligence reports indicated that a decisive strike on the Argentine forces could end the conflict swiftly but at the cost of significant civilian casualties in the Falklands. This was a moral and strategic dilemma. On one hand, a swift victory would secure Britain's control over the islands and solidify her leadership. On the other hand, the loss of innocent lives would tarnish Britain's reputation and haunt her legacy.

Thatcher's mind was a battlefield of conflicting emotions. She thought of the soldiers who had sacrificed their lives, the families waiting anxiously for their loved ones to return, and the principles of justice and humanity that she held dear. Her inner dialogue was fierce:

"What will history say of me if I authorize this strike? Will I be remembered as the leader who defended her nation's honour or as one who allowed innocent blood to be spilled? Can I justify this to myself, let alone to the world?"

Her advisors' voices faded into the background as she wrestled with her conscience. Then, a memory surfaced—her father's teachings about integrity and the value of every human life. She took a deep breath, her hands clasped tightly, and made her decision.

"We will find another way," she said, her voice resolute yet tinged with emotion. "Victory at the cost of our humanity is no victory at all."

Thatcher's decision to pursue a more measured approach marked a turning point in the conflict. Instead of escalating the war, she authorized a strategy that prioritized minimizing civilian casualties while maintaining military pressure. The British forces eventually succeeded in reclaiming the Falklands, and the war ended on June 14, 1982, with minimal additional loss of life.

This decision cemented Thatcher's reputation as a decisive and principled leader. While she was celebrated for her victory, she carried the weight of the war's sacrifices for the rest of her life. In her memoirs, she reflected on the conflict, writing, "Every decision I made during the Falklands War was guided by a single principle: to act in the best interest of my country while upholding the values that define us as a people."

Even years later, as she walked past the Cenotaph on Remembrance Sunday, the faces of the fallen lingered in her mind. She would pause, bow her head, and whisper a silent prayer—not just for the soldiers who had died, but for the families who bore the pain of their absence.

In her later years, Thatcher reflected more deeply on the personal cost of leadership. She confided in close aides that the war had changed her—hardened her resolve but also deepened her understanding of sacrifice. She had won a war but had also witnessed first-hand the weight of every decision.

One afternoon, as she sat in quiet contemplation, a call arrived from Buckingham Palace. Her Majesty, Queen Elizabeth II, wished to see her. It was not an unusual summons, but there was an air of formality in the tone of the messenger.

Dressed in her signature blue suit, Thatcher arrived at the palace, her mind swirling with possibilities. When she entered the Queen's private chamber, she was greeted not just as a former Prime Minister but as a leader who had shaped Britain's course.

The Queen, composed and regal as ever, gestured for her to sit.

"Margaret," the Queen began, "I have decided to bestow upon you the Order of Merit."

For a brief moment, Thatcher said nothing. The Order of Merit was not merely an honor—it was a distinction given to only twenty-four living individuals at a time, reserved for those who had rendered exceptional service to the Crown, to the nation, and to humanity. No commoner had ever received it before.

Thatcher's hands trembled slightly as she folded them in her lap. She should have felt honored. She should have felt proud. Instead, she felt undeserving.

"Your Majesty," she said carefully, her voice softer than usual. "I am deeply grateful. But I must ask... after all that happened in the Falklands, after all the lives lost... do I truly deserve this?"

The Queen's gaze was unwavering. "Margaret, you must let go of the burdens you still carry."

Thatcher inhaled sharply.

"You are not being honoured because of war," the Queen continued. "You are being honored because of the choices you made during it. Because you carried the weight of difficult decisions and did not flinch. Because you ensured that Britain remained Britain."

The words settled into the silence between them.

Thatcher looked down, clasping her hands tightly. For years, she had shouldered the weight of every name on the casualty list. Every letter she had signed to grieving families. Every mother, father, wife, and child who had suffered loss.

But the Queen's words held a truth she could not ignore.

The world outside the palace walls faded. The war, the headlines, the expectations—they all dissolved into a moment of pure stillness.

And in those 30 seconds of introspection, she confronted the one truth she had refused to face.

She had never sought war. She had sought to protect her nation. She had done what was necessary, not what was easy. She had chosen restraint over destruction, strategy over vengeance. And yet, for years, she had punished herself for it.

Had she truly been carrying the weight of the fallen, or had she been carrying the weight of guilt?

As the realization sank in, her shoulders, once rigid with the burden of history, relaxed just slightly.

She looked up at the Queen, her expression no longer clouded with doubt.

"Thank you, Your Majesty," she said, her voice steady now.

As she walked out of the palace that day, Margaret Thatcher carried with her not just an honour, but something she had struggled to embrace for years.

The understanding that letting go did not mean forgetting. It meant allowing oneself the grace to move forward.

And in that one defining pause, those 30 seconds of reflection, she finally did.

Reflection: Choosing Release Over Resentment, Growth Over Grief

In life, we all face moments that test us—moments that demand choices, not just of action but of spirit. These moments force us to confront our deepest fears, challenge our beliefs, and define who we truly are. The stories of Amira, Nelson Mandela, and Margaret Thatcher serve as powerful reminders that letting go is not about weakness or forgetting—it is about finding the strength to move forward unburdened.

Amira's journey was not just about grief, but about releasing guilt—the kind that imprisons us in endless 'what-ifs' and 'if-onlys.' Letting go of her pain did not mean letting go of Aarav's memory; it meant honouring him by choosing life instead of endless mourning. Her moment of realization—that survival was not betrayal—became her path to healing. In allowing herself to step beyond sorrow, she found a way to carry love without being crushed by loss.

Nelson Mandela's story illuminated an even greater paradox: that true power lies not in retaliation but in reconciliation. After 27 years of imprisonment, he had every reason to seek vengeance, to purge the government of those who had upheld apartheid. The weight of injustice was enough to justify resentment. And yet, as he stepped into his role as the first Black President of South Africa, he chose unity. He understood that holding onto the past, no matter how justified, would only build new walls of division. His moment of introspection led him to a decision that shaped history—not to punish, but to heal. His leadership was defined not by what he had endured, but by what he was willing to release.

Margaret Thatcher's struggle was of a different nature—one that revealed the quiet, internal battle of leadership. The Falklands War had tested her resolve, and though Britain emerged victorious, she carried the weight of every life lost. In her later years, as the Queen bestowed upon her the Order of Merit, she found herself still shackled by guilt. But in that moment of pause, she realized that letting go was not about dismissing the sacrifices made—it was about acknowledging them without being consumed by them. She had not sought war; she had sought to protect her nation. She had led not with recklessness, but with responsibility. And in finally detaching from the guilt she had carried for years, she found peace.

Together, these stories remind us that letting go is an act of courage. It is not about erasing the past, but about refusing to let it dictate the future. In those fleeting moments of introspection, we hold the power to break free from what binds us—be it grief, anger, or guilt. And when we choose to let go, we do not surrender. We rise.

So, when your moment comes—when life presents you with a choice that challenges your heart and your convictions—will you have the courage to pause, to detach, and to make the choice that truly matters?

A Moment to Introspection: The Strength in Letting Go

As you turn this page, take a moment to reflect-how often have you held onto something long after it served you? How many times has the weight of the past shaped the way you see the future?

- Have you ever clung to pain, believing that letting go would mean forgetting?

- Have you ever carried guilt for something that was never truly in your control?

- Have you allowed anger or resentment to define your choices, even when they no longer served you?

- Have you ever been afraid that releasing something meant losing a part of yourself?

- Have you ever mistaken holding on for strength, when true strength lay in the ability to move forward?

- Have you ever paused-just for a moment-to consider what might happen if you let go?

Because sometimes, the hardest thing to release is not the past itself, but the version of ourselves that refuses to move beyond it. Letting go is not about weakness, nor is it about erasure. It is about making space-space for healing, for growth, for new beginnings.

So, what is it that you are holding onto today? And more importantly-are you ready to let it go?

Finding Purpose in Chaos

Bhagavad Gita - Chapter 2, Verse 48

योगस्थः कुरु कर्माणि संगं त्यक्त्वा धनञ्जय।

(Perform your duties with steadfastness in yoga, without attachment.)

The Search Within: Redefining Success and Meaning

In the hustle and bustle of life, it's easy to get lost in the chaos of work, success, and ambition. We often find ourselves consumed by the desire to achieve, to be someone, and to leave a mark on the world. But in all this striving, we forget one crucial thing—the real purpose of it all.

The Bhagavad Gita teaches us to engage fully in our duties, but to detach from the outcomes. It encourages us to act with dedication, but without letting the pursuit of success define us. True peace and purpose come not from the things we accumulate or the titles we achieve, but from the relationships we nurture and the love we share.

Amidst the noise of daily responsibilities, the unpredictability of life often throws us into moments of uncertainty—times when plans unravel, setbacks strike, and everything we've worked toward seems to lose meaning. In these moments, purpose can feel distant, almost invisible. But perhaps, purpose is not something we find in perfectly laid-out plans or external validation. Perhaps it is something we create in the way we respond to life's disruptions. True purpose is not about having all the answers; it is about embracing the questions, finding clarity in the mess, and anchoring ourselves in something deeper than fleeting success. It is about learning that even in the midst of chaos, we can still choose meaning, we can still choose love, and we can still choose to show up for what truly matters.

Aryan & Augustya: Chasing Perfection, Losing What Matters

Aryan had spent his life chasing success, believing it was the answer to everything. From the time he was young, he was told that success was the highest form of love—a way to provide, to secure a future for the ones he cared about. He held onto that belief with everything he had, pushing himself relentlessly, never stopping, never slowing down.

In his mind, every meeting, every deal, every long night at the office was for his family. But somewhere along the way, he had forgotten something so simple, yet so vital: his family didn't just need his success. They needed him.

His son, Augustya, had grown up with the quiet absence of a father who was physically present but emotionally distant. Aryan had been in the house, but his mind was always elsewhere. Augustya had wanted so many things—his time, his words, his warmth—but Aryan was too absorbed in his own world to see that.

Maya, his wife, had always been there, picking up the pieces, filling in the gaps. She was both mother and father to Augustya, while Aryan was too busy building an empire. Every day, he told himself that this was temporary, that once the business was stable, once they had everything they could ever need, things would be different. But the truth was, the moments that mattered were slipping through his fingers, one by one.

Yet, Augustya had carried a burden heavier than Aryan had ever imagined. From his teenage years, he had known that he was different. He had known that his heart, his love, his identity did not fit within the narrow mould his father had constructed of what was right and acceptable. He was gay, and for years, he had kept this truth locked inside him, fearing that Aryan would never understand.

He had seen the way his father measured everything by society's standards. To Aryan, success was not just about money—it was about being *right*, about being perfect in the eyes of the world. And Augustya? He had never felt perfect. He had spent years hiding parts of himself, terrified that the moment he spoke his truth, he would lose his father forever.

Maya knew. She had always known. She had held him through the nights when he was too scared to speak, had wiped his tears when he had struggled with self-doubt, and had whispered to him that he was enough, exactly as he was. But no matter how much she reassured him, the fear remained. Would his father ever accept him? Would he ever see him for who he truly was?

When the time came for Augustya to choose his future, he decided to study in the United States—not just for the education, but to escape the suffocating expectations of his father. In the U.S., he found a world where he didn't have to pretend, where he could be himself without fear of judgment. He built a life that was his own, a life outside the perfect definition his father had imposed. When he received a job offer there, he accepted it without hesitation. He was finally free, finally able to embrace the world that felt like home.

Then, one evening, the phone call came.

"Dad, I need to tell you something," Augustya said, his voice quieter than usual.

Aryan didn't hear the sorrow in his son's tone at first. He was too distracted, already thinking about the next meeting, the next deal, the next thing that needed his attention. But something in his son's voice made him pause. A weight in those words that made him stop and listen.

"What is it, son?" Aryan asked, his mind still divided between the call and the mountain of work that awaited him.

"I've decided to stay here in the U.S. I've accepted a job offer, and I don't think I'll be coming back," Augustya's words were slow, deliberate, and heartbreaking.

Aryan's world stopped. The words seemed to freeze in his chest. "What do you mean? You were supposed to come back. I've worked all these years for you, for our future," Aryan's voice cracked as the panic set in.

For a moment, silence stretched between them, like a vast chasm that he could not cross. Then, Augustya spoke again, his voice quieter, but the pain sharper.

"For whom, Dad? You weren't really there. I grew up without you. Mom did everything for me. You always said you were doing it for us, but I never felt it."

The words hit Aryan like a punch to the gut, and for the first time in his life, he was speechless. He had been so caught up in his own ambition, so consumed by the idea of giving his family everything, that he had forgotten the one thing they truly needed from him: his presence.

"There's something else I need to tell you," Augustya continued, his voice trembling slightly. "I've wanted to tell you for so long, but I was scared. Scared of how you'd see me, scared that I'd never be enough in your eyes."

Aryan's breath caught in his throat. "Augustya, what is it?"

"Dad… I'm gay. And I'm happy to be in my imperfect world."

Silence. A heavy silence that stretched on for what felt like an eternity. Aryan felt his pulse quicken, his mind racing to find a response. This wasn't part of the plan. This wasn't the son he had imagined. This wasn't—

No. He stopped himself. *This is your son. This is the same boy you held in your arms when he was born, the same child who once looked at you with wide, adoring eyes. This is the son who waited for you to come home, who longed for your presence, who feared your rejection.*

His throat tightened. "Augustya… I… I don't know what to say."

"I know," Augustya said softly. "And that's why I didn't tell you before. Because I knew you wouldn't understand. Because to you, being *right* has always been more important than being *real* with me."

Aryan clenched his fist, feeling a sting behind his eyes. He had spent his whole life trying to build something great, but in doing so, had he destroyed the most important thing of all? His own son's trust?

His eyes drifted to the portrait hanging on the far wall of his office, the words "Perform your duties with steadfastness in yoga, without attachment" inscribed in elegant Sanskrit beneath an image of Krishna and Arjuna on the battlefield. It had been there for years—a mere decoration, something he barely acknowledged between meetings and decisions. He had seen the words countless times, but never truly understood them. They had been nothing more than ink on a canvas.

But today, they were no longer just a verse. They were a truth he had ignored, a lesson that had been waiting for him to see it. And now, in the wake of his son's pain and his own realization, the meaning of those words stood before him—clear, undeniable, and deeply personal. His hands trembled as he grabbed his phone, staring at the screen for a moment before typing.

"Son, I know I've failed you. I've missed so many moments with you. But if you ever give me the chance, I want to make things right. I love you. And I'm here. Whenever you're ready."

The words felt inadequate, but they were all he could offer.

As Aryan hit send, something inside him shifted. It wasn't a fix for everything. It didn't erase the years of neglect. But in that moment, he made the decision to try, to change, to show up for his son the way he had never done before.

For the first time in years, Aryan felt peace. And in the quiet space between those 30 seconds of decision, Aryan chose to make things right.

As Aryan sat in silence, the weight of his own expectations pressing down on him, he realized that he had spent his entire life chasing an illusion of perfection—one that had cost him the very thing that mattered most. Success, wealth, achievements—none of it meant anything if it came at the cost of love, of understanding, of being present in the lives of those who truly mattered.

His duty was not to mold his son into a version of perfection that existed only in his mind. His duty was to love Augustya as he was, without expectation, without conditions.

In those thirty seconds, Aryan made a choice—not to hold on to the past, not to resist the truth, but to step forward with love. His son had found his own world, his own happiness, and Aryan's journey now was not to change it, but to honor it.

He exhaled, typing out the only words that truly mattered.

"I love you, son. And I'm proud of you. Just as you are.

Steve Jobs: The Real Measure of a Life Well Lived

Steve Jobs had always been a man of relentless ambition. From the moment he co-founded Apple in his parents' garage, he had one goal: to change the world. And he did. His vision reshaped technology, making devices not just functional but personal, intuitive, and, in many ways, an extension of the human experience. But in the pursuit of innovation, something had been left behind—something he would only realize when time was no longer on his side.

Back in the early days of Apple, Jobs was consumed by the thrill of creation. He spoke with an almost prophetic certainty about his mission. In a 1980s interview, he famously said, "Being the richest man in the cemetery doesn't matter to me. Going to bed at night saying we've done something wonderful—that's what matters to me." He believed in his work with the fervour of a missionary, convinced that every waking moment should be spent pushing boundaries, creating, revolutionizing.

Success came fast and hard. By 25, he was worth over a hundred million dollars. But that was never the goal. "I was worth over a million dollars when I was 23, and over ten million dollars when I was 24, and over a hundred million dollars when I was 25, and it wasn't that important because I never did it for the money," he once said in a 1995 interview. It was never about wealth; it was about legacy. Yet, as Apple flourished, the cracks in his personal life widened.

His relationships suffered. He had a complicated history with his first daughter, Lisa, initially denying paternity. His obsessive work habits left little time for deep personal connections. He chased perfection in his products but overlooked the imperfections in his personal relationships.

Then came the fall. In 1985, he was forced out of his own company. The company he had built, nurtured, and sacrificed everything for had turned its back on him. It was a brutal wake-up call. For the first time, he was forced to pause.

But Jobs was never one to dwell on defeat. He founded NeXT and later acquired Pixar, transforming it into the most successful animation studio in history. In those years, something shifted in him. He met Laurene Powell, the woman who would become his wife, and started a family. He began to see that life wasn't just about the next big innovation—it was about the people who stood by you, the ones who loved you not for what you created but for who you were.

It was during this time that Jobs' inner transformation began to deepen and the understanding of success began to evolve. The pursuit of external accomplishments, the thrill of victory, no longer held the same allure. Instead, he started to realize that the moments spent with those who mattered most were what truly defined his life.

When he returned to Apple in 1997, he was a different man. Still brilliant, still demanding, but more aware of the fleeting nature of time. At the Stanford Commencement speech in 2005, he shared a hard-earned realization: *"Your time is limited, so don't waste it living someone else's life. Don't be trapped by dogma – which is living with the results of other people's thinking."* This was a clear shift from the man who once believed that success was solely about creating revolutionary products and changing the world. Now, he spoke about living authentically, true to one's own passions and values.

In 2005, Jobs had the courage to admit: *"Remembering that you are going to die is the best way I know to avoid the trap of thinking you have something to lose. You are already naked. There is no reason not to follow your heart."* This statement revealed a profound understanding of life's impermanence, something Jobs had come to terms with after years of obsessive work and professional success.

The contrast between the young Jobs, consumed with ambition, and the more introspective Jobs that emerged after years of failure, loss, and family life is stark. His 2009 speech at Stanford was a pivotal moment. Reflecting on his cancer diagnosis, he acknowledged how close he had come to losing everything that mattered. He said: *"I've looked in the mirror every morning and asked myself: If today were the last day of my life, would I want to do what I am about to do today?"* This daily introspection served as his compass, guiding him toward a life where his priorities were realigned with love, relationships, and a deeper purpose.

As his health continued to decline, the once ambitious and driven CEO became a father, a husband, and a man facing mortality. His final words—*"Oh wow. Oh wow. Oh wow."*—are believed to have reflected his final moments of clarity, perhaps a realization of the fleeting nature of life and the importance of love and connection above all else.

In his last moments, Jobs was surrounded by his family. His sister, Mona Simpson, later shared that his final words were: *"Oh wow. Oh wow. Oh wow."* No one knows exactly what he saw in those final moments, but perhaps, for the first time, he saw life not as a race to the next innovation, but as the sum of all the love, connections, and experiences he had gathered along the way.

Steve Jobs changed the world, but in the end, his greatest realization was not about technology or business—it was about love, presence, and the fleeting nature of time. The 30 seconds that matter most in life are not those spent chasing success, but those spent in the quiet presence of those who truly matter. His journey teaches us that amidst the chaos of ambition, there is a deeper purpose waiting to be discovered—a purpose that lies in the hearts of the people we love and the moments we choose not to miss.

Keikeyi: The Price of Righteousness

The sun hung low in the sky, casting an amber glow across the dense forests of Chitrakoot. The towering trees whispered with the evening breeze, their leaves murmuring secrets of the ages. Birds called to one another in the distance, their songs a melancholic echo of a world left behind. Lord Rama stood still, gazing at the horizon, where the golden light faded into a quiet dusk. The exile weighed upon his soul, not as a burden, but as a silent question.

Though his heart was heavy with sorrow, he held no bitterness. The promise his father had made to Kaikeyi had led to his banishment, yet he had embraced his fate. He had left his home, his throne, and his family to live as a hermit. He was a man bound by duty, not desires.

The forest, though serene, was also a place of solitude and reflection. It often became an echo chamber of his inner turmoil. The rustling leaves and birdsong did little to silence the questions that whispered through his mind.

Why must I suffer this fate? he pondered. Why must I live in this wilderness, far from my kingdom, far from my people? How much longer must I endure this torment?

A pair of footsteps snapped him from his thoughts. Lakshmana approached, his expression clouded with concern.

"Rama," he said, his voice carrying the weight of unspoken sorrow, "how much longer must we endure this exile? How much longer must we bear this pain?"

Rama met his gaze, his own eyes shadowed by grief. But he could not falter.

"Lakshmana, our lives are not our own," he said, his voice steady but tinged with sorrow. "We are bound by duty. I did not choose this exile, but I have accepted it. Resisting it would mean defying the will of the universe. We must endure, for in our suffering, we may find our true purpose."

Lakshmana's hands curled into fists. "And what of injustice, brother? What of the pain inflicted upon us unfairly? Must we simply bow to it?"

Rama placed a firm hand on his brother's shoulder. "To fight the course of fate is like trying to hold back the tide with bare hands. We do not bow to injustice, but we must rise above it. Our dharma is not to lament, but to act when the time is right."

Then, tragedy struck. One day, as Rama and Lakshmana ventured deeper into the forest, Sita was taken—snatched away by Ravana, the demon king of Lanka. The news shattered Rama's heart. The weight of exile had been heavy, but the weight of her absence crushed him.

The days that followed were filled with torment. His heart bled for Sita, yet his mind remained clear. He had a duty—to rescue her and restore dharma. There was no room for self-pity.

"Lakshmana," he said, his voice steady but strained, "we must find Sita. The world is out of balance without her. My heart aches, but grief cannot cloud my purpose. We must act swiftly."

Thus began his journey—not just across lands but within himself. He forged alliances, gathered an army, prepared for war. The burden of responsibility grew heavier with each passing day. His was not an army of kings but of vanaras, bears, and sages—beings drawn to his righteousness. And yet, as the battle neared, so did his doubts.

Why must I fight this war? Must blood be shed to restore dharma? Is there no other way?

Then, standing before the great fortress of Lanka, bow in hand, Rama found himself at a crossroads. The war drums echoed, the air thick with the anticipation of battle. He had spent months preparing for this moment. And yet, for a brief, fleeting thirty seconds, his mind wavered.

He closed his eyes. He saw Sita—not just as a queen to be rescued, but as the embodiment of love, of sacrifice, of all that he had lost. Would saving her truly bring him peace? Would victory justify the destruction that lay ahead?

Must I kill to restore order? Must I become what I seek to destroy?

Lakshmana, sensing his brother's hesitation, stepped forward. "Brother, do not waver now. This war is not about revenge. It is about righteousness."

Rama sighed. "I do not seek vengeance, Lakshmana, but I cannot ignore the suffering this battle will bring. So many will perish today. Even Ravana, for all his sins, was a son, a brother, a king."

Lakshmana's voice was firm. "And Sita? Is she not suffering? Will you not end her torment?"

The weight of duty bore down on him, pressing against his soul like an unshakable force. He had fought for righteousness, for dharma, for the truth his father had taught him. But now, in this brief, suspended moment, he questioned whether he could detach himself from the outcome. Could he fight without seeking victory? Could he act without being consumed by the war itself?

A sudden gust of wind stirred the battlefield dust, carrying the scent of burning incense from the distant temples. He opened his eyes.

"I will fight," he whispered, his voice no longer uncertain. "Not for victory. Not for power. But because it is my path. And I must walk it without attachment."

The battle raged. When the final confrontation came, it was not a moment of triumph. There was no joy in slaying Ravana, no celebration in victory. As the demon king fell, Rama stood over him, his heart heavy. He had done what was necessary—but at what cost? He had lost Sita once to Ravana, and now he feared he had lost her to fate itself.

For a moment, he looked at Ravana's fallen form, and a deep sadness crept into his heart. Despite his arrogance, his cruelty, Ravana had been a king, a scholar, a devotee of Lord Shiva. A man of immeasurable knowledge, undone by his desires. In another life, perhaps, they might have been allies, even friends.

As the smoke of battle cleared, Rama turned inward. The exile, the loss, the battles—each had tested him, each had been a step on his path. He had performed his duty without attachment, and yet the hollowness remained.

He had restored dharma, but had he found peace? Ravana, in his final moments, had smiled—a knowing, defiant smile. Had he, too, been a victim of fate, bound by the strings of destiny?

As Rama journeyed back to Ayodhya, a thought lingered. The weight of dharma is eternal, but so is its pursuit. He had walked his path with righteousness, but peace? Peace was not in the victory, nor in the throne. It was in knowing that he had stayed true to himself, despite it all. And yet, he wondered—was dharma a path one chooses, or a path that chooses its seeker? Or was it merely another name for the chains that bound even the noblest of men?

Reflection: The Clarity Within Chaos

Life rarely follows a straight path. It twists, turns, and often throws us into chaos—unravelling the plans we once held tightly. Yet, it is in these moments of uncertainty that we are forced to confront the deeper questions: What truly matters? Where does our purpose lie? These stories show that purpose is not found in control or certainty, but in our response to life's disruptions. When ambition, expectation, and even duty blur our vision, chaos becomes the unexpected teacher, forcing us to redefine what truly holds meaning.

Aryan spent years believing that success meant security, that his relentless pursuit of achievement would be his greatest act of love for his family. But in chasing perfection, he lost sight of what mattered most. It took his son's painful truth to make him realize that success was never about wealth or societal validation—it was about presence, about truly seeing the ones he loved. In that moment, Aryan's understanding of purpose shifted. It was never in the deals he closed, but in the connections he had neglected. And when he finally let go of the illusion he had built, he found what had been waiting for him all along—a chance to show up, to accept, and to love without conditions.

History, too, has seen men lose themselves in the chaos of ambition, only to realize their greatest lessons in moments of stillness. A visionary who changed the world, Steve Jobs built an empire with his brilliance, but at the cost of broken relationships and personal loss. He spent his youth believing that innovation was the greatest measure of a life well-lived, but as he neared the end, his definition of success transformed. In his final days, he saw that the true legacy he left behind was not in technology, but in the love he shared with those closest to him. The chaos of his journey had led him to clarity—an understanding that the moments spent with loved ones were far more valuable than any invention.

Even in the realm of duty and righteousness, purpose is often forged in the fires of doubt. The weight of dharma led a king into exile, stripped him of his throne, and forced him into battles he never sought. Through suffering, loss, and war, he upheld his duty without hesitation. But in the quiet moments before battle, when the world expected him to be unwavering, even he questioned the path ahead. Was righteousness only about fulfilling duty, or was it about something greater—about understanding the cost of action, about choosing to fight without hatred, about walking a path without attachment? In those moments of chaos, purpose did not come from the throne he had lost or the war he had to fight. It came from knowing that his journey was never about victory, but about standing firm in his truth.

In all these stories, chaos was not an obstacle—it was the catalyst. It shattered illusions, challenged beliefs, and forced them to look beyond what they thought defined them. Purpose was never in the title, the power, or the control they once held—it was in the choices they made when everything else fell apart. And perhaps, that is where purpose is truly found—not in certainty, but in the courage to embrace the unknown, to redefine what matters, and to keep moving forward, even when the path is unclear.

Finding Purpose in Chaos: A Moment of Introspection

As you reach the end of this chapter, take a moment to reflect. In the rush to create stability, success, and meaning, we often try to control the chaos around us. But what if purpose isn't about controlling life, but about embracing it as it comes? What if the moments of uncertainty, disruption, and doubt are not distractions, but the very path to clarity?

- Have you ever mistaken busyness for purpose, believing that constant movement means meaningful progress?

- Have you ever chased success so relentlessly that you lost sight of why you started in the first place?

- Have you ever resisted life's detours, not realizing that they may be guiding you to something greater?

- Have you ever been so consumed by an outcome that you forgot to be present for the moments unfolding before you?

- Have you ever felt like you were losing control, only to realize later that the unraveling was actually leading you toward something more real?

- Have you ever paused—just for a moment—to ask yourself: If everything I've built were taken away, would I still know who I am?

Because sometimes, the search for purpose isn't about finding the perfect path—it's about learning to walk forward, even in uncertainty. True purpose isn't in the plans we create, but in the choices we make when those plans fall apart. So, as you step forward, ask yourself—are you willing to find meaning, even in the mess?

Turning Moments Into Paradigm Shifts

Bhagavad Gita, Chapter 13, Verse 27:

समं सर्वेषु भूतेषु तिष्ठन्तं परमेश्वरम्।
विनश्यत्स्वविनश्यन्तं यः पश्यति स पश्यति।।

(He who sees the Supreme Lord equally present in all beings, the
imperishable within the perishable, truly sees.)

From Reflection to Transformation: Moments That Matter

There are moments in life that shift the ground beneath our feet, altering our understanding of the world in profound and unexpected ways. These paradigm shifts are not always grand or loud—sometimes, they unfold in quiet pauses, in fleeting 30-second reflections, where we choose to see things differently. In those moments, we find ourselves standing at the edge of a deeper truth—one that invites us to step beyond surface appearances and limited perspectives to embrace the bigger picture.

This chapter explores how those 30 seconds can trigger profound shifts in awareness, whether in the face of global crises or intimate personal struggles. Through stories of transformative decisions and realizations, it reveals the life-altering power of choosing to see the unity within diversity, and how that simple shift in perception can change the way we understand the world—and our place within it.

The Cuban Missile Crisis: The Power of a Moment in the Face of War

The year 1962 was a time when the world seemed to teeter on the edge of disaster. The Cold War had already divided the globe into two camps: the

United States, with its capitalist ideals, and the Soviet Union, upholding the tenets of communism. The arms race between the two superpowers was escalating, with both nations amassing nuclear weapons capable of obliterating the world many times over. For years, the leaders of these nations had engaged in a delicate dance, each step calibrated to avoid open conflict while seeking to gain the upper hand.

But now, the world was about to face its most terrifying test.

It began with the discovery that the Soviet Union, under Premier Nikita Khrushchev, had placed nuclear missiles in Cuba—just 90 miles off the coast of Florida. The United States had long been concerned about Soviet influence in Latin America, but this new development was a game-changer. The proximity of the missiles meant that the U.S. could be within striking distance of nuclear attack. This was no longer a matter of ideological differences; it was a matter of survival.

For President John F. Kennedy, the weight of the situation was crushing. He had only been in office for less than two years, yet now, he found himself facing a decision that could determine the fate of millions, perhaps even billions, of lives. The discovery of the missiles in Cuba brought his presidency to a crossroads. Kennedy had to act—swiftly and decisively—but how?

Inside the Oval Office, Kennedy sat at his desk, surrounded by his closest advisors. The room was thick with tension as the military generals and CIA officials made their case. The voices clamoured around him, urging him to take immediate action. "We must strike now, Mr. President," General Curtis LeMay, the head of the Air Force, insisted. "We cannot let this stand. If we do nothing, we appear weak. If we wait, the Soviets will only strengthen their position."

Kennedy's brow furrowed as he listened to the barrage of voices, each one advocating for a different course of action. He was surrounded by men who had devoted their lives to strategy and war, men who saw the situation in black and white. But Kennedy knew better than to make a rash decision. He had been briefed on the stakes of the situation—an airstrike followed by a full-scale invasion of Cuba would surely provoke retaliation from the Soviet Union, possibly triggering World War III. The question loomed large: What was the right choice?

As the voices continued to clash in the room, Kennedy felt the weight of history pressing down on him. He was the leader of the free world, but what did that mean in this moment? Was he to be the man who started a nuclear war, or was he to find a way out of the crisis—without losing face? The conflict within him was intense.

- *"If I back down now, if I appear weak, the world will lose confidence in us,"* he thought. *"How can I live with that? We've spent years building this power. What if this moment defines us, and we fail?"*

- *"But if we strike, and the Soviets retaliate, we could lose everything— millions of lives, cities reduced to ashes. The guilt would be unbearable. Would it be worth it?"*

- *"Khrushchev is a leader like me. What if he's just trying to protect his country too? What if we're not so different after all?"*

Kennedy's mind raced, caught between pride and fear, between the pressure to act decisively and the realization that every choice he made would have consequences far beyond his own lifetime.

In that moment, Kennedy felt an overwhelming urge to stop the noise. He raised his hand, signalling for the room to quiet down. The advisors, surprised by his sudden calmness, fell silent.

"Give me a moment," Kennedy said, his voice steady but firm.

He stood up from his desk and walked toward the window, the weight of his decision pulling him down with every step. Outside, the sun was setting, casting long shadows over the White House lawn. The breeze rustled the autumn leaves, a quiet, peaceful contrast to the storm that raged within him. Kennedy closed his eyes for a moment and took a deep breath.

For 30 seconds, he stood still, allowing the swirling emotions to settle. The panic in his chest began to ebb, replaced by something more subtle—a clarity that had eluded him moments before. He could see the bigger picture now, the long-term consequences of his decisions. He thought of the families on both sides, the innocent lives that could be lost, the children who might never grow up. He thought of his own children, of Caroline and John, and how he would want to protect them from the horror of nuclear war.

As he stood there, the voices in his head quieted. He knew what he had to do.

When he turned back to the room, his face was calm, but his eyes burned with determination. The weight of the decision no longer felt like a burden but a responsibility—a responsibility to humanity.

"No," he said simply, his voice clear and unwavering. "We will not strike."

There was a stunned silence. His advisors were not prepared for this. General LeMay's face reddened with frustration. "But, Mr. President, if we don't act now, the Soviets will take us for fools."

Kennedy shook his head. "This isn't about appearing weak or strong. It's about survival. We will find another way."

The room erupted in protest, but Kennedy remained calm, his mind made up. He had seen the way forward—not through aggression, but through dialogue. He immediately ordered backchannel communications with Soviet Premier Nikita Khrushchev. What followed were tense days of negotiation, with both leaders on the brink of making a catastrophic mistake.

On the other side of the world, the weight of the crisis bore heavily on Khrushchev as well. The days passed in agonizing silence, the world holding its breath. Behind closed doors, the tense negotiations continued, each side calculating its next step. It wasn't until Khrushchev, too, experienced his moment of clarity—when he realized that the risk of total annihilation far outweighed the pursuit of political dominance—that the crisis finally began to de-escalate.

On October 28, 1962, Khrushchev publicly agreed to remove the missiles from Cuba in exchange for a U.S. pledge not to invade the island. The world exhaled in relief.

Had Kennedy not paused, had he succumbed to the pressure to act in haste, the world might have faced a nuclear war. But by taking **those 30 seconds of introspection**, Kennedy had chosen peace, ensuring the survival of millions. And in doing so, he had not only reshaped history but had also demonstrated the power of perspective in moments of crisis.

A Love Lost in the Absence of a Pause

Rajeev's anger surged as he stormed out of the house, slamming the door with a force that echoed through the empty hall. His breath came in short, furious bursts, his mind racing through the harsh words that Meera had thrown at him. "You've given up on us!" Her voice had been sharp, accusing, cutting into him like a dagger.

"Given up?" he had roared back. "I have done everything for this family! And you—you stand there blaming me?"

"Everything except being present, Rajeev!" Meera shot back, her eyes brimming with hurt. "Except loving me the way you used to."

The words stung, but instead of pausing, instead of breathing, his rage took over. His hand lashed out before he even realized it, the sharp crack of his palm against Meera's cheek ringing through the room. She stumbled back, her hand flying to her face, shock and disbelief flashing in her eyes.

But Rajeev didn't feel sorry. Not then. His anger blinded him, drowned out the guilt trying to creep in. Instead, he grabbed her by the arms and shook her violently. "You always push me!" he shouted, his fingers digging into her skin. "You always blame me for everything! You make me do this!"

Meera gasped, trying to pull away, but Rajeev wasn't done. In a fit of uncontrollable rage, he shoved the table, sending glasses shattering to the floor. He grabbed a vase and hurled it across the room, watching it explode against the wall. He swept his arm across the kitchen counter, sending dishes crashing onto the floor. His breaths were ragged, his chest heaving, his vision blurred with fury.

Meera stood frozen, tears streaming down her face, her body trembling. "This isn't you, Rajeev," she whispered through her sobs. "You don't even see what you're becoming."

But Rajeev didn't stop to see it. He turned and stormed out, slamming the door behind him, his heart pounding with fury.

His hands gripped the steering wheel tightly as he sped through the city, his knuckles turning white against the smooth leather. The streets blurred, his mind fixated on the words that still reverberated in his ears. "She deserved it," he told himself. "She had no right to say those things. After everything I've done?"

But another voice, quieter yet persistent, gnawed at him. "You crossed a line." He shook his head violently. No. He wouldn't allow himself to feel guilt. Not now.

Days turned into weeks, and the fights escalated. Meera grew distant, her voice colder, her presence a ghost in their home. Words they could never take back were hurled in moments of fury. Love became a distant memory, buried under resentment and unspoken pain. When Meera finally uttered the word "divorce," Rajeev did not protest. His pride, his anger, his refusal to pause had chained him to a path he never thought he'd walk.

Months later, on a dreary afternoon, Rajeev stood outside the courthouse, holding the final divorce decree in his trembling hands. The cold wind bit at his skin, but he barely felt it. Meera stood a few feet away, silent, her eyes downcast. The woman he had once loved beyond words, now just a shadow in his life.

Rajeev wanted to say something, anything. To take back the anger, the harsh words, the nights filled with silence. To take back the slap, the way he had shaken her, the way he had shattered everything in his rage. But it was too late. The ink had dried. The moment had passed.

For the first time, he allowed himself to think—really think. What if he had taken just 30 seconds that night to reflect on his actions? What if, instead of storming out, he had paused, taken a breath, and truly listened? What if he had chosen restraint over rage, comfort over conflict? Would they still be standing on opposite sides of a broken past?

A lump formed in his throat, the weight of his choices crushing him. "Meera," he whispered, his voice barely audible. She looked up, her eyes filled with an emotion he could no longer reach.

"Take care, Rajeev," she said softly, and with that, she turned and walked away.

Rajeev stood frozen, the decree crumpling in his grip, his vision blurred by unshed tears. He had lost her. Not because of fate, not because of destiny. But because he had refused to pause.

A deep void settled in his chest, one he knew would never be filled. The love of his life was gone—forever. And the regret, the sorrow, the unbearable ache in his heart—that would never leave him.

Those 30 seconds could have changed everything. But now, they were just a haunting reminder of what could have been.

Beyond Resentment: A Bond Reclaimed in Silence

The sterile scent of antiseptic filled the hospital room, mingling with the rhythmic beeping of the ventilator. The dim fluorescent light cast a ghostly glow over the frail figure lying in the hospital bed. Priya stood at the doorway, gripping the cold metal frame, her feet frozen in place. The sight before her was almost unrecognizable. Her father—once a towering figure of discipline and dominance—now lay weak, his chest rising and falling with the support of a machine.

A war raged inside her. She should feel something—grief, concern, sadness. But all she could summon was an ache that burned deep, a resentment that had taken root years ago. Her fists clenched as old wounds resurfaced.

"Why am I even here?" she thought bitterly. "He never truly loved me. He only wanted control. Why didn't he ever just love me? Why was I never enough?"

Her heart pounded in her chest as memories flooded in—uninvited, unwelcome. She closed her eyes, reliving them as if they were happening all over again.

She was eight years old, clutching her drawing with excitement. "Papa, look! I made this for you!" She held up the colourful paper with trembling hands, heart racing. Her father barely glanced at it before shaking his head in dismissal. "The lines aren't straight. You should practice more." His voice was cold, dismissive. Her chest tightened. The paper, once vibrant with her love, felt like a crumpled failure in her small hands.

"I tried so hard for him to be proud," she thought, her voice shaky. "Why couldn't he just see it? I wanted him to say he loved me... just once."

She was ten when she came home with her school report, brimming with excitement. "I got ninety-two, Papa!" she had beamed, expecting praise. But his face remained expressionless. He didn't even look at her, only at the report. "What happened to the other eight marks?" he asked, his voice sharp. "You should have done better."

"I could never get it right. Nothing was ever enough for him," she whispered to herself, her voice breaking. "Why did he never see me for who I was? Why did he always tear me down instead of building me up?"

At fifteen, she gathered the courage to tell him she wanted to study literature. "Literature won't feed you," he scoffed. "Choose something practical or don't expect my support." His words hit her like a slap. Her dreams, her hopes—they were nothing to him. "I spent so many nights crying myself to sleep, wondering if he would ever love me for me."

Every moment she sought his approval, he met her with indifference or disappointment. Every time she tried to shine, he dimmed her light. The suffocating rules, the endless expectations, the way he dismissed her passions like they were childish whims. He had never tried to understand her. Never cared to see her for who she was.

And now, here he was, lying helpless, unable to dictate, unable to control. A part of her should have felt victorious, relieved. But instead, she just felt hollow. Empty. "Is this what it took for him to be vulnerable? This sick, frail body? Why did he never let me in? Was it so hard to just love me?"

She took a hesitant step forward, the faint hum of the machines filling the silence. Her father's chest rose and fell in slow, uneven movements. The mask covering his face muffled any sound he might have made. He looked so… small. So fragile.

She reached out, her fingers trembling as they grazed the side of the bed. "Papa," she whispered, her voice thick with the years of silence and sorrow between them. "I spent my whole life waiting for you to love me the way I needed. I always thought you didn't care. But now… now I'm not so sure. Maybe you loved me in your own way… but it was never enough for me. And I… I couldn't bear it anymore."

Her heart ached with every word. "Why couldn't he just tell me? Why couldn't he just say that he loved me? Was it really that hard?"

A tear slipped down her cheek, landing on the rough skin of his hand. "I forgive you, Papa," she whispered, her voice cracking. "I forgive you for all the pain, all the missed chances, all the moments you let me down. I forgive you, because I don't want to carry this weight anymore."

She squeezed his fingers lightly, and for the briefest moment, she felt it—a faint pressure, barely there. But it was real. A silent response. A final moment shared between father and daughter.

Her breath hitched as she saw a weak tear escape from the corner of his closed eyes. His eyes—those eyes that had always been filled with so much authority, so much pride, so much anger—now held nothing but vulnerability. He had heard her. He had understood.

A sob broke free from her lips as she rested her forehead against his hand. The years of resentment, the weight of bitterness—it all dissolved in that instant. The air in the room seemed to thicken, her heart shattering in a million pieces. "I've wanted you to apologize for so long," she cried softly. "But I never thought I could forgive you. Not like this. Not when you're lying here. But now… now I just want peace."

She didn't know how long she stayed there—time seemed to bend and stretch, each second pregnant with emotion. But in that moment, something in her shifted. Something deep within her broke free. Forgiveness. It wasn't for him. It wasn't to absolve him of his wrongs. It was for her.

What if I hadn't forgiven him? she thought suddenly, her heart clenching. What if I had just walked away with all this anger still inside me? What would I have carried with me? What would this ache have felt like?

Her mind reeled at the thought. I would have carried this pain forever, the bitterness would have poisoned me, even after his death. The 'could haves' and 'should haves' would haunt me. I would've spent my life asking, 'Why didn't I just forgive him when I had the chance?' And I would never have found peace. I would have lost the opportunity to heal myself, to let go of this weight that has crushed me for so long.

A long, flat beep suddenly echoed through the room.

Priya looked down at his hand, lifeless now, and felt the heaviness of it all settle into her chest. It wasn't relief. It wasn't triumph. It was peace—finally, a deep sense of quiet that she had longed for, even without realizing it. Her heart no longer felt as if it was trapped under the weight of endless years of anger and resentment.

Forgiving him didn't mean excusing his actions. She knew that. But it meant choosing to let go of the past, choosing to forgive herself too—for holding on to so much pain for so long. It meant reclaiming her own heart from the darkness that had lingered there. In forgiving him, she had found a new strength. She had found freedom from her own self-imposed prison.

She stood there, the weight of the moment heavy, but her heart lighter. I had the power to let go. The realization hit her like a flood.

Later that night, as she walked out of the hospital, she looked up at the sky. The same stars she had gazed at as a child, wondering why her father never told her bedtime stories, now twinkled with a quiet knowing. The silence of the night was deafening, yet comforting.

She could have walked away. She could have let her anger keep her distant. But those 30 seconds—the choice to pause, to reflect, to let go—had changed everything. In that brief moment, she hadn't just forgiven him; she had finally understood him. And in understanding, she had built a bridge where a wall once stood.

She had lost her father. But in those final moments, she had found something far more lasting—a love that had always been there, just hidden beneath unspoken words.

Reflection: The 30 Seconds That Shaped Their Lives

In a world that moves at an unforgiving pace, we often let our emotions dictate our actions, allowing anger, pain, and pride to cloud our judgment. In these fleeting moments, we react instead of reflect, and in doing so, we risk making choices that leave behind scars—some visible, some buried deep within. But as these stories remind us, sometimes, all it takes is 30 seconds to change everything.

For President Kennedy, that pause was the difference between war and peace, between destruction and diplomacy. In those 30 seconds of quiet contemplation, he chose not just to protect his nation but to uphold the survival of millions across the world. He saw beyond pride and power, beyond the immediate need to act, and in doing so, he reshaped history.

For Rajeev, the pause never came—until it was too late. He let his anger speak for him, let his pride build walls too high to tear down. The moment to stop, to reflect, to hold back from saying or doing something irreversible—it was there, but he ignored it. And by the time he allowed himself to think, the damage had already been done. His 30-second pause became a lifetime of regret.

For Priya, those 30 seconds in the hospital room gave her something she never thought she would **have—peace.** In that silence, she realized that forgiveness wasn't about excusing the past; it was about freeing herself from it. Had she walked away in anger, she would have carried that burden forever. Instead, she paused, she listened—not just to her father's unspoken words, but to her own heart. And in those final moments, she didn't just reclaim the bond they had lost—she reclaimed herself.

Each of these moments—a decision, a regret, a reconciliation—was shaped in the space of 30 seconds. It's a reminder that we all stand at these crossroads, more often than we realize. A pause before lashing out. A breath before walking away. A moment before making a choice that cannot be undone.

It's not easy. In the heat of the moment, rage feels justified, silence feels unbearable, and pain feels permanent. But what if we allowed ourselves those 30 seconds—to step back, to see the bigger picture, to ask ourselves: Is this really what I want? Will this bring me closer to the life I want to live?

Because in those 30 seconds, we don't just make decisions. We define who we are.

A Moment to Pause, A Lifetime to Introspection

As you turn this page, ask yourself—how many moments in your own life have been shaped in just 30 seconds?

- Have you ever said something in anger that you wished you could take back?

- Have you ever made a decision that felt right in the moment, only to regret it later?

- Have you ever held onto resentment for so long that it weighed heavier on you than the person you resented?

- Have you ever let pride stop you from saying something your heart wanted to?

- Have you ever walked away when you could have chosen to stay, or stayed when you knew you should have walked away?

- Have you ever paused just long enough to see the situation differently, to choose understanding over assumption, love over ego, or peace over conflict?

Because in the end, it's not just about the moments we act on—but also the ones we pause for.

Because sometimes, all it takes is 30 seconds—not just to make a decision, but to see differently, to shift perspectives, and to turn fleeting moments into lasting paradigm shifts.

The Illusion of Control

प्रकृतेः क्रियमाणानि गुणैः कर्माणि सर्वशः।

(All actions are performed by the modes of material nature,
but the soul deluded by ego thinks itself the doer.)

The Power of Acceptance

Life is a delicate dance between effort and surrender. We chase success, plan meticulously, and work tirelessly, believing we are the architects of our fate. Yet, time and again, we are humbled by forces beyond us—unexpected setbacks, shifting circumstances, and moments that refuse to unfold as we envisioned. The more we try to hold on, the more life reminds us that control is, at best, an illusion.

The Bhagavad Gita teaches us that while action is essential, attachment to the outcome leads to suffering. We believe we are in command, but in reality, we are part of a much larger flow—one governed by time, fate, and the unseen forces that shape our journey. In those fleeting moments of realization—those "30 seconds" of clarity—we recognize that true strength is not in controlling every outcome but in knowing when to let go.

This chapter explores the stories of individuals who stood at the edge of their perceived control, grappling with uncertainty, loss, and the unpredictable nature of life. It is in these moments—when resistance fades and acceptance takes hold—that they found something far greater than control: freedom, peace, and the ability to move forward with grace.

When Skill Meets the Limits of Destiny

Dr. Anjali was a renowned heart surgeon, known not just for her precision but for her unshakable confidence in her abilities. Having studied at an elite international college on a scholarship—an institution where admissions were nearly impossible—she carried an air of superiority. She was the one senior doctors consulted, the one whose patients never succumbed. To her, medicine was not just a profession; it was a conquest, and she was its master. Life and death were decisions she orchestrated with her scalpel.

Over the years, she had saved hundreds of lives, cementing her belief that skill and intelligence could overcome anything. She prided herself on her unyielding dedication, convinced that effort and expertise alone determined fate—until one fateful night shattered that belief and forced her to confront a truth she had long ignored.

A young boy, Rudra, was rushed into the emergency room. His tiny body had suffered a sudden cardiac arrest, and the odds were stacked against him. Yet, Anjali did not believe in odds. She believed in action. With the confidence of years of practice, she scrubbed in, ready to fight for him.

For hours, she worked tirelessly, her hands moving with the expertise of a master. Every stitch, every incision was calculated, precise. Her world narrowed down to the rhythmic beeping of machines and the fragile heart she was trying to save. Sweat trickled down her forehead, stinging her eyes, but she blinked it away. Her fingers ached from the relentless precision, but she ignored the pain. Exhaustion clawed at her muscles, her breathing grew shallow, yet she pushed on. *I can do this. I have to do this.* Her pulse pounded in her ears, her stomach clenched with urgency. She was the healer. She was the savior. She had never lost a battle before—why should this be any different?

And yet, fate had its own designs.

The machines let out a long, hollow sound. A sound she had heard before, yet never learned to accept.

She stood frozen, staring at the lifeless form on the operating table. *No. This wasn't supposed to happen.* Her fingers, still trembling, hovered above the boy's chest, as if willing life back into him. The sterile white light above her suddenly felt blinding, suffocating. A chill crawled up her spine, her body turning rigid with disbelief. The beeping monitors had fallen silent, yet the echoes of failure roared in her ears. Her throat tightened, her breath coming in shallow bursts, as if the room itself were closing in on her. Her legs wobbled, her knees threatening to give way beneath her. Her hands, once so steady, clenched into fists at her sides. *How? How could I fail?*

Stepping out of the operating room, her scrubs heavy with sweat and failure, she faced Rudra's parents. His mother clutched her husband's arm, desperation in her tear-streaked eyes. "Doctor… he's going to be okay, right?"

Anjali swallowed the lump in her throat. "We did everything we could. His heart was too weak. I'm so sorry."

The mother stared at her, motionless for a moment. Then, as realization dawned, her eyes widened in horror. "No… NO! You're lying! You're Dr. Anjali! You're the one who never loses a patient! You were supposed to save him! Everyone said you were the best!"

Her voice cracked as she clutched at Anjali's arm. "I prayed to God for my son's life, but everyone told me I didn't need to… because *you* were his savior! They called you a miracle worker! You let them believe it! You let *me* believe it! If you can't save him, who can?"

Her sobs turned into desperate, angry wails. "You're not a doctor—you played god! And today, you failed!"

Anjali took a step back, her vision blurring as her hands began to shake. The mother's broken cries cut through her, sharper than any scalpel she had ever held. Her breath hitched, her chest heaving as if the weight of her own arrogance was pressing down on her. The room spun for a second, her grip loosening on reality. *I thought I controlled fate. But did I ever?* Her entire identity—the invincible, infallible surgeon—shook beneath the weight of that moment. It was a moment that would change her forever.

She turned away, retreating to the hospital terrace. The cold wind bit at her skin, but she barely felt it. Her hands clutched the railing, her knuckles white. Looking up at the sky, she asked the question that had haunted her for years, the one she never dared voice aloud: *Who decides?*

Was it medicine? Was it science? Was it something greater, beyond her reach?

Memories of past patients flooded her mind—the ones she had saved, the ones she had lost. She had always taken their survival as proof of her competence, their deaths as a failure of her skill. *But had I ever truly been in control?*

She thought back to her years in medical school, the relentless pursuit of perfection. She had pushed herself beyond limits, refusing to let a single mistake define her. She had convinced herself that mastery over her craft meant mastery over life and death.

But life had proved otherwise.

Later that night, as she sat alone in her office, staring at the city lights blurred by rain, a soft knock interrupted her thoughts. Rudra's father stood at the door, his face etched with sorrow but his voice steady. "Doctor," he said, "we know you tried. Sometimes, it's not in our hands. Thank you for giving him a chance."

Anjali opened her mouth to speak but hesitated. *Not in our hands.* The words struck her deeply. She had spent her life believing she was in control. But the truth was humbling—she was merely an instrument, not the master of fate. The boy's life was never hers to save or lose. She had played her part, but nature had its own course.

She sat in silence long after he left, her fingers tracing the edge of her desk. For the first time, she understood. She was not the doer. She was the vessel. The burden she had carried for years, the belief that she alone dictated outcomes, began to ease.

That evening, as she walked through the hospital corridor, she noticed a junior doctor sitting alone, distressed after losing his first patient. She saw in him the reflection of her younger self. Taking a deep breath, she walked over and sat beside him.

"It wasn't supposed to happen," he muttered, his voice shaking. His hands were clenched into fists, his breath shallow, as if he were suffocating under the weight of his emotions. "I thought I could save him."

Anjali placed a reassuring hand on his shoulder. A warmth spread through her chest, a lightness she had never felt before. She exhaled deeply, as if releasing a burden she had carried for too long. A faint, knowing smile touched her lips. "We do our best, but the results are never ours to decide. All we can do is serve with everything we have."

And in that surrender, she found peace.

The Fall of Napoleon Bonaparte

The Russian winter was merciless. Snow-covered fields stretched endlessly, swallowing the horizon in a vast, indifferent whiteness. The once-mighty

French army, reduced to shadows of their former selves, staggered through the frozen wasteland. The air was thick with the scent of death—horses lay frozen mid-stride, soldiers clutched their frostbitten limbs, their eyes hollow with despair. The Grand Armée, which had once marched with unshakable confidence into the heart of Russia, now retreated in broken silence, leaving only suffering in its wake.

Napoleon Bonaparte stood at the edge of a dwindling campfire, his piercing eyes scanning the desolate horizon. Born in 1769 on the island of Corsica, Napoleon had risen from humble origins, the son of a minor noble family, to become the Emperor of France. His brilliance in military strategy had propelled him to greatness, allowing him to rewrite the map of Europe and challenge the mightiest monarchies of his time.

Napoleon's ascent to power was deeply entwined with the French Revolution. The revolution, which began in 1789, was a violent upheaval against the monarchy and the old feudal order. The people of France, exhausted by famine, heavy taxation, and the opulence of the aristocracy, overthrew King Louis XVI, ultimately executing him and his queen, Marie Antoinette. The revolution promised liberty, equality, and fraternity, but it soon spiraled into chaos. The Reign of Terror followed, with thousands guillotined as the revolution devoured its own leaders.

Amidst this turmoil, Napoleon emerged as a rising star. Trained as an artillery officer, he first gained prominence during the Siege of Toulon in 1793, where his tactical ingenuity led to a decisive victory against royalist forces. His triumphs in Italy and Egypt further cemented his reputation. By 1799, France was in disarray, with corruption and instability plaguing the government. Sensing an opportunity, Napoleon orchestrated a coup d'état, seizing power and establishing himself as First Consul. In 1804, he declared himself Emperor, a move that defied tradition and demonstrated his unrelenting ambition. Under his rule, France expanded its influence across Europe, toppling ancient dynasties and redefining the balance of power.

The war that had led him here was the fateful Russian campaign of 1812, an ambitious invasion meant to bring Tsar Alexander I to his knees. Confident in his army of over 600,000 men, Napoleon had underestimated the vastness of Russia and the brutal winter that would soon decimate his forces. Now, as he and his men trudged back from Moscow in the grip of an unforgiving blizzard, he faced the bitter consequences of his ambition.

A gust of wind howled through the camp, carrying with it the distant cries of suffering men. Footsteps approached, crunching against the frozen ground. Marshal Michel Ney, "the bravest of the brave," stood before him, his face gaunt, his eyes hollow. Ney had fought beside Napoleon through countless battles, rising through the ranks due to his unwavering courage and tactical brilliance. Once a common soldier, he had become one of Napoleon's most trusted commanders, renowned for his fearless leadership on the battlefield. Even now, despite his exhaustion, he stood resolute.

"Your Majesty," Ney's voice was hoarse, his breath visible in the frigid air. "The men can go no further. We are dying here. We must turn back."

Napoleon remained silent, his gaze locked on the horizon. To retreat was to admit failure. It was to accept that he had gambled and lost. His pride, the very thing that had propelled him to greatness, screamed in protest. How could the great Napoleon retreat? How could he allow himself to be bested— not by an army, not by a general, but by the land itself?

His mind reeled back to his rise—a Corsican boy mocked for his accent, underestimated by the nobility, yet determined to carve his name into history. He had risen through the ranks, a general by twenty-four, an emperor by thirty-five. He had shattered coalitions, crowned himself in defiance of the Pope, and commanded the greatest army Europe had ever seen. The world had bowed before him.

Yet here he stood, powerless before an enemy he could not command.

He looked at Ney—at the desperation in his eyes, at the thousands of men who still clung to life, waiting for his command. And then, for the first time, something shifted within him. A voice, cold and unyielding, whispered in his mind: This is not about you anymore.

His fingers curled into fists. His heart pounded against his ribs. The weight of the moment pressed down upon him, suffocating and inescapable. His entire life had been spent in defiance of limits, yet here he stood, face to face with an undeniable truth: there were forces greater than his will. Nature. Fate. The currents of war. He was but a man in their grip.

For thirty agonizing seconds, Napoleon battled himself. His mind became a battlefield of memories—a blur of his childhood in Corsica, the boy who had once dreamed of greatness, the man who had ascended from obscurity to command an empire. He saw the sunlit fields of Austerlitz, where he had once stood victorious, the deafening cheers of his men filling the air. He heard the echoes of his coronation in Notre Dame, where he had crowned himself emperor, defying the Pope and the very order of the world. He felt again the thrill of conquest, the sweet intoxication of absolute power.

But as swiftly as these visions came, they began to disintegrate. The cheers turned to wails, the triumph to despair. The golden halls of his empire crumbled into ice and darkness.

A wave of dizziness overtook him. He stumbled, gripping the hilt of his sword for support. In his mind's eye, he saw a shadow of himself standing tall on a grand pedestal, only to watch it crack and collapse, reduced to rubble beneath an indifferent sky.

And then, the deepest fear of all struck him: How will history remember me? Would he be a visionary or a tyrant? A ruler who shaped Europe or a fool who led his men to ruin? Would his name be spoken in reverence or as a cautionary tale?

The whispers in his mind grew louder. You are not immortal. You are not invincible. You are a man like any other.

He clenched his jaw, his breath ragged. The realization cut deeper than any enemy's blade. The world he had built was slipping through his fingers, and for the first time in his life, he could not command it back into place.

"We retreat," he finally said, his voice barely above a whisper.

Ney exhaled sharply, relief washing over his weary features. "Thank you, sire."

Napoleon turned away, his expression unreadable. As the order spread through the camp, soldiers collapsed in quiet gratitude, knowing they would live to see another day.

And in that moment, Napoleon Bonaparte, conqueror of Europe, understood the cruellest truth of all: Power is fleeting. Control is an illusion. He had spent his life believing he was the master of his fate, but in the end, he was merely a vessel, carried by the tides of history, just as the Gita had foretold—not the doer, but merely an instrument of forces beyond his control.

Nalayani: The Price of Perfection

The flickering flames of the yajna kund danced in the still night as a young woman sat in deep meditation, her eyes closed, her heart whispering a single wish. This was no ordinary woman. This was Nalayani, the daughter of the virtuous sage Mudgala. She had been born into a life of devotion, yet fate had not been kind to her.

Her husband, the sage Maudgalya, was a man of great wisdom and a learned scholar of the Vedas. He was deeply immersed in ascetic practices and the pursuit of spiritual knowledge. However, he had been cursed with a diseased and feeble body, making his physical existence frail and burdensome. Despite his wisdom, he was known for his unpredictable temperament—sometimes deeply immersed in serene contemplation, at other times testing Nalayani's patience with his erratic behavior. Their marriage was filled with trials, as Nalayani remained steadfast in her duty despite her husband's deteriorating condition. However, deep within, she yearned for a companion who embodied strength, virtue, and divine grace.

Maudgalya's condition was not just a natural ailment; it was the result of a powerful curse. In his youth, he had once displayed arrogance in his knowledge, mocking the teachings of an aged and revered sage—none other than Sage Chyavana. Enraged by his disrespect, Chyavana cursed him, saying, "You, who think yourself superior, shall suffer a body that fails you, so you may learn humility and the true purpose of wisdom." From that day forth, Maudgalya had been afflicted with a weak and diseased form, a reminder of his past arrogance.

Determined to seek divine intervention, Nalayani turned to the ultimate source of power—Lord Shiva. With unwavering devotion, she renounced all worldly pleasures and retreated into the depths of the forest, surrendering herself to years of rigorous penance. She endured harsh climates, fasting for months, surviving only on leaves and water. She stood on one leg in deep meditation, her mind fixed solely on Mahadev. Her prayers echoed in the heavens, her heart unwavering in its plea. Night after night, she folded her hands, surrendering herself to the supreme will.

But Lord Shiva did not appear.

Years turned into decades. Her voice grew hoarse from calling out to him. The seasons changed, the forests withered and bloomed, but she remained unmoved. Her feet bled, her body weakened, yet her resolve remained unshaken. At times, doubt crept into her heart—had her prayers gone unheard? Was she unworthy of an answer? But each time despair threatened to consume her, she gritted her teeth and called out again.

"Mahadev! If you do not answer me, who will? Have I not surrendered everything? Have I not burned away every desire except this one? Why do you remain silent?"

She fell to her knees, tears streaming down her face. "Oh Mahadev! You haven't heard my prayers! I am only asking you to grant me a husband who is the embodiment of dharma, the pinnacle of strength, the master of war, the epitome of charm, and the wise scholar. Let him be patient like the earth, fierce like the storm, and loving like the moon. Let him be a reflection of you in every way!"

Nalayani bowed deeply, her heart soaring with hope. The best husband in the world—one who would embody all virtues of the divine! What more could she ask for?

Atop Kailash Parvat, the divine abode of Lord Shiva and Goddess Parvati, a heated discussion unfolded.

Parvati paced, her eyes blazing with frustration. "Mahadev, this is absurd! How can you even consider granting her wish? This is not devotion; this is sheer obstinacy! Does she even understand what she asks for?"

Shiva remained seated in serene contemplation, his expression unreadable. "Her penance is unwavering, Devi. Such determination cannot be ignored."

Parvati let out an exasperated sigh, her patience fraying. "But at what cost? Look at her! She is not seeking wisdom, she is not praying for the greater good—she is demanding a husband who fulfils her idea of perfection! This is not surrender; this is selfishness in disguise!"

Shiva's gaze remained steady. "Desire is a path to understanding, Parvati. One must experience fulfilment to comprehend its emptiness."

Parvati clenched her fists, her divine energy crackling in the air around her. "And what if she never understands, Mahadev? What if she is born again with the same longing? You are giving her what she wants, but not what she needs! Love is not a possession, not a reward for stubbornness!"

Her voice grew sharper, edged with bitter amusement. "Shall we then grant every mortal's relentless desire? Perhaps the ocean should turn sweet for the fisherman who despises salt! Or the sun should dim for one who cannot bear its light! Where do we draw the line?" She turned to Shiva, her frustration evident. "You call me your equal, your Shakti. Then listen to me, Mahadev—this is folly!"

Shiva sighed, his voice calm yet firm. "Her soul's journey is hers to undertake. Even if she does not learn in this life, she will, in time. That is the nature of existence."

Parvati threw her hands up, a wry smile playing on her lips. "Then let it be known—this wish will not bring her peace. Mark my words, Mahadev. She will not find joy in what she so desperately desires. She believes she is asking for happiness, but she is blind to the burden she invites. When her heart shatters under the weight of this wish, I hope she remembers that we tried to warn her."

Shiva turned his gaze toward the mortal world, where Nalayani remained deep in penance. His lips curved into a knowing smile. "So be it."

Finally, one night, after years of relentless devotion, the Lord appeared before her, his divine presence illuminating the darkness.

"My child, your devotion is unparalleled," Shiva's voice resonated like the chime of a temple bell. "Your wish shall be granted."

Before Shiva could utter another word, Goddess Parvati, standing beside him, crossed her arms. "You persist in this wish despite all warnings, Nalayani. Do you understand what you ask for? This is not a boon—it is a path laden with trials beyond mortal comprehension. To love a being who embodies divinity is to suffer the burden of separation, conflict, and loss. Are you prepared for such a fate?"

Nalayani's eyes glowed with determination. "Yes, Devi. No suffering will shake my devotion. I only wish for a husband who embodies all virtues of the divine."

Parvati's expression darkened, her voice cold. "So be it. But know this—destiny never unfolds as we imagine. You may have prayed for perfection, but what you receive may break you before it makes you whole."

Shiva smiled, his deep eyes holding the mysteries of the cosmos. "Your wish shall be granted."

Born as Draupadi in her next life, she found herself standing before a blazing fire once again—only this time, she was emerging from it, born of sacred flames, a princess destined to change the course of history. She was originally named Krishnaa by her father, King Drupada, due to her dark complexion and divine beauty. However, as was customary, her identity became linked to her lineage, and thus, she came to be widely known as Draupadi—'the daughter of Drupada.'

As years passed, she was wedded not to one man, but five. Yudhishthira, the embodiment of dharma; Bhima, the pinnacle of strength; Arjuna, the master of archery; Nakula, the epitome of charm; and Sahadeva, the wise scholar. Together, they were unparalleled.

Yet, Draupadi's heart ached with confusion.

Years later, as Draupadi, she stood by the banks of the Ganges, gazing at her reflection in the still waters. Her fingers curled into fists, her breath uneven.

"Why, Mahadev?" she whispered, her voice thick with anguish. "Why did you deceive me?"

For years, she had believed herself wronged—trapped in a fate she had not chosen, bound to five husbands, torn by duty, honor, and sacrifice. Had she not prayed for the perfect husband? Had she not surrendered everything for a single wish? And yet, here she was, battle-worn, carrying the weight of countless expectations.

A faint glow shimmered in the mist. Lord Shiva's ethereal form emerged, his presence calming yet unshakable.

Shiva's voice, calm as the still night, resonated in the air.

In the silence of the night, the waters trembled, and a divine glow surrounded her. Lord Shiva's ethereal form emerged from the mist, his serene gaze meeting hers. "Did I not fulfill my promise, Draupadi?" his voice was both gentle and firm.

"You did not, Mahadev," she argued, her voice quivering. "I wished for a single husband with all your virtues, not five."

A knowing smile graced Shiva's lips. "Tell me, my child, is there any one man who can contain all of me? My strength, my wisdom, my patience, my detachment, my fury?"

Draupadi fell silent, her mind racing.

"No single human can embody the entirety of the divine," he continued. "The laws of the universe are not dictated by personal desires. You prayed for the best husband, and you were granted not one but five, each bearing a part of my essence. It was never about control, Draupadi. It was about surrender."

Her breath hitched. She had spent years believing she had the power to dictate fate, that her devotion gave her authority over destiny. But in that moment, she realized—she was never the doer. She was merely an instrument in the grand design of the cosmos.

A soft breeze whispered through the trees as realization dawned upon her. She bowed her head, a smile breaking through her tears. "I was under the illusion that I controlled my fate," she murmured. "But the truth is, we are all bound by the unseen threads of karma and dharma."

"You spent years believing you were deceived, Draupadi. But tell me—was it deception, or was it the unraveling of a greater truth? You wished to control your fate, to shape it to your will. But destiny is not a script written by mortals—it is the river that flows, carrying you where you need to go, not where you wish to be."

Draupadi's heart pounded. "No. No, Mahadev. I fought, I bled, I suffered. Was that destiny? Was that where I 'needed' to be?" Her voice trembled, anger and grief rising like a storm within her.

Shiva's gaze held hers, unwavering. "The greatest illusion is that we have control. The moment you let go, you will understand—true strength lies in surrender, not in resistance."

She shook her head, her breath ragged. "Surrender?" The word felt foreign, impossible. She had never surrendered—not to her fate, not to her enemies, not even to the gods. How could she?

Her reflection in the river rippled. And in that instant, something shifted.

She saw herself—not as a victim, not as a queen, not as a wife torn between duty and love—but as a soul that had journeyed through lifetimes, learning, growing, becoming.

Her knees buckled. A shuddering breath escaped her lips. She had spent lifetimes fighting, clawing, resisting. But now… now, in this moment, she felt the weight lift.

She closed her eyes. And for the first time in lifetimes, she let go.

A strange peace flooded her being. The battle within her stilled.

She whispered, voice barely above the wind, "I see now, Mahadev. It was never about what I wanted, but what I needed to learn."

Shiva smiled. "And that, my child, is the wisdom of surrender."

Reflection: Beyond the Illusion - When Control Gives Way to Wisdom

Life often makes us believe that control is within our grasp—that through intelligence, strategy, and willpower, we can dictate outcomes. But there are moments when even the most capable, the most powerful, and the most devoted are humbled by forces beyond their reach. These stories reveal that true wisdom does not lie in mastering fate but in recognizing when to surrender to it.

Dr. Anjali spent years believing that skill alone could triumph over destiny. Every successful surgery reinforced her illusion of control, making her believe that life and death were decisions that lay in her hands. But one night, when even her unmatched expertise could not save a young boy, she was forced to confront a truth she had long ignored—she was not the doer. The burden of perfection shattered, and in that moment of helplessness, she found clarity. It was not about controlling fate; it was about serving with everything she had, while knowing that the outcome was never hers to dictate. In that surrender, she discovered peace.

History, too, has witnessed men who believed they could command destiny—only to realize they were merely instruments of forces greater than themselves. Napoleon Bonaparte, the conqueror of Europe, built an empire on the foundation of his ambition, his intellect, and his indomitable will. He had defied monarchies, rewritten maps, and bent nations to his command. But in the frozen wastelands of Russia, he met an enemy he could not defeat— nature itself. As his once-mighty army crumbled, so did the illusion that he was invincible. In those desperate moments of retreat, Napoleon faced the cruelest truth of all: power is fleeting, and control is an illusion. No matter how great the man, no one bends the will of fate.

And then, there are those who mistake devotion for control, believing that prayers and penance can shape destiny to their desires. Nalayani, who later became Draupadi, spent lifetimes yearning for a husband who embodied perfection. She surrendered everything for her wish, believing that unwavering devotion would grant her control over fate. But when she found herself married to not one, but five husbands—each bearing fragments of the divine qualities she had longed for—she realized her folly. Fate had given her what she needed, not what she had wanted. And in that painful, humbling moment, she saw the greater truth: life is not meant to be commanded, only lived with grace.

In all these stories, control was not the answer—it was the illusion. The surgeon, the emperor, and the devoted seeker all faced moments that shattered their belief in their own power. And yet, in that surrender, they found something far greater: wisdom. The wisdom to serve without attachment, to lead without arrogance, to love without possession.

Perhaps that is the greatest lesson of all. Life is not a battle to be won, nor a script to be written by our own hands. It is a river that flows, carrying us where we need to go, not where we wish to be. The only choice we have is whether to resist or to surrender—to fight the current or to trust that it will take us exactly where we are meant to be.

The Illusion of Control: A Moment of Introspection

As you reach the end of this chapter, take a moment to reflect. We often believe that control is the key to success, that with enough effort, intelligence, and willpower, we can shape outcomes to our desire. But what if true wisdom lies not in controlling life, but in knowing when to surrender to forces beyond us? What if the moments when we lose control are the very moments that reveal what truly matters?

- Have you ever believed that mastery over a skill or profession gave you control over life itself, only to be humbled by an outcome beyond your reach?

- Have you ever mistaken power for permanence, only to realize that even the strongest empires can crumble overnight?

- Have you ever prayed for something with unwavering devotion, convinced that your faith could dictate fate, only to find that destiny had its own design?

- Have you ever resisted an inevitable change, fearing that letting go meant failure, only to realize later that surrender brought unexpected clarity?

- Have you ever held onto an identity so tightly that you struggled to see who you were without it?

- Have you ever been so sure of your path, only for life to take an unexpected turn—one that ultimately led you to something far greater?

Because sometimes, control is the greatest illusion of all. The real power lies not in forcing outcomes, but in trusting the flow of life. So, as you move forward, ask yourself—are you still trying to control what was never yours to command, or are you ready to surrender and see where life takes you?

The Strength of Virtue

Bhagavad Gita, Chapter 6, Verse 40.
न हि कल्याणकृत्कश्चिद्दुर्गतिं तात गच्छति॥
(One who engages in virtuous actions never meets
with a bad end.)

Righteousness Never Goes Unrewarded

In life, challenges may seem insurmountable, casting shadows of doubt and fear. Yet, in these moments, a brief pause can bring clarity. It reminds us that our journey is not defined by setbacks but by our choices. The past does not bind us, nor do our struggles dictate our future. No effort made in goodness is ever wasted, and no righteous action leads to ruin.

Crisis often feels like an end, but in truth, it is a passage—a doorway to transformation. The hardships that seem to break us are, in reality, shaping us, urging us to release old limitations and step into something greater. With every challenge, we are given an opportunity—to learn, to grow, and to rise.

Like a river carving new paths after a storm, we too have the ability to reshape our destiny. When we act with integrity, perseverance, and faith, we align ourselves with a force far greater than immediate success or failure. The journey may be difficult, but the universe does not forsake those who walk the path of righteousness. Even when outcomes remain uncertain, the pursuit of virtue ensures that we are always moving forward—never truly lost, never without purpose.

By embracing this understanding, we can see every setback as a lesson, every hardship as preparation, and every moment of doubt as an invitation to trust. For in the grand scheme of existence, no act of goodness goes unanswered, and no soul that walks the path of righteousness is ever abandoned.

The Courage to Walk Away

Maya stood at the door, the suitcase still in her hand, but her heart was no longer heavy. She could feel the tears threatening to spill, but she held them back. The moment was now. She had chosen herself.

Just as she reached for the door handle, Vishesh's voice, raw with desperation, shattered the silence. "Maya, please," he cried, his voice breaking. "You can't leave me. I can't live without you."

She turned, watching him fall to his knees. The man who had once been so confident, so powerful in her eyes, now appeared so small, so broken. His eyes were wide with fear, his hands trembling. "Please don't leave me," he begged, his words nearly inaudible as his voice cracked. "I'll change. I'll do anything. Don't leave me. I love you."

Maya's chest tightened as she saw him—the man who had hurt her so much, now reduced to a shell of the person she once knew. He crawled toward her, his face wet with tears, and before she could react, he grabbed her feet, pressing his forehead to the floor in utter humiliation.

"Maya, please," he sobbed. "I've been a fool. I didn't know what I had until now. I was wrong, I was stupid. Please don't leave me. You're everything to me. You're all I have."

Maya recoiled, her heart aching, but the pain in her chest wasn't the same as it had been before. This wasn't love—it was desperation, manipulation. She pulled her feet away gently, her heart heavy with the realization of how far he had fallen.

Vishesh's hands grasped at the air, his sobs becoming louder, more frantic. "No! Don't leave me! Don't do this!" His voice became a guttural cry, filled with anguish as he began hitting his head against the wall in a fit of rage and self-pity. He threw a chair across the room, smashing it against the wall, his breath ragged and uneven.

"Please, Maya!" He stumbled to his feet, still crying uncontrollably, his hands reaching out in desperation, his eyes pleading with hers. "I can't live without you. You don't understand… you'll never find anyone who loves you like I do. Don't leave me like this. I'll change. I swear I will!"

Maya's heart twisted at the sight of him, but the decision had already been made. She had spent so many years looking for validation, searching for love in a place that could never give it back. She could feel the weight of the years of pain and disappointment—the years she had spent trying to fix him, trying to hold onto something that was never hers to begin with.

"I am not the woman you think I am," Maya said quietly, her voice steady despite the emotional turmoil inside her. "I'm not the one who can be fixed by your empty promises. You've hurt me too much, Vishesh. And this... this isn't love. This is control."

Her words stung him deeply, but he didn't seem to hear them. He was lost in his tears, his panic consuming him. He collapsed on the floor, sobbing uncontrollably, hitting his fists against the ground as if the pain would somehow make her stay.

Maya's hand trembled as she reached for the door once more. She could feel her chest tightening with grief, but also with the realization that she was stronger than she had ever been before. She wasn't walking away from love—she was walking toward it, toward herself.

With one last look at him, broken and pleading, she stepped out into the unknown, her heart heavy but resolute. For the first time in years, she felt like she was breathing again. The door clicked behind her, the finality of it ringing in her ears.

And though she didn't know what awaited her, she knew she was choosing herself. No longer would she live in the shadow of his promises or his threats. She was free.

Two years had passed since that fateful day when Maya had walked away from everything she had known—away from the suffocating weight of betrayal and pain. As the airplane soared into the sky, her heart fluttered with a mix of excitement and quiet satisfaction. The familiar hum of the engines was a reminder of how far she had come.

She glanced at the little girl sitting beside her, her four-year-old adopted daughter, who had her small hands pressed against the window, gazing out in wonder at the clouds. Maya smiled softly, feeling an overwhelming sense of gratitude. This child—her daughter—was the new beginning, the joy she never knew she needed.

The memories of the past felt distant now. There was no longer a yearning for validation, no more fear of how society would view her. She wasn't defined by the expectations of others, not by the roles of a wife or a perfect woman. She was Maya, and she was enough. She was finally living for herself, and for the first time in a long while, she felt free.

As the plane made its way toward Barcelona, a place she had once dreamed of visiting with Vishesh, she didn't feel the sting of that lost dream. It had morphed into something better. She wasn't alone in the physical sense—she had her daughter beside her—but more importantly, she was no longer alone in her spirit. She had discovered a happiness that was her own, independent of anyone else's approval.

Maya leaned back in her seat, closing her eyes for a moment. She thought about the 30 seconds that had changed everything—the stillness that allowed her to finally make the choice to let go, to let herself breathe again. Those moments of clarity, when the weight of fear and doubt had been replaced with the power to move forward, had been the catalyst.

Now, as she gazed out the window, she realized that the journey ahead was not just one of physical travel, but a journey into herself. She wasn't just visiting Barcelona; she was living in the moment, embracing the freedom she had fought so hard to find.

She held her daughter's hand, squeezing it gently, and whispered, "We're going to be okay. We're going to live this life on our terms."

And for the first time, Maya truly believed it.

There was no longer any concern about what others would think. She no longer feared being judged or pitied. No longer did she feel the weight of expectations to be a perfect wife or a woman who fit neatly into society's boxes. She was a mother. She was a woman who had taken control of her destiny, and she was at peace with the choices she had made.

Maya smiled softly as the plane dipped into the clouds, making its way toward Barcelona, a place she had once hoped to visit with Vishesh. But today, she didn't feel sadness or regret. Instead, she felt gratitude. Gratitude for the life she had reclaimed. Gratitude for the 30 seconds that had given her the strength to walk away and choose herself. And above all, gratitude for the journey that had brought her here, to this moment—content, fulfilled, and unburdened.

Draupadi: From Humiliation to Retribution

The great hall of Hastinapura trembled, not with sound, but with the weight of unspoken truths. The scent of burning oil lamps mingled with the quiet rustle of silk, but for Draupadi, there was only the stench of betrayal. The walls, carved with the deeds of past kings, bore witness to an atrocity that history itself would shudder to recall.

The Pandavas had been stripped of everything—their kingdom, their wealth, and their freedom—all lost to a game of dice rigged by Shakuni's cunning hands. Yudhishthira, bound by his unwavering faith in dharma, had walked into the trap blindly. Yet, the final wager had been the cruellest. Draupadi—not a jewel, not a land, but a living, breathing queen—had been staked and lost. A murmur had passed through the court when her name was uttered as a bet, but none had dared stop the horror from unfolding.

Dushasana dragged her into the assembly, his fingers tangled in her long, dark hair, yanking her forward like a hunter displaying his prey. She stumbled but did not fall, though her body screamed in protest. The silken fabric of her saree had torn in the struggle, slipping from her shoulders, leaving her vulnerable before the sea of lustful, indifferent, and averted gazes.

A roar of laughter shattered the silence. Dushasana, emboldened, his grip cruel, seized what little remained of her dignity. The air was thick with jeers. The men who claimed to uphold dharma sat frozen, their silence an abyss more damning than words.

Draupadi lifted her chin, defiance flashing in her tear-rimmed eyes. "Is this the court of Hastinapura?" Her voice rang out, raw, unyielding. "A court where righteousness is measured in silence? Where honor bends before power?" She turned to the elders—Bhishma, Drona, Kripacharya. "You, who have sworn your lives to dharma, is this how you honor it? Will you let a woman be torn apart before your very eyes?"

No answer. Only the heavy weight of shame, the shifting of gazes, the unbearable hush of cowards.

Her eyes burned into Yudhishthira—her husband, her king, the man who had staked her like a possession. "Tell me, my lord," her voice trembled, the betrayal cutting deeper than any wound, "do you still believe that dharma guides you? Or is your dharma but a hollow excuse, a shield behind which you hide your own helplessness?"

Yudhishthira flinched but did not answer. Inside him, a storm raged. He had always believed that righteousness was above all, but today, that belief lay in shambles at his feet. He had thought he was protecting dharma, but had he merely been protecting his own sense of duty at the cost of justice? Had he become a prisoner of his own virtue? The weight of his silence crushed him, yet he could not bring himself to break it. "I thought I was doing what was right," he whispered finally, his voice barely audible. "But perhaps I have failed you, Draupadi."

She turned to Bhima, her voice a dagger. "And you, Bhima, who swore to protect me with your strength. Where is that strength now? Were your words mere drunken boasts, spoken in the heat of bravado but abandoned in the face of duty?"

Bhima's fists clenched, his breath ragged, but still, he did not move. His voice, raw with restrained fury, escaped through gritted teeth. "If I rise now, I will tear them apart limb by limb. But my hands are tied by my elder's word. And yet, I swear—one day, Draupadi, I will drink Dushasana's blood for this."

Her gaze swept over Arjuna. "And you, Arjuna? The warrior who conquered the world with his bow. Where is the man who won me at my swayamvar? Do you only raise your Gandiva against enemies on the battlefield, but not against injustice in your own home?"

Arjuna's face darkened with pain. "I am bound by dharma, Draupadi. I am helpless before my brother's word. But know this—I would rather burn in hell than forget this day. The arrows of my bow will one day answer for this silence."

Her piercing eyes turned to Nakula and Sahadeva. "And you? The sons of Madri? You who pride yourselves on honor and virtue? Does your righteousness allow you to watch in silence while your wife is humiliated? Did you ever truly love me, or was I only an object for your desire, a trophy to be shared?"

Nakula's voice was hoarse, his head bent low. "I would rather die than see you suffer, but dharma... dharma holds my hands captive. Yet I promise, Draupadi, we will reclaim your honor."

Sahadeva, always the quiet one, spoke in a voice that trembled with pain. "A time will come when these sins will be answered for. And when that time comes, we will not be silent."

Then, her gaze fell upon another—Karna. The man she had once admired. The man whose words had cut her down before, branding her unworthy, undeserving. Yet, she had seen the flicker of conflict in his eyes.

"Karna," she whispered, and in that whisper was not accusation, but something raw and devastating. "You, too, have been humiliated. You know the sting of rejection, the pain of being cast aside. And yet, you stand among those who strip me of my dignity?"

Karna clenched his jaw, his fingers curling into a fist. He had cast his lot with Duryodhana. He had mocked her. But now, standing before her unwavering gaze, something within him cracked. A part of him screamed to stop this madness, but he did nothing. He had chosen his side, and his silence was its price. And yet, deep inside, he wondered—was he truly a warrior of dharma, or had he allowed his bitterness to turn him into its enemy? In the pit of his soul, a voice whispered that he had become the very thing he had once despised.

Draupadi's heart pounded. The walls of the great hall seemed to close in, suffocating her in an ocean of despair. A single thought clawed at her mind— Is there no justice in this world? Does dharma exist only in fragile words?

And then—in that abyss, in that breath, something shifted.

She closed her eyes. Not in surrender. Not in prayer. But in defiance.

She sought no salvation from gods, no miracle to save her. Instead, she turned inward, into the depths of her own being. The shlokas she had heard, the ideals she had upheld, rose like a whisper from the ashes of her despair.

Her faith did not waver. If dharma was real, it did not exist in the silence of those who claimed to uphold it. It existed in her own stand, in her refusal to be broken. And she swore—this injustice would not be forgotten.

A storm was brewing.

The court of Hastinapura believed the moment had passed, that the humiliation inflicted upon her would be buried in history. But karma is not blind, nor does it forget.

That day, a vow was taken—one that would shape the fate of the kingdom.

Bhima clenched his fists and roared, "I vow that I will tear open Dushasana's chest and drink his blood for what he has done to you!"

Arjuna swore, "I will ensure that Karna falls to the ground, never to rise again, for the words he spoke against you!"

Nakula and Sahadeva promised, "The day of reckoning will come, and none who wronged you shall escape it!"

Even Yudhishthira, bound by his ideals, stood witness to the fire that had been ignited that day—the fire that would burn Hastinapura to its roots.

And in time, dharma answered.

The Pandavas, once humiliated, rose again—not as exiles, not as defeated men, but as warriors who reclaimed their honor. On the battlefield of Kurukshetra, justice was delivered.

Bhima crushed Dushasana's ribs, tearing them apart, fulfilling his oath as the Kaurava's blood spilled upon the earth. Karna, the warrior who once mocked her, fell lifeless, struck down by Arjuna's arrows. The court that remained silent that day was silenced forever by the war that followed.

Draupadi, who had once stood alone, dishonoured in that hall, stood again—not as a victim, but as the queen of a kingdom reclaimed, a testament to the truth that righteousness never goes unrewarded.

Hastinapura had ignored her cries, but dharma had listened.

And justice had prevailed.

Orpheus & Eurydice: The Whisper That Wasn't Heard

Orpheus was no ordinary man. Son of Calliope, the muse of epic poetry, his music was a divine gift. With his lyre, an instrument given by Apollo, Orpheus wove melodies so enchanting that rivers changed course, trees leaned closer, and wild beasts grew tame. Revered across the land, his heart belonged only to Eurydice.

Eurydice, a beautiful and kind-hearted nymph, was his soulmate. Their love seemed to transcend the world itself. Their wedding day was joyous, blessed by nature. Yet fate was cruel. As Eurydice danced through the meadow, she stepped upon a venomous serpent. The bite was swift, the poison merciless. Before Orpheus could reach her, she collapsed—lifeless, her soul claimed by the underworld.

Orpheus fell to his knees, grasping at her as if he could will warmth back into her. He called her name, voice cracking with desperation. But her skin had grown cold. The world, once vibrant, blurred into grief. Birds no longer sang, the breeze withered, and even the sun seemed to dim. His cry of anguish was so raw that the heavens themselves seemed to shudder.

But grief was not enough. Orpheus could not accept this cruel separation. His love was too deep, his pain unbearable. He resolved to do the unthinkable—descend into the underworld and plead for her return. With his lyre in hand, he crossed into the realm of Hades. The River Styx loomed before him. Charon, the boatman, hesitated, but the first note of Orpheus' song moved him to pity. He granted passage.

Before the throne of Hades and Persephone, Orpheus played. His music poured forth his grief, love, and longing. Each note spoke of the emptiness Eurydice had left behind. The underworld wept—the tormented souls, the merciless Furies, even Persephone, who knew the pain of longing.

Orpheus fell to his knees before Hades. "I ask for nothing but mercy," he implored. "If love has meaning, if devotion holds power, let Eurydice return with me. If she must return to you one day, so be it—but not yet."

A heavy silence filled the air. Hades' gaze was unreadable. Then, after what felt like eternity, he spoke.

"You may take her," Hades declared. "But only on one condition."

Orpheus held his breath.

"She will follow you," Hades continued. "But you must not look back until you have crossed into the world of the living. If you turn, she will be lost forever."

Hope and dread filled Orpheus. He agreed.

The path was long, winding through an abyss where lost souls whispered regrets. The silence pressed upon Orpheus like an invisible weight. Each step echoed. Was she truly behind him? Or had the gods tricked him?

"Eurydice," he whispered. No reply. His pulse quickened. Was he alone? What if they had deceived him? Doubt seeped in like poison. The surface was close—just a few more steps. Trust.

Then his mind faltered. What if Hades mocked him? She was dead—how could she follow? Had he been a fool, his love mere entertainment for the gods? He slowed. The air grew colder.

"Orpheus," a voice, delicate as a falling petal, reached him. His breath hitched.

"I am here, my love," Eurydice reassured. "Do not doubt me."

Her voice was soft yet urgent. "Orpheus, please. You must trust me. I am with you. Just as I have always been. Do not let fear cloud your heart."

She sensed his hesitation. "You once told me that love is not about seeing, but feeling," she continued. "Feel me, Orpheus. I am yours. Believe in me."

The silence stretched between them. Every fiber of her being willed him forward. "If you love me, do not look back," she whispered. "Choose trust over doubt."

But doubt was relentless. At the threshold, where the light of the living world beckoned, uncertainty consumed him. The choice—to believe or to question, to trust or to waver—collided in a single moment. And in that instant, he lost it all.

He turned.

A breath. A gasp. A whisper of wind.

Eurydice's eyes widened in shock, her lips parting to cry out. But no sound came. Her fingers reached for him—then the shadows swallowed her whole.

"Orpheus!" Her voice rang with agony. "Why? Why did you not trust me? Did you doubt our love?"

Her hands, inches from his grasp, faded. Orpheus lunged forward, but it was too late. The abyss claimed her, silencing her pleas. A final whisper of his name lingered before vanishing into the void.

Orpheus fell to his knees, hands grasping at empty air. He had doubted. And in that doubt, he had lost her forever.

His mind reeled, a storm of regret crashing upon his soul. Why did I not trust? Why did I falter? Those thirty seconds consumed him, swallowed his reason. His fear had outweighed faith. He could still hear her voice, still feel the ghost of her presence. The torment was unbearable—had he not loved her enough to believe?

He clutched his lyre. Was my love not strong enough? Was my faith so weak?

Eurydice's words echoed. Why, Orpheus? Did you not trust me? Did you not trust yourself?

The choice had been his, and he had chosen wrong. Now, he was alone.

Eurydice was gone—not merely lost, but erased, as if the universe itself had reclaimed her. The space she once occupied felt hollow, yet thick with an absence so profound it crushed the air around him. He could still see the way her form had blurred, dissolving into the shadows, her desperate hands reaching, reaching—only to be swallowed whole. The underworld had taken her back, severing her from him with a finality that was both cruel and inevitable. The echoes of her last whisper clung to the silence, fading into nothingness. And Orpheus, standing at the threshold of light, realized he had never truly known what it meant to be alone—until now.

He wandered the earth, his music now filled with sorrow. And though the world still listened, though rivers still wept for him, Orpheus knew—without Eurydice, the melody of his soul had been lost.

Yet grief was not his only legacy. He had changed. His heart bore the weight of trust broken, but also the understanding of what it meant to truly believe. He no longer wandered aimlessly, consumed by sorrow; instead, he sought meaning in his loss. His music, once filled with lament, transformed—carrying the wisdom of trust, the pain of doubt, and the resilience of love. His story became a timeless reminder—that love demands faith, and sometimes, the greatest tragedies are those we bring upon ourselves. But even in loss, one can choose to rise, to change, to truly understand what it means to believe.

Orpheus had not used those thirty seconds wisely. In the end, his doubt and distrust had overpowered his faith in love, in Eurydice. Perhaps, in those fleeting moments, it was not fate but his own hesitation that sealed their doom. Perhaps love, no matter how deep, could not survive the weight of uncertainty. Had he trusted just a little longer, believed just a little stronger, she would have been his once more. But doubt had stolen his resolve, and in doing so, had stolen her from him forever. And for that, he paid the ultimate price—a lifetime of regret, a song forever unfinished, and a love lost to the abyss.

Reflection: The Strength of Virtue

Virtue is often tested in moments of crisis—when the easy path calls, when doubt whispers, and when surrender seems inevitable. But true virtue is not just about moral ideals; it is about the strength to act in alignment with them, even when the cost is high. The stories of Maya, Draupadi, and Orpheus reveal that righteousness is not merely a principle—it is a force that demands courage, conviction, and faith.

Maya spent years trapped in the illusion of love, believing that patience and sacrifice would mend what was broken. But love, she learned, is not endurance in the face of betrayal—it is the strength to walk away when dignity is at stake. In the moment that mattered most, she chose herself. She chose to break free from the weight of empty promises and define her own future. The path was uncertain, but virtue demanded that she honour her own worth. And in that choice, she found the happiness she had once thought impossible.

History, too, has shown how virtue must often stand-alone before it is vindicated. Draupadi stood in the grand court of Hastinapura, surrounded by silence, shame, and cowardice. She could have begged. She could have surrendered. But she chose to defy. When no one spoke for her, she spoke for herself. And though justice was not immediate, her righteousness was not in vain. The humiliation she endured did not break her—it forged the fire that would one day bring down a kingdom. The silence of that day was deafening, but the echoes of her resistance shaped the war that restored dharma.

Yet virtue does not only demand courage—it demands trust. Orpheus, despite his love, faltered in his faith. He had fought against the impossible, defied death itself, and won back Eurydice with the power of his devotion. But in the final moment, when all he had to do was believe, doubt overtook him. That single moment of hesitation cost him everything. His love was real, but his faith was not strong enough to sustain it. Virtue is not just about the battles we fight—it is about the choices we make in the quiet, when no one is watching, when the test is not of strength but of trust.

In all these stories, virtue was not an abstract ideal—it was a trial by fire. It was the unwavering belief in self-worth, the resilience to stand against injustice, and the faith to hold on when doubt beckoned. Strength is not just in the ability to endure—it is in the courage to act, to trust, and to uphold what is right, even when the path ahead is unknown. Because in the end, virtue is not always rewarded immediately, but it is never in vain.

The Unshakable Power of Virtue: A Moment of Introspection

As you reach the end of this chapter, take a moment to reflect. Strength is often mistaken for force, for dominance, for winning against all odds. But true strength—the kind that lasts, the kind that defines destinies—lies in virtue. It is the ability to hold your ground when the world pushes you to compromise, to trust when doubt is easier, and to choose righteousness even when it costs you everything.

- Have you ever stayed in a situation, believing patience was strength, only to realize that walking away required greater courage?

- Have you ever witnessed injustice and remained silent, convincing yourself that it was not your battle to fight?

- Have you ever doubted your path, questioning whether doing the right thing was worth the struggle?

- Have you ever allowed fear to dictate your choices, only to regret not having trusted yourself more?

- Have you ever compromised your values to avoid conflict, only to later feel the weight of that decision?

- Have you ever been tested by life, where virtue seemed like a burden rather than a guiding force?

Because strength is not in the absence of struggle; it is in the choices we make despite it. Virtue is not always rewarded immediately, nor does it always shield us from pain. But it ensures that when the storm passes, we stand unshaken—free, whole, and at peace with the choices we made.

So, as you move forward, ask yourself—when your moment of choice comes, will you have the courage to stand firm in your virtue? Will you trust that righteousness, though difficult, never truly goes unrewarded?

The Illusion of Identity

Bhagavad Gita, Chapter 12, Verse 17:

न मे द्वेष्टि न काङ्क्षति।

(One who neither hates nor desires is at peace.)

Releasing the False Self to Embrace Truth

In the Bhagavad Gita, Lord Krishna teaches that peace arises from shedding the burdens of ego and desire. The mind, clouded by worldly attachments and the need to define oneself through external labels, is far from peace. In this chapter, we explore how the 30-second pause can allow us to break free from the illusion of identity and reconnect with our true self.

From the moment we enter the world, we are given labels—names, roles, identities shaped by society, expectations, and personal ambition. We define ourselves by what we achieve, how we are perceived, and the validation we receive. But beneath these layers of identity, beyond the need for approval or distinction, lies our true self—untouched by ego, unaffected by external recognition. The challenge is that we spend so much of our lives holding onto these labels that we forget who we are without them. In those rare moments of stillness, when we pause long enough to let go of pride, resentment, and craving, we glimpse something profound—peace not tied to success, validation, or comparison, but to an unshakable inner truth.

The Awakening: A Son's Return to What Matters

Shibhya sat at his desk in his plush corner office, the floor-to-ceiling windows offering a panoramic view of the bustling city skyline. His desk was a shrine to his success—awards, certificates, and photographs of him shaking hands with influential figures. At 35, he was the youngest vice president in his company's history. His peers envied him, his parents were proud, and the world seemed to affirm that he had "made it."

Yet, something gnawed at him. In the stillness of the night, when the city's roar dulled to a whisper, an emptiness clawed at his heart. His phone was filled with unread messages, but none that truly mattered. The laughter of his childhood seemed like a distant echo, drowned out by the constant hum of emails, deadlines, and board meetings.

One evening, as he reviewed a critical presentation for an upcoming client meeting, his phone buzzed. The screen lit up with his mother's name.

For a moment, he hesitated. It wasn't unusual for her to call, but he had ignored many of her calls in the past, brushing them off with promises of "I'll call you later." He glanced at the clock. He had another hour before his next meeting.

"Maybe later," he thought, his hand hovering over the mute button. But something made him pause. Her name on the screen stirred a faint ache in his chest. With a sigh, he picked up the call.

"Ma?" he answered, his voice carrying the faint impatience of someone too preoccupied.

"Shibhya, beta, I need to talk to you," her voice trembled, each word weighted with emotion.

Shibhya's fingers instinctively moved to his laptop trackpad, his eyes scanning through an email notification. "What is it, Ma? Is everything okay?" he asked, his tone brisk.

"Shibhya… I… I went to the doctor two months ago," she began, her voice cracking. "They found something. I have cancer."

The words struck like a thunderclap, scattering his thoughts. "What?" he asked, leaning back in his chair as if the distance could soften the blow. "Why didn't you tell me earlier?"

"I didn't want to disturb you," she said, her voice laced with guilt. "You've been so busy building your career. I didn't want to be a burden."

"A burden?" Shibhya's voice rose, tinged with disbelief. "You're my mother! How could you even think that?"

"I see your life, Shibhya. You're so successful, so important. I didn't want to pull you away from that," she replied softly.

The weight of her words bore down on him. His mother's voice, once a source of comfort, now filled him with guilt. He had spent years chasing accolades and titles, oblivious to the growing distance between him and his family. And now, the very foundation of his identity felt like a fragile facade.

Later that night, Shibhya sat alone in his apartment, staring blankly at the city lights. His mother's words echoed in his mind: "I didn't want to be a burden."

When had his priorities become so skewed? He thought about the nights he had ignored her calls, the excuses he made to avoid visiting home. He told himself it was all for the greater good—building a life that would make his parents proud. But what good was it if they felt neglected in the process?

His thoughts spiraled as he replayed their conversation.

"Why didn't I call her more often?" he asked himself, his voice trembling. "Why didn't I make time?"

He remembered his childhood vividly—the way his mother would stay up late to help him with school projects, the warmth of her hands as she applied balm to his forehead when he had a fever. She had been his anchor, his safe space, and yet, in his quest to "succeed," he had let that bond fray.

His chest tightened, a sharp pang of realization cutting through him. He had spent so much time proving his worth to the world, but in doing so, had he forgotten what truly mattered? His identity—his name, his titles, his achievements—felt meaningless in that moment. He wasn't just Shibhya, the youngest VP. He was a son. A son who had forgotten how to love the one person who had loved him unconditionally.

The next morning, Shibhya made the decision to take a leave of absence from work. It wasn't easy—his team relied on him, and there were critical projects in the pipeline. But for the first time in years, his career didn't feel like the most important thing in his life.

He booked a flight to his hometown that same day. As the plane descended, the familiar landscape brought a wave of nostalgia. The bustling streets, the aroma of street food, the laughter of children playing in narrow lanes—it all felt like a world he had left behind.

At the hospital, he found his mother resting in a chair by the window. The sight of her frail figure sent a pang through his heart. She looked up as he entered, her face lighting up with a mixture of surprise and joy.

"Shibhya! You didn't have to come so soon," she said, attempting to rise.

He rushed to her side, placing a gentle hand on her shoulder. "Ma, please. Don't say that. I'm here now," he said, his voice cracking.

For the next few days, Shibhya stayed by her side, rediscovering the essence of his family's love. He listened to stories of her youth, laughed at her sharp wit, and found solace in the simplicity of their conversations.

But the guilt lingered. One evening, as they sat together watching the sunset, he finally voiced the thoughts that had been tormenting him.

"Ma, I've been a terrible son," he said, staring at the horizon. "I was so blinded by my ambition that I forgot what really mattered."

She reached for his hand, her touch as comforting as ever. "Shibhya, we all get caught up in life. What matters is that you're here now. That's what counts."

"But I wasted so much time," he said, his voice barely above a whisper. "Time I can never get back."

"Then don't waste any more," she said firmly. "The past is gone, beta. What you do with the present is what defines you."

As the night deepened, Shibhya settled into a chair next to his mother's hospital bed. The rhythmic beeping of the monitors, the soft hum of the air conditioning, and the distant murmur of hospital staff filled the silence. He watched his mother sleep, her breathing steady yet fragile. The exhaustion of the past few days weighed on him, and before he realized it, his eyes drifted shut.

In the quiet of his subconscious, his mother's words echoed:

"What you do with the present is what defines you."

A scene unfolded in his mind—not the boardrooms, not the awards, not the deals he had closed. Instead, he saw himself as a child, running into his mother's arms after school, his tiny fingers gripping her hand, his laughter unrestrained. He saw the joy in her eyes when he brought home his first school trophy, the pride in her voice when she introduced him to neighbors.

When had he let go of that version of himself?

Then, in those first 30 seconds upon waking, reality hit him with staggering clarity.

His identity was not tied to his job title or achievements. It was not measured by how many people admired him at work or how impressive his

LinkedIn profile looked. His true identity was in his ability to love, to connect, and to be present for the people who mattered most.

For the first time in years, he saw through the illusion. The race for external validation had led him nowhere. In chasing an identity crafted by ambition and status, he had almost lost the most authentic part of himself—the son who once believed that love was more important than success.

He sat up, rubbing his temples as the weight of the realization settled in. His mother stirred slightly but remained asleep. Looking at her peaceful face, he made a silent vow.

He would no longer chase the illusion of success at the cost of his relationships. He would no longer measure his worth by titles and achievements, but by the depth of his connections and the presence he brought to those he loved.

And he would start with her.

A quiet sense of peace washed over him. The illusion of identity had shattered, and in its place was something far more real—love, connection, and a purpose that transcended ambition.

For the first time in years, he didn't feel like the youngest vice president of his company. He felt like a son who had finally come home.

Beyond the Illusion: The Search for Truth

Thousands of years ago, in the prosperous kingdom of Kapilavastu, a young prince lived in the lap of luxury. Siddhartha Gautama, heir to King Śuddhodana, had never known hardship. His father, determined to keep him shielded from suffering, surrounded him with beauty and pleasure. Musicians played sweet melodies in his court, scholars imparted the finest education, and his every need was met before he even had to ask. The prince had a loving wife, Yasodhara, and a newborn son, Rahula. His life, by all worldly standards, was perfect.

Yet, something within him remained unsettled.

As days passed, Siddhartha felt suffocated by the confines of his palace. His heart yearned for something beyond the silken robes and grand feasts. He often found himself standing at the palace balcony, gazing toward the horizon. What lay beyond these walls? What truths remained hidden from his view?

One fateful day, his curiosity led him to venture beyond the golden gates. Accompanied by his charioteer, Channa, Siddhartha rode into the bustling streets of the city. There, he encountered four sights that shook him to his core: an old man, frail and bent with age; a sick man, groaning in agony; a corpse, lifeless and still; and a wandering ascetic, clad in rags but radiating an aura of peace.

For the first time, Siddhartha truly *saw* the world. Suffering was not an anomaly; it was an undeniable truth of existence. And no amount of wealth or power could shield him from it. That night, as he lay beside Yasodhara, listening to Rahula's soft breathing, an unbearable restlessness consumed him.

In those quiet moments before dawn, Siddhartha realized that his identity as a prince, a husband, and a father was a mask. Beneath it, he was just a soul, burdened by ignorance. Could he continue playing this role, knowing it was built upon illusion? Could he ignore the suffering he had now witnessed? He closed his eyes and exhaled. This was his moment—the decision that would define his life.

Rising silently, Siddhartha walked to where Channa awaited with his horse, Kanthaka. He paused, looking back at his wife and son one last time. A war raged within him. Was he abandoning them? Or was he setting them free from the burden of a man who could no longer live a lie? His heart ached, but he knew the truth. If he stayed, he would never be at peace. Clutching Kanthaka's reins, he whispered, "Let go."

And he did.

Under the cover of night, Siddhartha rode into the wilderness. At the edge of the forest, he dismounted. With steady hands, he cut his long locks, shedding the last symbol of his princely identity. He exchanged his silk garments for a simple robe. Turning to Channa, he said, "Go back. This is a journey I must take alone."

Siddhartha wandered through forests, seeking wisdom from ascetics and sages. He subjected himself to severe austerities, believing self-denial would bring enlightenment. He fasted for days, reduced himself to mere skin and bones, meditated through storms, and endured suffering beyond measure. But instead of clarity, he found himself teetering on the edge of death.

One day, weakened and exhausted, Siddhartha collapsed by a riverbank. A kind-hearted village girl, Sujata, saw him and offered a bowl of rice milk. As he ate, a realization dawned upon him: extreme suffering was no more a path to wisdom than indulgence had been. He had been trapped in another illusion. There had to be another way—a middle path.

Determined, he made his way to Bodh Gaya, where he sat beneath a Bodhi tree. He vowed, "I will not rise until I have found the truth." Months passed in deep meditation, his mind unwavering in its pursuit of enlightenment.

Then, sensing the nearing of his awakening, Mara, the lord of illusion, appeared. He whispered doubts into Siddhartha's mind: Who are you to seek enlightenment? Turn back. You are just a man. He conjured temptations, sent terrifying visions, and unleashed an army of demons. But Siddhartha remained unmoved. He had let go of fear. Let go of doubt. Let go of desire.

Then, as the first rays of dawn touched the earth, clarity descended upon him. The illusions shattered. He saw the cycle of suffering, the cause of attachment, and the path to liberation. In that moment, Siddhartha became the Buddha—the awakened one.

Years later, Buddha returned to Kapilavastu. The city that once celebrated his birth now buzzed with whispers. He was no longer the prince they had known. Draped in a saffron robe, barefoot and serene, he walked through the streets, his gaze steady.

His father, King Śuddhodana, was the first to confront him. "Why did you do this? You were destined to be a king, yet you abandoned your throne!"

Buddha smiled gently. "Father, a kingdom built on illusion is no kingdom at all. True peace is not found in gold and power, but in wisdom."

Then came Yasodhara. Her voice trembled. "Did we mean so little to you? You left without a word. You left Rahula without a father."

Buddha's gaze softened. "I did not leave out of neglect, Yasodhara, but out of necessity. I had to find the truth—not just for myself, but for all who suffer."

Tears welled in her eyes. "And what of Rahula?"

A small voice interrupted. "Father."

Rahula, now a young boy, stood before him. Buddha knelt and held his son's hands. "Rahula, I have found a path free from suffering. If you wish, I will teach you."

Rahula hesitated, then nodded. "Teach me."

The palace that once felt like a cage now felt like a distant memory. Buddha had relinquished everything: his name, his title, his past. And in return, he had found something greater—a truth untainted by identity, a peace beyond desire and hatred.

His journey was not one of abandonment, but of liberation. And his story remains a timeless lesson: When we let go of who we think we are, we uncover the truth of who we have always been.

King Henry III: The Birth of a New Order

The 13th century was a turbulent time in England. The feudal system was under strain, and the power of the monarchy faced growing challenges from the barons and nobility. King Henry III, who reigned from 1216 to 1272, inherited the throne at the tender age of nine after the death of his father, King John. His early reign was marked by regency governance, but as he grew older, Henry sought to assert his authority.

King Henry III was deeply devoted to religion, art, and architecture, believing that his rule was divinely sanctioned. Unlike his warrior predecessors, he lacked military prowess and instead sought to define his legacy through grand construction projects, particularly the rebuilding of Westminster Abbey in the Gothic style. This extravagant vision, while culturally significant, came at a steep financial cost. His continuous lavish spending on religious and artistic endeavours drained the royal treasury, forcing him to levy heavy taxes on the nobility and commoners alike.

At the same time, Henry's increasing reliance on foreign advisors and courtiers, particularly his Lusignan half-brothers and other foreign allies, alienated the English barons. These foreign influences dominated royal decision-making, securing lands and privileges at the expense of native English lords. The barons, who had long expected to hold a central role in governance, found themselves side-lined.

One of the most prominent figures opposing Henry's rule was Simon de Montfort, a nobleman of French descent who had initially been a loyal supporter of the king. However, disillusioned by Henry's favouritism toward foreign advisors and his disregard for baronial rights, Simon became a staunch advocate for reform. He led the barons in drafting the Provisions of Oxford in 1258, a set of reforms that sought to limit the king's power and establish a parliamentary system. Henry's refusal to fully accept these provisions led to civil war, known as the Second Barons' War.

Throughout this period of turmoil, another key figure in Henry's court was William de Valence, his half-brother and one of his most trusted advisors. Unlike Henry, William was a skilled military strategist, fiercely loyal to the monarchy, and deeply committed to restoring the king's authority through force. Yet, even he recognized the delicate nature of the crisis and often urged Henry to negotiate with the barons rather than rely solely on suppression. But Henry, blinded by his belief in the divine right of kings, repeatedly dismissed these warnings, underestimating the strength of the opposition.

As the rebellion escalated, the once-powerful King Henry III found himself increasingly isolated. His faith in absolute monarchy had left him vulnerable, and his inability to compromise had turned even once-loyal nobles against him. The war reached a turning point in 1264 at the Battle of Lewes, where Henry suffered a humiliating defeat at the hands of Montfort's forces. Captured and forced to submit to the barons' demands, the king became little more than a figurehead under Montfort's control.

Now, in the dimly lit chamber of the Tower of London, Henry sat alone, the weight of his crown pressing heavily on his brow. The once-proud monarch, who had once ruled with unchecked authority, now bore the marks of age and defeat. His robes, once symbols of majesty, felt like chains binding him to a role he no longer knew how to fulfill. The vision of kingship he had clung to so tightly had crumbled, leaving behind the stark realization that power—without the wisdom to wield it—was nothing more than an illusion. Outside the thick stone walls, the city of London murmured with unrest. Simon de Montfort's victory at the Battle of Lewes had not just humiliated the king; it had shattered the illusion of absolute monarchy. The barons' demands for reform had grown louder, and Henry's son, Prince Edward, had been taken hostage. The kingdom he had sworn to protect now felt like a distant dream.

As Henry stared at the flickering candle on the table before him, memories flooded his mind. He thought of his coronation, the cheers of the people, the weight of the scepter in his hands. He had been so young, so full of hope. "I was meant to be their shepherd," he whispered, his voice cracking. "How did it come to this?"

The door creaked open, and his trusted advisor, William de Valence, entered. "Your Majesty, the barons demand an audience tomorrow. They wish to finalize the terms of your surrender."

Henry's hand tightened around the armrest of his chair. "Surrender," he said bitterly. "Is that what they call it? Stripping a king of his crown and binding him in chains?"

"Your Majesty," William began cautiously, "it is not the crown that makes a king. It is the wisdom to know when to fight and when to yield."

Henry's gaze hardened. "Yield? Have I not yielded enough? They've taken my lands, my authority, my son. What more do they want?"

William hesitated, then said softly, "Perhaps they want you to see, Sire. To see beyond the crown and the throne. To see the people you've sworn to serve."

Henry dismissed him with a wave of his hand. "Leave me," he said curtly. William bowed and exited, leaving the king alone with his thoughts.

That night, sleep eluded Henry. He paced the chamber, his mind a battlefield of conflicting emotions. "A king without power is no king at all," he thought. Yet, another voice whispered, "But what is power if it brings only discord and suffering?"

He thought of his son, Edward, brave and headstrong, now a prisoner because of his father's stubbornness. "Did I let my pride become my prison?" he muttered. "Did I cling to the throne so tightly that I forgot why I sat upon it in the first place?"

He thought of his wife, Eleanor, who had stood by him through every storm. "She sees my failures and yet remains. Is that not love? Or does she stay only because duty binds her?"

He thought of the crown, that cold, lifeless object that had dictated his entire life. He picked it up and stared at it, turning it over in his hands. "This? This is what I have fought for? A piece of gold and jewels?"

In that moment, the door opened slightly, and Eleanor stepped in. She looked at him with quiet sadness. "Henry," she said gently, "what do you fear more—losing your kingdom, or losing yourself?"

Her words struck him like a blow. He looked at her, then back at the crown. Slowly, he placed it down. "Perhaps I have already lost myself," he admitted.

The next morning, Henry entered the hall where Simon de Montfort and the barons awaited him. The room was tense, the air thick with anticipation. As Henry took his seat, he looked around at the faces of his adversaries. He saw not enemies, but men fighting for what they believed was right.

Simon de Montfort stood. "Your Majesty," he began, "we are here to restore balance to the kingdom. This is not about dethroning you but about creating a system where justice prevails. Will you listen to reason?"

For a moment, Henry said nothing. The room seemed to hold its breath. Then, he rose slowly from his chair. "I have spent my life believing that the crown gave me power," he said, his voice steady but tinged with sorrow. "But power without wisdom is a curse. I see that now."

A hush fell over the hall. Then, slowly, Simon nodded. "Then let us build a kingdom where wisdom guides us all."

The events that followed forever changed the course of England's governance. Simon de Montfort, now effectively ruling in Henry's name, summoned a council in 1265 that included not only barons and church leaders but also representatives from towns and boroughs—a radical shift that laid the foundation for what would later become the House of Commons.

The illusion of absolute monarchy had shattered, but in its place, something stronger emerged—a government where the king no longer ruled alone but alongside his people. The seeds of parliamentary democracy had been sown, and England would never be the same again.

Henry had spent his life clinging to power, consumed by his desires and resentments. But in that moment, as he relinquished his struggle, he found a deeper truth. Peace was never in the throne—it was within him.

Reflection: Beyond the Mask - Shattering the Illusion of Identity

From the grand halls of power to the quiet corners of self-reflection, the illusion of identity shapes and confines us in ways we rarely recognize. Whether in the modern corporate world, the palaces of ancient royalty, or the pursuit of spiritual enlightenment, these stories reveal how we define ourselves by external markers—titles, achievements, wealth, and even the roles we play—only to realize that true fulfillment lies beyond them.

Shibhya's relentless pursuit of success made him believe that his identity was bound to his status as a high-ranking executive. Yet, in the stillness of a hospital room, as he sat beside his ailing mother, the illusion shattered. He saw clearly that his worth was never in his accolades but in his ability to love, to connect, and to be present for those who mattered. The race for validation had blinded him to the simplest truth: he had always been a son first, and it was in that role, not his professional success, that his life found its deepest meaning.

Centuries earlier, a prince named Siddhartha Gautama faced a similar awakening. Born into royalty, his world was shaped by privilege, comfort, and expectation. Yet, one glimpse beyond the palace walls revealed a reality he had never known—suffering, impermanence, and the fleeting nature of material success. Shedding the identity imposed upon him, he walked away from everything he had been told to cherish. It was only when he abandoned the illusion of self—neither prince nor pauper, neither ruler nor subject—that he found the truth that lay beyond all labels, emerging as the Buddha, the awakened one.

Even kings, who command armies and nations, are not immune to the trappings of identity. King Henry III believed that his divine right to rule was absolute, his crown the ultimate symbol of his authority. Yet, his unchecked power, misguided priorities, and refusal to adapt led to his downfall. When the barons stripped him of his authority and forced him into submission, he was confronted with a painful realization: his crown was just an object, and his throne just a seat. True power did not come from the title of 'king' but from wisdom, humility, and the ability to serve his people. The illusion of absolute monarchy had crumbled, and in its place, a new reality emerged—the foundation of parliamentary democracy.

In all these stories, the moment of awakening comes not through force, but through introspection—when ambition, status, and power are seen for what they are: fleeting and insubstantial. When the illusions fall away, what remains is something far greater: love, wisdom, and the freedom to live not by the labels imposed upon us, but by the truth of who we are.

Introspection: Beyond the Labels - Uncovering Who You Truly Are

As you reach the end of this chapter, take a pause. How much of who you are is truly you, and how much is a reflection of the labels, expectations, and validations you have accumulated over time?

- Have you ever mistaken success for self-worth, believing that titles and achievements define your value?

- Have you ever felt lost when a role you identified with—be it a job, a relationship, or a status—was taken away?

- Have you ever chased recognition, only to realize that external approval never truly fills the void within?

- Have you ever resisted change because it threatened the identity you had built for yourself?

- Have you ever wondered who you are beyond the labels given to you by society, family, or circumstance?

- Have you ever paused—just for a moment—to ask yourself: If I strip away everything I do, everything I own, and everything I am known for, what remains?

Because sometimes, the greatest illusion is not what the world sees—it is the one we create for ourselves.

True identity is not found in titles, power, or validation. It is not something to be earned or proven. It is something to be uncovered. So, as you step forward, ask yourself—are you ready to let go of who you think you are to discover who you truly are?

Commitment Over Consequence

Bhagavad Gita, Chapter 2, Verse 47

कर्मण्येवाधिकारस्ते मा फलेषु कदाचन।

(You have the right to perform your duty, but never to
the fruits of your actions.)

The Freedom of Effort Over Outcome

In a world obsessed with success and recognition, we often tie our worth to results—seeking validation in applause, promotions, or measurable achievements. But what happens when the outcomes don't meet our expectations? When effort goes unnoticed or success takes longer than expected? If our purpose is driven by external rewards, we risk frustration, fear, and self-doubt.

The Bhagavad Gita offers a liberating perspective: "You have the right to perform your duty, but never to the fruits of your actions." Krishna does not ask us to abandon ambition but to shift our focus—from results to sincere effort. True fulfilment comes from giving our best, without being consumed by expectations.

When we detach from outcomes, we gain:

- Freedom from doubt – No longer asking "What if I fail?" but instead "Have I done my best?"

- Freedom from fear – Taking bold steps without the burden of success or failure.

- Freedom from disappointment – Viewing setbacks as part of the journey, not as defeats.

Every great revolution, invention, or act of courage was fueled by unwavering commitment, not guaranteed success. So, the next time you feel trapped by expectations, pause and ask: Am I giving my best? Because true greatness lies not in what we receive, but in how wholeheartedly we give.

Karna: The Unbroken Oath

Karna had spent his life fighting battles long before he ever held a bow. The world never let him forget that he was the son of a charioteer, a man meant to serve, not to rule. As a boy, he had watched princes like Arjuna train under the greatest masters, their lineage granting them access to knowledge that remained forbidden to him. He had the heart of a Kshatriya, the hands of an archer—but no one saw beyond his birth. No one, except himself.

But Karna's true birth was far nobler than the world believed. He was not the son of a charioteer. He was the son of the Sun God himself.

Long before he was born, Kunti, a young princess, had been granted a divine boon—she could invoke any god and bear his child. Out of curiosity and innocence, she called upon Surya, the Sun God. Bound by the power of the boon, he appeared before her, bestowing upon her a son—a child as radiant as the sun, adorned with golden armour and divine earrings.

But Kunti was unwed. Terrified of the consequences, she placed her newborn son in a basket and set him afloat on the river, praying the waters would carry him to safety.

It was fate that brought the infant to the banks of Hastinapur, where he was discovered by Adhiratha, a humble charioteer in the service of the royal court. He and his wife, Radha, took the child in, raising him as their own. They named him Karna and showered him with love, but the world was not so kind.

Despite his brilliance, Karna was constantly reminded of his low birth. He was denied the right to learn warfare alongside the Kuru princes. When he sought knowledge from Dronacharya, the revered guru of the royal family, he was humiliated and turned away. The doors of greatness were closed to him—not because he lacked skill, but because he lacked lineage.

But Karna refused to accept his fate. If one path was blocked, he would carve another.

And so, he set out in search of a teacher who would recognize his worth, not his birth. His journey led him to the ashram of Parashuram, the greatest warrior-sage of all time.

Parashuram was no ordinary teacher. He was an incarnation of Vishnu, a being of both divine wisdom and unmatched fury. Once, he had waged war against the Kshatriya race twenty-one times, erasing entire dynasties from the face of the earth. His rage was born from betrayal—his father had been wronged by a Kshatriya king, and in retaliation, Parashuram had sworn to rid the earth of arrogant warriors who had forgotten their dharma. He had slaughtered them without mercy until there were none left who could stand against him.

But over time, his hatred took another form. He no longer sought blood, but he vowed never to pass on his knowledge to the warrior caste, fearing they would misuse it. His disciples were few but chosen—Brahmins alone, those he deemed worthy of upholding dharma through knowledge, not conquest. To them, he taught the greatest secrets of warfare: the divine astras, the art of battle, the wisdom of a true warrior.

And then came Karna.

A boy with fire in his soul but humility in his words. A boy who did not demand but begged for knowledge.

"I am a Brahmin, Guruji," Karna had said, bowing low.

Parashuram had studied him. Unlike the arrogant Kshatriyas he had once fought, this boy was eager, devoted. There was no entitlement in his eyes, only hunger. And so, the great sage had accepted him.

Under Parashuram's guidance, Karna thrived. He learned to summon celestial weapons, to strike without hesitation, to read the battlefield like an open book. His skill rivaled even the greatest Kshatriyas of his time. But no training, no mastery, could change the truth of his birth. And fate had a cruel way of revealing secrets.

One afternoon, Parashuram sat in meditation, his breathing deep and steady. Karna sat beside him, motionless, his mind sharpening his lessons. It was then that a sharp sting burned through his thigh. He glanced down and saw a scorpion digging its pincers into his flesh, its venom seeping into his skin.

Pain exploded through his body, raw and searing. His muscles tensed, his breath caught in his throat. His first instinct was to move—to crush the creature, to pull away, to gasp aloud. But Parashuram was still deep in meditation, unaware.

His fingers twitched.

He could wake him. He should wake him.

But then, a thought struck him like a blade.

Is it really worth it?

Why am I enduring this? Will Guruji even recognize this sacrifice?

What will I gain from suffering in silence?

The venom burned deeper, spreading through his veins. His jaw clenched, his vision blurred.

What if he wakes and sees my pain? Will he admire my strength or suspect the truth?

What if he realizes I am not a Brahmin?

What if he finds out that I am a Kshatriya?

The thought sent a chill through him. He had spent years protecting this secret, holding onto it as tightly as his bow.

Will I lose more than I gain?

Yet, another thought rose above the pain.

No. If I cannot endure this, then what right do I have to dream of being the greatest?

Pain is temporary. Knowledge is forever. I will not break.

And so, he did not move.

When Parashuram finally opened his eyes, he turned to Karna and saw his pale face, the beads of sweat lining his brow, the trembling of his limbs. Then, his eyes fell to the blood pooling around his thigh.

A deep frown creased his forehead.

"Why did you not wake me?"

Karna swallowed, his voice tight with pain but unwavering. "Because my duty as your disciple is greater than my suffering."

Parashuram's sharp gaze did not waver. "No ordinary Brahmin can endure such torment in silence." His voice darkened, suspicion flickering in his eyes. "Tell me, Karna—who are you?"

Karna felt the weight of the question press down on him.

He took a slow breath.

"I am a Kshatriya, Guruji."

Silence stretched between them.

Parashuram's expression turned to stone. The kindness in his eyes vanished, replaced by cold fury.

"A Kshatriya," he repeated, his voice heavy with betrayal. "You deceived me."

Karna immediately fell to his knees. "Guruji, I did not mean disrespect. No one else would teach me. I only wanted to learn—I wanted to be worthy."

For the first time, a flicker of sadness passed through Parashuram's face. For a moment, he saw the boy, not the lie.

And for that moment, he hesitated.

But then, the pain of his own past—the betrayals, the arrogance of the Kshatriyas he had once trusted—hardened his heart again.

"You think dharma is a thing to be stolen? You think knowledge is yours to take through deception?" His voice was cold, but a trace of sorrow lingered.

Karna bowed his head. "I have lived my life being told I am not worthy. If my birth denies me my dharma, then what choice do I have but to fight for it?"

Parashuram closed his eyes for a brief moment. Then, his voice rang with divine power. "In your moment of greatest need, your knowledge will betray you."

The words struck deeper than any weapon ever could.

Karna felt the weight of Parashuram's words settle upon him like an iron chain. *In your moment of greatest need, your knowledge will betray you.*

The finality of the curse struck deeper than any wound he had ever suffered. The very thing he had sacrificed everything to gain—the knowledge, the power, the mastery—was now a fleeting illusion, destined to slip through his fingers when he needed it most.

A part of him wanted to protest, to beg his guru to reconsider, to plead that his deception was not out of malice but out of desperation. But even as the words formed on his tongue, he swallowed them.

What would be the point?

He had lied. He had broken the trust of the one man who had given him what the world had denied him. And though his heart burned with regret, another truth stood unshaken within him.

He had no choice.

Was it wrong to seek one's dharma when the world refused to acknowledge it? Was it a sin to chase one's destiny when fate itself conspired against it?

Karna's hands curled into fists. The pain in his thigh throbbed with every heartbeat, but it was nothing compared to the ache in his soul.

He had endured humiliation. He had endured rejection. He had endured a life of being told he was not enough.

But today, he had endured something worse.

For the first time, he wondered if it was all in vain.

Parashuram had seen the fire in him, had shaped him into something greater than any ordinary Kshatriya. But now, his teacher had cast him aside, sealing his fate with a curse that could not be undone.

Was it worth it?

A bitter laugh nearly escaped his lips. What a cruel joke. Even when he had done everything right—even when he had bled, suffered, endured—he was still denied what he had rightfully earned.

Would the gods ever let him win?

Slowly, he raised his head and looked at Parashuram, who now stood rigid, his face unreadable. For a moment, Karna thought he saw something flicker in his guru's eyes—was it sorrow? Regret? Or was it just the fading embers of whatever trust had once existed between them?

Karna exhaled, steadying himself. He had lost a teacher, lost a part of himself. But he had not lost his resolve.

No, he would never lose that.

Yet, Karna did not regret his choice.

He was still Karna.

The world had denied him his place, but he would carve it with his own hands.

His knowledge might betray him, but his will never would.

If this was his fate, so be it. He would embrace it with his head held high.

"If I am to fall, let it be as a Kshatriya, not as a man who turned away from his own truth."

Radha's Last Dance

The news had spread through Vrindavan like wildfire—Krishna was leaving.

Radha, the daughter of Vrishabhanu and Kirti, was no ordinary maiden. She was born not just of the earth but of divine love itself. The people of Barsana whispered that she was a goddess in human form, a being of celestial grace. From childhood, her heart beat to the rhythm of Krishna's flute, long before she even saw him.

And Krishna—Kanha, the dark-skinned boy of Gokul—was not merely a prince of cowherds. He was the eighth avatar of Lord Vishnu, the preserver of the universe, born to restore dharma. His birth was no ordinary event; he was the son of Devaki and Vasudeva, born in the prison of Mathura under the shadow of prophecy and danger. To save him from the tyrant Kansa, he was carried across the Yamuna to Gokul, where he was raised by Yashoda and Nanda, growing up amidst the simple joys of a cowherd's life.

Yet, Krishna was never just a child of Gokul—he was the very essence of existence, the divine in mortal form, a child of destiny. His purpose was to restore righteousness, to guide lost souls, and to lead the world through love and wisdom.

But when he first met Radha, it was not as god and devotee, but as two souls who had always known each other. It was at the banks of the Yamuna, where Krishna's laughter danced like ripples on the water, and Radha, draped in the golden hues of dusk, felt her heart surrender without resistance.

From that moment, they became inseparable, each the incomplete verse of the other's poetry, the echo of a song only they could hear. They did not need words; their silences spoke more deeply than any conversation. When Krishna played his flute, it was as if he called only for her, and when Radha heard it, she knew she had no choice but to follow. He was the moon to her night, the storm to her fire, the boundless sky to her unending ocean.

Yet, for all their love, fate was not theirs to command.

Radha's heart ached, not with despair, but with the weight of an unspoken truth. She had always known Krishna was never meant to stay, yet every stolen glance, every whispered promise under the moonlit sky had become etched into the very fabric of her soul. They were not two beings but one—a melody and its rhythm, the river and its current, the sky and its boundless blue.

From the first time Krishna had called her name, Radha had known she belonged to him, just as he belonged to her. Not in the way the world understood love, but in the way the soul recognizes its reflection. Their love was not bound by the laws of mortals; it was not meant to culminate in a union of flesh but in the eternal embrace of spirit.

She remembered the way he looked at her—as if she was the universe itself. The way his fingers had traced the edge of her veil, how his voice melted into her being like the first drops of rain on parched earth. He had filled her days with laughter and her nights with dreams of infinity. They had danced in the meadows, their feet moving in perfect harmony, the world fading until only they remained. When his flute played, it was not mere music—it was a call, a prayer, a longing that only she could answer.

But now, the melody was fading.

Radha had known this day would come. She had always known. Krishna was never meant to stay; he was the keeper of the universe, bound by destiny beyond the forests of Vrindavan. And yet, as she stood beneath the Kadamba tree by the Yamuna, a part of her still wished time would stop.

The village was drowning in sorrow. The gopis wept, the cows refused to graze, the birds had stopped singing. Even the river seemed to hold its breath. But **Radha did not cry**. She did not run to Krishna to beg him to stay, nor did she seek promises of return.

Instead, she walked barefoot to the clearing where they had once danced under the moonlit sky. The place where their love had blossomed—not in the chains of possession but in the freedom of devotion. The breeze carried the echoes of their laughter, the melodies of Krishna's flute still lingering in the air.

"Radha," Krishna's voice was soft, filled with something deeper than longing.

She turned to face him, her eyes reflecting the golden hues of dusk. "You have to go," she said, a gentle certainty in her tone.

Krishna reached for her hand but stopped just short of touching her. "And you always knew I would."

Radha smiled, though it held the weight of a thousand unspoken goodbyes. "I was never yours to keep, just as you were never mine to hold back. But Krishna, you will miss me, won't you?"

Krishna's gaze darkened with emotion. "Every breath, Radha. Every moment. Yet, even when I am far away, your name will be called before mine. Krishna will never be spoken without Radha. You are my melody, my soul's first note."

She looked up at the sky, where the first stars had begun to shimmer. "I never wanted anything from you, Kanha. Not a promise, not a tomorrow. My love was never about having you—it was about knowing that I could love you, endlessly, without needing anything in return. I am blessed, Krishna, that I had the chance to see you, to touch you, to feel your presence, and to love you. If I could explain—my love is like the love one has for the Moon. Every night, you wait for it to appear, to bathe in its glow, but you can never hold it, never touch it, never keep it. And yet, you love it every single day. You are my Moon, Krishna. You are my kasturi."

Krishna exhaled, a slow, reverent breath. "And that is why your love is divine, Radha. Because it is not of this world—it is beyond body, beyond time. Radhe, your love is a universe, beyond any limits and imagination."

She stepped closer, letting the space between them fill with silence. "Do not carry sorrow for me. You are not leaving me behind, Krishna. Wherever you go, I will be there. In your laughter, in the wind, in the music of your flute. Because love does not end. You carry me in your memories, Krishna, but I am yours forever. So do not carry me only in your mind—I am with you in every breath, in every blink of your eye, in every sound you hear. You do not have to carry any sorrow or any burden. I never asked you to stay or take me with you. You are born for a reason, and for me, that reason is to be loved by Radha." She smiled, tears glistening in her eyes.

Krishna closed his eyes, as if imprinting this moment onto his soul. "And I will carry you with me, in every step, in every war, in every duty I must fulfill."

But after that, there were no more words—only silence. A silence filled with love, with longing, with the weight of separation. A silence that knew they would never be together again in this lifetime, yet one that carried the eternity of their bond.

Radha placed her hand over his heart for a fleeting moment. "Then go, my love. The world awaits you. And I… I will dance."

And so she did.

Radha closed her eyes.

Radha stood at the crossroads of her destiny—her heart pulling her towards Krishna one last time, yet her soul whispering to surrender, not to him, but to love itself. To let go, not because she wanted to, but because love, in its purest form, was never about possession. She could run to him, hold onto him, plead for one more moment. Or she could embrace the truth that had always been—Krishna was not leaving her, for he had always been within her. Love was not in staying, nor in leaving. It was in being. It was in surrender. It was in the very act of letting go.

And so, she danced.

Not for Krishna.

Not to stop him.

Not to be remembered.

But because love itself was her dharma.

Her feet moved with the rhythm of the wind, the earth, the river. The anklets that Krishna had once fastened around her feet jingled, but they were not calling him back. They were singing of devotion, of surrender, of a love that sought nothing in return.

Somewhere, far away, Krishna felt it. He paused on his chariot. His heart stirred, as if the universe itself had whispered to him. He did not turn back, for he knew—Radha was not losing him. She was becoming him.

As Radha spun in the golden dust of Vrindavan, her soul dissolved into the melody of Krishna's flute, into the very essence of existence. She no longer needed Krishna to be near—because she had never been separate from him.

By the time the dance ended, the village found her sitting beneath the Kadamba tree, eyes closed, a peaceful smile on her lips. Krishna was gone, but Radha had not lost him. She had loved without expectation, performed her duty without attachment to its fruits.

And in doing so, she had become eternal.

Ashoka: The Battle Within

The Mauryan Empire, under Emperor Ashoka, was at the peak of its power. Spanning from modern-day Afghanistan to Bengal, from the Himalayas to the southern reaches of India, it was one of the most formidable empires in history.

Yet, Ashoka was not satisfied. His ambitions stretched beyond the vast lands he already ruled. Unlike his grandfather Chandragupta Maurya, who built the empire through strategy and alliances, and his father Bindusara, who expanded it steadily, Ashoka's reign was marked by aggression and ruthless conquest. He had inherited not only their empire but also their thirst for dominance, though his methods were far more brutal. Raised in the shadow of war, he had learned early that mercy was a weakness and that power was seized, not given.

The Mauryan dynasty ruled during the 3rd century BCE, a time when India was a land of kingdoms and empires constantly at war. Ashoka's lineage was legendary—Chandragupta Maurya had overthrown the Nanda dynasty and laid the foundation of a vast empire with the guidance of Chanakya, the brilliant strategist. His son, Bindusara, had maintained stability and extended the empire's reach. But it was Ashoka who would make it the most feared force in the subcontinent.

His ascent to the throne was steeped in betrayal and bloodshed. He was not the first choice of Bindusara, nor was he the favoured heir. But he was the most ruthless. In a violent struggle for succession, he eliminated his brothers, securing his rule through force. His early rule was marked by sheer terror—he crushed rebellions, silenced dissent, and instilled fear among his own ministers. "Loyalty is born from fear, not kindness," he once told his advisors. "A king who is loved can be overthrown. A king who is feared is eternal."

He was a warrior-king, feared by his enemies and even his own people. His rise to the throne was bathed in blood—he had fought his way through rival claimants, even his own brothers, to secure his place as emperor. He was called Chand Ashoka (Ashoka the Fierce) for a reason. War was not just his strategy—it was his very identity.

When the kingdom of Kalinga refused to bow to Mauryan rule, Ashoka took it as an insult. His generals warned him, "The Kalingans are not warriors, but they will fight to the last man for their freedom."

Ashoka's eyes darkened. "Then let them fight—and let them perish. I will grind their defiance into dust."

He turned to his war council. "Burn their fields. Slaughter their men. Let their women weep over corpses, and let their children learn what it means to defy an emperor."

The silence in the war chamber was thick, but no one dared to oppose him. Ashoka had spoken—Kalinga would fall.

Ashoka's lips curled into a smirk. "Then they will die standing."

And so, the war began.

The morning sun cast a deceptive glow on the Daya River, its tranquil surface unaware of the storm of steel and screams that would soon turn its waters into a river of blood and sorrow. The air trembled with the war cries of the Mauryan soldiers and the desperate, defiant shouts of the Kalingans, who stood ready to fight despite knowing their doom was near. The scent of burning wood and flesh began to creep into the wind, an omen of the carnage that was about to unfold.

The Kalingans were not trained soldiers—they were farmers, merchants, artisans, potters, and scholars. Yet, they stood with fierce determination. Fathers fought alongside sons, women sharpened their sickles into weapons, and entire families chose to die rather than surrender. Their ruler, King Ananta Padmanabha, had refused to submit to Mauryan rule, believing that freedom was worth any price.

Kalinga, a prosperous and independent state, thrived due to its maritime trade and cultural richness. Nestled on the eastern coast of India, it controlled key trade routes along the Bay of Bengal, making it an economic powerhouse. The Kalingans were fiercely proud of their sovereignty and had successfully repelled invaders in the past. Unlike the Mauryan Empire, which thrived on centralization and military supremacy, Kalinga was built on a confederation of local governance, trade, and cultural unity.

"We are not just fighting for our land, we are fighting for our very existence," King Ananta Padmanabha had declared to his people. "We bow to no emperor, for our spirit is our crown."

The Kalingans, known for their seafaring prowess and artistic achievements, had lived in peace and prosperity, but now they had no choice but to become warriors overnight. They did not seek war, but they would not accept slavery either.

Ashoka's triumph over Kalinga was absolute, but as he surveyed the battlefield, victory felt hollow. The blood of thousands soaked the earth, their cries echoing in his mind. He had won—but what had he truly gained?

That night, he could not sleep. The faces of the slain haunted him. The voice of a dying warrior whispered in his ears, "Will your son die like mine, Ashoka?" He saw visions—ghosts of children, their hollow eyes staring at him, silent accusations carved into their faces. For the first time in his life, Ashoka felt fear—not of enemies, but of himself.

Then came the final blow—rumors that his own son, Tivala, had gone missing in the chaos. Panic gripped his heart as he searched for him, frantic, desperate. The thought of losing his child, even for a moment, unraveled him. And in that agony, he understood. This was the pain he had inflicted upon thousands.

When Tivala was finally found safe, the relief did not cleanse him. Instead, it solidified his resolve. He had conquered Kalinga, but in doing so, he had lost his own soul. His breath quickened, his hands trembled, and his knees buckled under the weight of realization. The cries of the dying still echoed in his ears, the blood on his hands felt as though it would never wash away.

History would remember him not as Chand Ashoka, the Fierce, but as Dhamma Ashoka, the Righteous—the emperor who conquered not kingdoms, but himself. And perhaps, in the end, that was the greatest victory of all. For what is power, if it is not wielded with wisdom? What is a ruler, if he does not serve? And what is an empire, if it is built on the ashes of the innocent?

His transformation was not sudden, nor was it easy. The weight of countless lives lost at Kalinga pressed upon his soul, their cries echoing in the corridors of his conscience. Blood had cemented his empire, but it could not grant him peace. The battlefield, once his proving ground, became his greatest regret. And so, he laid down the sword—not in weakness, but in the greatest act of strength. He turned away from conquest, not because he lacked the might to continue, but because he had seen the hollowness of victory drenched in suffering.

In the end, his greatest conquest was not of land, but of the human heart. He sought no more to subjugate, but to uplift; no more to destroy, but to heal. His empire, once expanded through force, now flourished through faith, compassion, and the principles of dhamma. His laws no longer spoke of punishment, but of righteousness. His messengers carried not decrees of war, but edicts of peace. He did not seek immortality in monuments of stone but in the goodwill of his people, in the kindness that rippled through generations because of the path he chose.

His story was a testament to the truth that power wielded without wisdom leads only to ruin, but a leader who seeks justice and peace leaves a legacy that time itself cannot erase. And so, for centuries to come, the world would speak of Ashoka—not for the battles he won, but for the war he chose to end. For in choosing peace over conquest, he became greater than any emperor before him. He became a legend, not of might, but of morality. And long after his kingdom faded, his ideals endured—etched not in stone, but in the soul of humanity itself.

Reflection: The Strength of Selfless Action

We live in a world where success is often measured by results—achievements, rewards, recognition. But what happens when we don't get what we worked for? When our efforts don't yield the outcomes we expected? The Bhagavad Gita reminds us of a deeper truth: our duty lies in sincere action, not in attachment to results.

Karna devoted his life to proving his worth, fighting against a world that refused to accept him. He endured humiliation, deception, and rejection, yet his commitment to his dharma never wavered. He sought knowledge, he sought honor, and he gave his loyalty freely—even when it cost him everything. But his greatest challenge was not in battle—it was in accepting that no amount of effort could rewrite his fate. He gave his all, and yet, the rewards were denied to him. Still, Karna's story is not one of loss, but of commitment—because he never stopped doing what he believed was right, regardless of what he received in return.

Radha's love for Krishna was never about possession. She loved, knowing she would never be his in the way the world defined love. She did not seek promises or assurances, nor did she expect anything in return. For her, the act of love itself was enough—pure, complete, unwavering. She did not love Krishna for the future they might have had; she loved him in the present, without attachment to an outcome. She teaches us that the truest form of devotion is not in expecting, but in giving wholeheartedly.

Ashoka sought power through conquest, believing that expansion was the ultimate purpose of an emperor. He fought, he won, and yet, when he stood amidst the blood-soaked land of Kalinga, he found only emptiness. His victory did not bring him the satisfaction he had envisioned—it only burdened him with guilt. It was in that moment that he understood the flaw in his pursuit. Power, when driven by the hunger for results, only leads to suffering. And so, he chose a different path—not to erase his past, but to dedicate himself to a greater cause without seeking personal gain. His transformation was not about renouncing action, but about shifting the purpose of his actions—from conquest to service, from ambition to duty.

All three stories reinforce the same truth: we are entitled to our efforts, not the rewards they bring. When we tie our happiness to results, we give away control of our inner peace. But when we act with sincerity, without being bound by expectations, we find true freedom.

And so, the question remains: Do we measure our actions by what we receive, or by the integrity with which we perform them? If success is not guaranteed, will we still commit to our purpose? If love is not reciprocated, will we still love? If our efforts go unnoticed, will we still give our best?

Because in the end, greatness is not defined by what we achieve—but by how we act, even when no reward is promised.

Introspection: The Freedom in Selfless Action

We often tie our happiness to outcomes—believing that success, recognition, or validation will bring us fulfilment. But what happens when life doesn't reward us as expected? When our dedication goes unnoticed? When our efforts don't yield the results we desire? Do we still act with the same sincerity, or do we let disappointment hold us back?

The Bhagavad Gita teaches us that our duty is to act, not to cling to the fruits of our labour. It is in this detachment that true freedom lies—not in apathy, but in the ability to give our best without being controlled by results.

When we surrender the need for a specific outcome, we free ourselves from fear, disappointment, and self-doubt.

As you reflect on your own journey, ask yourself:

- Do I measure my worth by my actions, or by the results they bring?

- Would I still put in the same effort if I knew there was no guarantee of success?

- Do I hesitate to act because I fear failure or lack of recognition?

- Can I give my best to something without expecting anything in return?

- When have I allowed the disappointment of an outcome to overshadow the sincerity of my effort?

- Am I willing to embrace the process, rather than obsess over the result?

Greatness lies in the act itself, not in its reward. A warrior does not step onto the battlefield for the assurance of victory, but because it is his duty. A leader does not serve only when applause is promised, but because service itself is meaningful. A lover does not give love expecting it in return, but because love is meant to be given freely.

So, the next time you hesitate because of fear, doubt, or uncertainty—pause and ask yourself: Am I doing this for the result, or because it is my path? If you can act with sincerity, regardless of what follows, then you have already won. Because in that moment, you have found true freedom—the power to act without being enslaved by expectation.

Rise Above Doubt

क्लैब्यं मा स्म गमः पार्थ नैतत्त्वय्युपपद्यते।
क्षुद्रं हृदयदौर्बल्यं त्यक्त्वोत्तिष्ठ परन्तप॥

(Abandon weakness. Rise with courage, for a warrior's
duty is to uphold righteousness, not be paralyzed by doubt.)

In life, we all face moments of hesitation—times when fear, self-doubt, or emotional turmoil make us question our choices. The weight of responsibilities, the fear of failure, or the pain of letting go can paralyze us, keeping us trapped between what we desire and what must be done. These moments can feel overwhelming, convincing us that waiting, delaying, or remaining in our comfort zone is the safer choice.

But true strength is not the absence of doubt—it is the ability to rise above it. It is not about never feeling fear but about choosing to act in spite of it. Strength is forged in the fire of uncertainty, and resilience is born when we refuse to let hesitation dictate our fate. The greatest warriors, leaders, and visionaries were not those who never questioned themselves, but those who refused to let their doubts control them.

Every time we let fear hold us back, we give up a piece of our potential. The mind will always whisper reasons to wait, to reconsider, to take the safer path. But clarity is not something we wait for—it is something we create through action. The moment we move forward, the fog begins to clear, and what once seemed impossible becomes merely the next step in our journey.

This chapter is about transcending uncertainty, shedding self-imposed limitations, and stepping into the power that already exists within us. Because in the end, it is not hesitation but decisive action that shapes our destiny. And when we learn to silence doubt with courage, we discover that we were always stronger than we believed."

Arjuna's Moment of Reflection

The battlefield of Kurukshetra stretched endlessly, a vast ocean of warriors shimmering under the scorching sun. The air was thick with the scent of sweat, dust, and impending bloodshed. Flags of a hundred clans fluttered in the wind, their symbols of valor swaying like restless spirits, torn between fate and fury. The conch shells had been blown; the war cries had begun, reverberating through the land like the call of destiny itself.

The ground trembled beneath the pounding of war elephants, their armored tusks glinting like harbingers of destruction. Chariots rolled forward in formation, their wheels carving deep scars into the earth. Thousands of soldiers shifted anxiously, their hands tightening around their weapons, their breaths merging with the heavy silence before the first clash. The sky above, once a witness to peace, now bore the tension of an era-defining moment, as if even the heavens awaited the first drop of blood to seal the fate of kingdoms.

Yet, in the heart of this impending storm, Arjuna stood frozen.

His fingers gripped the Gandiva, but his arms felt like lead. His chariot, positioned between the two armies at Krishna's behest, offered a perfect vantage point. He saw Bhishma standing tall, his silvered beard catching the sunlight, eyes filled with unshaken resolve. Dronacharya, his beloved teacher, held his bow with the same steady grip that had once trained Arjuna himself. Karna, his rival yet his blood, stared ahead, oblivious to the secret that bound them. Cousins, uncles, friends—faces he had known all his life—stood prepared to die by his hand.

His breath hitched.

"Krishna," he murmured, his throat dry. "How can I fight them? My own kin... my gurus... the ones I have worshipped?"

His voice wavered, but he continued, desperation creeping into his tone. "Tell me, Madhava, how do I strike down Bhishma, who cradled me as a child? How do I lift my weapon against Dronacharya, whose hands shaped me into the warrior I am today?"

He swallowed hard, his anguish spilling over. "What kind of dharma demands this? How do I silence my heart, which screams that this is wrong?"

His fingers tightened around the Gandiva, his knuckles white. "Would you call me a warrior if my soul shatters with every arrow I release? Would you call me righteous if I cannot bear the weight of my own actions?"

Krishna, his charioteer, turned to him, serene as ever. "Arjuna, what is troubling you?"

Arjuna exhaled sharply, his mind a tempest of emotions. "I look at them, and all I see is destruction. What is victory if it comes at the cost of my own blood? If I strike them down, how will I live with myself? Even if I win, won't I lose?"

His voice grew heavier, thick with sorrow. "What will I tell my mother, Krishna? That I was the hand that ended the lineage she bore in pain and sacrifice? What will I say to Draupadi? That the war fought in her name was waged by a man who could not even bear to meet her eyes afterward? And if anything happens to her sons, her grandsons—what then? How will I ever face her, knowing that I was the cause of her unending sorrow? Will my brothers look at me with pride or with grief, knowing the price we have paid?"

He clenched his fists, his breathing ragged. "I have trained my whole life to be a warrior, but today, my own strength disgusts me. What use is skill when it only leads to ruin? What honor is there in a throne that stands atop the bones of my kin? Tell me, Krishna! How do I carry this burden without it breaking me?"

He felt his body tremble, a cold sweat beading on his brow. His knees buckled, and he collapsed onto the floor of the chariot. The Gandiva slipped from his grasp.

"I see only despair," he whispered. "I cannot do this."

A heavy silence hung between them, stretching into eternity. The world outside was chaos—war drums pounding, warriors shouting—but within this chariot, time stood still.

Arjuna clenched his jaw, his hands gripping the edges of the chariot. His voice broke as he spoke again, anguish seeping through every word. "Tell me, Krishna, why must I do this? If I kill them, they will kill my brothers, my sons. This war will only birth more suffering, more hatred, more widows and orphans. What kind of duty demands such a sacrifice?"

His voice rose, almost desperate. "How can this be righteousness when my soul recoils from it? When every fiber of my being screams against it?" His breath came ragged now. "Tell me, Krishna, if someone is not convinced of a task, if his heart does not allow it, should he still do it? How can an action performed without will be called duty?"

Krishna looked at him, his gaze unwavering, his voice calm yet powerful. "Arjuna, you grieve for those who do not need grieving. You speak of love, of attachment, but do you not see the higher truth?" His voice was neither harsh nor soft—it was steady, like the river that carves through mountains. "This battle is not just about victory or defeat. It is about dharma."

Arjuna's breath quickened. "Dharma? Is dharma to slay those who raised me? To strike down the ones who have loved me?"

Krishna's eyes softened, filled with a divine patience. "Dharma is not dictated by personal attachment. It is the path of righteousness, even when it wounds the heart. If you abandon this war, thinking you will find peace, you deceive yourself. The weight of inaction is heavier than the burden of war."

He paused, his voice steady yet filled with quiet urgency. "And what of your teachers, Arjuna? Do you not owe an answer to Dronacharya, the one who shaped you into the warrior you are? To Kripacharya, your mentor, whose wisdom guided you? To Bhishma Pitamaha, the very embodiment of duty and sacrifice? If you walk away, what will you say to them? Will you meet their gaze and tell them you abandoned the battle they dedicated their lives to prepare you for? Will you let their teachings go in vain? You must decide now, Arjuna. Look ahead and predict—what will you say to those who built you, trusted you, and believed in your purpose?"

Krishna then gestured toward Yuyutsu, the lone Kaurava who had chosen to fight on the side of righteousness. "Look at him, Arjuna. Yuyutsu was born on the other side, raised as a Kaurava. Yet, he saw the truth. He understood his duty and where he was needed. He did not let blind attachment dictate his actions. Do you not owe an explanation to those who trust in this vision? To those who believe in justice?"

Arjuna's fists tightened as Krishna continued. "What will you say to Draupadi? The woman who was humiliated in a court of elders while you stood powerless? Should she not expect an explanation from you, her husband? Should a wife not expect her husband to protect her pride and honor? What will you say to the countless souls who look to you for justice? Will you tell them that your heart wavered, that your duty was too heavy to bear? What will happen to those who have placed their faith in this war? If you falter now, Arjuna, what will remain of righteousness?"

Arjuna clenched his fists, his inner turmoil a raging storm. The voices in his head screamed conflicting truths—justice or mercy, obligation or conscience?

Krishna, sensing his turmoil, gestured toward the magnificent chariot they stood upon. "Do you see this chariot, Arjuna? It is not mere wood and metal—it is symbolic of your journey, of every warrior's journey. The five horses pulling it represent the five senses—sight, sound, touch, taste, and smell—constantly pulling the mind in different directions. The reins that hold them together signify the intellect, the power of discrimination. The charioteer, guiding them, is wisdom, steering one toward the right path. And you, Arjuna, are the warrior—the soul that must choose whether to let the senses control you or to master them through wisdom."

Arjuna's eyes flickered to the golden reins in Krishna's hands, his mind racing. "Then what of this battlefield, Krishna? If my senses pull me toward compassion, toward love for my family, does that not mean I should turn away from this war?"

Krishna shook his head, his eyes steady. "Compassion without wisdom is weakness, Arjuna. A warrior does not abandon battle because his senses make him hesitate. He uses intellect to see beyond momentary pain and act with righteousness. Even the greatest chariot must be led with discipline, or it will crash. Will you let your chariot be guided by sorrow, or will you take the reins and steer it toward dharma?"

The words struck deep. Arjuna inhaled sharply, staring at the great battlefield stretched before him. The war, the destruction, the pain—had he only been looking at the storm, not the purpose behind it? He felt the Gandiva in his hands, no longer as a burden, but as a tool of fate. He closed his eyes for a moment, letting the meaning of Krishna's words settle within him.

His heart pounded like a war drum. Images flashed before his eyes—his mother's gentle hands, his childhood laughter with his brothers, the lessons of his gurus, the battles he had fought, the oaths he had sworn. He felt his soul pulled in every direction, tethered by love, duty, fear, and faith.

Then, suddenly, everything shifted.

Arjuna gasped as a vision took hold of him. The battlefield blurred, and he saw a future drenched in blood. Hastinapura lay in ruins, the cries of widows echoing through the empty corridors. The bodies of countless warriors lay unburied, the price of a war waged in hesitation. He saw his brothers lifeless, their sacrifice meaningless, the throne a cursed relic of a broken kingdom.

But then, another vision emerged—a kingdom reborn from the ashes. Justice restored, dharma reigning supreme. The children of those lost in battle growing up in peace, learning the ways of righteousness. The sacrifices had not been in vain; they had paved the way for a future where war was no longer necessary. The vision burned into his mind, a truth he could not unsee.

And then, a voice.

"Fight, Parth."

Arjuna's head jerked up. Across the battlefield, Karna stood tall, staring directly at him. His voice was low, but it reached Arjuna's soul.

"If not for yourself, then for those who believe in you," he said. Then, after a pause, his voice grew sharper, more resolute. "You speak of grief, Arjuna, but have you considered mine? I have fought my whole life for a place that never accepted me, and yet, I stand, unwavering. Do you not owe your brothers the same? The men standing behind you, ready to die for righteousness—do you not owe them your courage?"

Arjuna swallowed hard, his throat dry. Karna's words pierced through his doubts like arrows.

Karna stepped forward, his gaze unyielding. "You think this war is cruel? So is fate. But fate does not ask—it demands. What will you do, Parth? Stand here questioning the heavens while the world crumbles around you? Or will you rise, as destiny has willed?"

Arjuna's breath hitched. Karna… his rival, his unknown brother. Was this fate? Was this dharma speaking through the very one he was destined to fight?

Thirty seconds.

His breathing slowed. The war cries became distant echoes. The weight of indecision that had shackled him began to lift. He looked again—not at his family, but at warriors, each bound by their own fates. He saw not a war of vengeance, but a battlefield where dharma must prevail.

The storm inside him quieted.

His trembling hands steadied.

He reached for his Gandiva once more, feeling its familiar weight in his grasp. The bow that had once felt like a burden now felt like an extension of himself. He inhaled deeply, his chest rising with newfound resolve.

"I understand now, Krishna," he said, his voice no longer shaking. "I was blind with sorrow, unable to see the greater truth. This war is not about me. It is about dharma. And I… I will fight."

A small smile played on Krishna's lips. "Then fight, Arjuna. Not with anger, nor with hatred, but with the clarity of duty."

As Arjuna raised his bow, the battlefield seemed different. The chaos remained, but his mind was still. The hesitation was gone. His heart no longer wavered. The cries of warriors, the pounding of war drums, the clashing of steel—all faded into a distant hum. A strange serenity filled him, as if he had finally stepped into the role he was meant to embrace. The weight of doubt lifted, replaced by an unshakable purpose. He was no longer just a prince, a brother, or a disciple—he was the wielder of dharma, the force that would restore balance. And in that one moment of resolve, everything changed.

The warrior in him had returned, his soul now aligned with the path of dharma. The echoes of Krishna's wisdom resonated within him, intertwining with the truth that righteousness is never in vain. In that moment, Arjuna understood his karma, his duty, and the profound realization that dharma transcends personal grief. He stood tall, his doubts shed like a discarded shell, and with renewed purpose, he lifted his Gandiva, ready to fulfill his destiny.

And in that one moment of balance, Arjuna felt the weight of his hesitation dissolve, replaced by an unshakable clarity. He saw not just a battlefield but the course of destiny unfolding before him. His past, his doubts, his grief—all surrendered to the call of dharma. With a steady hand and a resolute heart, he embraced his duty, knowing that righteousness, once realized, leaves no room for retreat. The warrior in him had awakened, and the path ahead was now unmistakably clear.

But in this clarity, a question lingered—one that he knew would remain long after the war had ended. In a world where righteousness and duty often demanded sacrifice, was there ever a path that did not leave wounds in its wake? And if the price of dharma was always paid in blood, who truly bore its cost?

Bhagat Singh: The Sound of Revolution

The dimly lit room smelled of ink, old books, and burning candles. Papers were scattered across the wooden table—pamphlets calling for freedom, maps of British administrative buildings, and notes on their upcoming act of defiance. The weight of revolution hung heavy in the air, mixing with the hushed murmurs of urgency. The flickering candlelight cast shifting shadows on their faces, reflecting the fire that burned within them. Every rustle of paper, every sharp intake of breath carried the tension of an irreversible decision. The world outside was unaware, but in this room, history was being rewritten—one act of defiance at a time.

Bhagat Singh, just 22 years old, sat at the center, his intense eyes scanning his comrades—Shivaram Rajguru and Sukhdev Thapar. They weren't just friends; they were brothers in arms, bound by one dream—a free India. But Bhagat Singh's fire had been ignited long before. At just 12 years old, he had rushed to the site of the Jallianwala Bagh massacre, his small hands gathering soil soaked in the blood of innocent martyrs. That soil, that sacrifice, had stayed with him, shaping his every thought, every action. The horror of that day had etched itself into his soul—the sight of bullet-ridden bodies, the cries of the wounded, the stifling silence of helplessness. He had vowed that day that he would not live as a slave. He would fight, not just for freedom, but for justice. The massacre was not just a tragedy; it was a call to arms, a moment that turned a boy into a revolutionary.

Shivaram Rajguru, born in Maharashtra, was different. He was fire—impatient, relentless, fearless. Where Bhagat Singh strategized, Rajguru acted. He was an expert marksman, ready to take down any British officer who dared to oppress his people. Raised in a country where British rule had crushed the spirit of his people, Rajguru had resolved to fight, no matter the cost.

Sukhdev Thapar was the soul of the group. A native of Ludhiana, Punjab, he was deeply involved in the Hindustan Socialist Republican Association (HSRA), the secret revolutionary group they all belonged to. He was meticulous, thoughtful, and deeply committed to the cause. He had worked closely with Bhagat Singh, planning protests, writing fiery articles, and mobilizing young revolutionaries.

The three revolutionaries sat in tense silence, the weight of history pressing down on them. The dim glow of the lamp flickered against their determined faces as they pored over the latest decree issued by the British government. The Public Safety Bill and the Trade Disputes Act were not just laws—they were shackles, designed to crush the voice of India's revolutionaries. They had tried petitions, protests, and hunger strikes, yet the colonial rulers remained deaf to their cries for justice. They all knew it—if the movement was to survive, if the people were to wake up, they needed something that would shake the nation to its core.

But now, the fight had reached a turning point.

The British had introduced a new bill—The Public Safety Bill and the Trade Disputes Act. Under these laws, the government could silence anyone who dared to speak against them. It would crush the voices of workers, revolutionaries, and students—ensuring that no one could question British rule.

Bhagat Singh slammed the newspaper down on the table, his jaw clenched in frustration. The flickering candlelight made his eyes gleam with intensity as he looked up at his comrades. "They don't just want to rule us. They want to silence us forever."

Sukhdev exhaled sharply, rubbing his temples. "Every time we raise our voice, they tighten their grip. We protest, they arrest us. We speak, they shut us down. We write, they burn our words."

Rajguru leaned forward, fire burning in his eyes. "Then maybe it's time we make them listen in a language they can't ignore."

Bhagat Singh let the words settle before speaking. "No random violence. No reckless killings. That is not who we are. But we must do something so powerful, so unshakable, that they have no choice but to hear us."

Sukhdev nodded slowly, understanding. "Something that shakes the very foundation of their arrogance."

Bhagat Singh met his gaze. "Yes. And I know exactly what that is."

Sukhdev clenched his fists. "We have protested, marched, written, spoken. Nothing has changed."

Rajguru's eyes burned with rage. "Then maybe words aren't enough anymore."

The room was silent for a moment. Then Bhagat Singh exhaled and leaned forward. "No. We will not kill. Violence without purpose is not revolution—it is anarchy. We must do something bigger. Something that will wake up the entire nation."

His fingers tapped on the table as he thought. Then his eyes lit up.

"The British are deaf. It takes a loud noise to make the deaf hear."

Sukhdev's brows furrowed. "You're talking about—"

"A bomb," Bhagat Singh interrupted. "Not to kill. Just to make them listen."

Rajguru grinned. "Now that… that is an idea."

Sukhdev hesitated, his fingers gripping the edge of the table. "We will get caught," he said, his voice barely above a whisper. He looked at Bhagat Singh, searching for reassurance, for some way out of the inevitable.

Rajguru, arms crossed, exhaled sharply. "Then what happens next? What's the plan after that?"

Bhagat Singh leaned in, his gaze steady. "Then we stand trial. We use the courtroom as our battlefield. We let the entire nation see our resolve, hear our voices, and witness our sacrifice."

The Assembly hall was packed with British officials, their expressions smug and indifferent as debates droned on. Some shuffled papers, others whispered among themselves, confident in their unchecked authority. The scent of cigars filled the air, curling in lazy tendrils as they chuckled among themselves, making offhanded jokes about the "helpless natives." A few leaned back in their chairs, their polished boots propped up arrogantly as they dismissed the discussions with amused smirks. The air was thick with the monotony of colonial rule—until it was shattered.

BOOOOOM! A deafening explosion ripped through the chamber, shaking the very walls of colonial authority. The roar of the blast drowned out every sound, followed by an eerie silence before chaos erupted. Smoke coiled through the air, swallowing the room in a suffocating grey haze. Papers flew like frantic birds, chairs toppled over, and startled gasps turned into panicked shouts. The laughter and arrogance of the British officials vanished in an instant, replaced by shock and fear. The scent of burning gunpowder mixed with the fading smoke of cigars, now abruptly extinguished. Officers stumbled back, their monocles falling, their hands gripping the table for support. "What in God's name—?!" a voice choked out, but no answer came. The empire had been shaken to its core.

Amidst the swirling smoke, Bhagat Singh and Batukeshwar Dutt stood firm, their faces calm, their eyes blazing with purpose. The scent of burning parchment and gunpowder mixed with the acrid smell of cigars, now extinguished mid-puff. A few officers clutched their ears, dazed by the sudden explosion, their hands trembling as they reached for their weapons. "What in God's name—?" a voice choked out before being drowned by the growing uproar.

And then, in the midst of the chaos, their voices rang out, unwavering, unshaken—

""Inquilab Zindabad! Bharat Mata Ki Jai!" they roared, their voices thundering through the smoke-filled chamber. Again and again, their cries rang out, each repetition a hammer striking at the chains of oppression The words echoed off the towering walls, drowning out the panicked orders of the British officers. Their defiant chant refused to die, growing stronger, overpowering fear itself."

Guards stormed forward, their boots pounding against the marble floor, but they hesitated—if only for a second. Bhagat Singh and Dutt did not waver. They stood tall amidst the smoke and chaos, their fists raised in defiance. Their voices, fierce and unyielding, thundered through the assembly hall—

"Inquilab Zindabad! Bharat Mata Ki Jai!"

A commander barked, "Seize them!" Arrest them! but his voice was laced with something he would never admit—hesitation. The guards moved, yet their steps faltered. These were not men begging for mercy. These were warriors who had already conquered fear itself. The British officials scrambled, their chairs screeching against the marble floor, their faces pale with disbelief. The scent of gunpowder still lingered in the air, mixing with the acrid smoke from extinguished cigars. Panic gripped the room.

Bhagat Singh and Dutt exchanged a glance—a silent understanding passing between them, a moment of unshaken resolve. A slow, knowing smile flickered on their lips, as if they had already seen history being written. And then, in unison, their voices rang out once more, shaking the very foundation of the Assembly—

With a firm voice that cut through the commotion, Bhagat Singh shouted, "We did not come here to kill. We came here to awaken! To make the deaf hear!" "We did not intend to harm! Only to be heard!" But his words were lost in the fury of the moment.

His voice echoed in the chamber, defiant and unwavering. For a brief moment, even the British hesitated, staring at the young men who had walked into fire without flinching. The very foundation of British arrogance trembled as the echoes of the blast reverberated through the hall.

Dragged into court, their hands bound, they faced a panel of stern, unyielding judges. The newspapers painted them as criminals, but outside, the people whispered their names in reverence. The moment was electric—two men, facing an empire, unshaken in their purpose.

Their trial began with fervor, the courtroom brimming with tension as British judges and lawyers attempted to break their spirit with sharp questioning and accusations. Bhagat Singh, Rajguru, and Sukhdev stood firm, their voices unwavering, their responses laced with biting wit and defiant idealism. A British lawyer slammed his fist against the table. "You planted bombs in the Assembly! You intended to kill!" he accused.

The prosecution hurled allegations, but Bhagat Singh, with a slight smirk, countered with sharp retorts that left even the British stunned. "We are not criminals, we are revolutionaries. We fight for a cause greater than your laws," he declared. "We planted bombs, yes, but not to kill. If we had wished to kill, not a single official in that chamber would be alive today. Our aim was to make the deaf hear! To shake the very foundation of this oppressive rule!"

Sukhdev stepped forward, his voice calm yet resolute. "We do not regret our actions. We have not come here to plead for mercy. We have come to tell the world why we did what we did."

Rajguru smirked, his eyes gleaming with defiance. "You call us criminals. But what of the British, who have looted this land, spilled innocent blood, and crushed the spirit of our people for decades? If fighting against injustice is a crime, then yes, we are guilty. And we are proud."

"You are accused of sedition against the British Empire," the judge declared, his voice echoing through the chamber. "How do you plead?"

Bhagat Singh lifted his chin. "We do not plead to an unjust system. We challenge it."

A murmur rippled through the crowd. The British officials shifted in their seats, their arrogance momentarily disturbed. The prosecutor smirked, stepping forward. "Challenge it? With what? Your empty hands? Your poetry?"

Rajguru scoffed. "With ideas. Ideas that have already begun dismantling your empire, brick by brick."

The prosecutor leaned in. "You admit to the bombing, then?"

Sukhdev met his gaze, unflinching. "We admit to making the deaf hear."

The judge struck his gavel once more. "Enough! You are revolutionaries, yes, but revolution ends at the gallows. Your fate is sealed."

Bhagat Singh smiled. "Martyrdom is not the end. It is the beginning."

The air in the courtroom grew heavier as the days passed. British officers exchanged frustrated glances; they had expected fear, not unbreakable resolve. "These men should tremble before the Empire!" one of them muttered, slamming his fist against the table. But Bhagat Singh and his comrades only exchanged knowing smiles, their silence louder than any argument.

The British government realized—no amount of debate, no trial, no words could shake these men. The sessions grew quieter. The revolutionaries stood stronger. And then, one day—the trial stopped. The courtroom fell into an eerie silence. The waiting began. Days turned into an agonizing stretch of uncertainty, each moment thick with an unspoken verdict. The revolutionaries exchanged glances; they knew. This was not a delay. It was a decision.

Finally, the sentence was passed. Death. But fear never touched their faces. As they were led away, Bhagat Singh turned to the people in the courtroom. His voice was calm, steady.

"You may kill us, but our voices will thunder through generations."

And they did.

When the news spread through the prison that Bhagat Singh, Sukhdev, and Rajguru were to be hanged on March 23, 1931, an eerie silence descended upon the inmates. These young men, once mere faces among many, had become symbols of resistance, their unbreakable spirit inspiring all who came into contact with them. Now, their once-determined expressions were etched with grief, as if the walls of the prison itself bore the weight of their impending sacrifice.

"Why them?" a prisoner sobbed, clutching the cold iron bars. "What did they do wrong, except dream of a free land?"

"They didn't even get a chance to defend themselves!" another shouted, his voice thick with anger and disbelief.

"Is there no justice left in this world?" asked a trembling voice, its sorrow reverberating through the heavy air.

Even some British officers, who had long dismissed them as nothing more than rebellious youths, now felt a strange, unexpected sorrow. Yet, others stood firm, convinced that the empire's rule must be preserved at any cost. The prison walls bore witness to this moment of history, heavy with the burden of injustice and unanswered questions.

The final day arrived—the day they would be forced to surrender their lives for a cause they believed in so fiercely.

In their dimly lit cell, the air felt thicker than ever. Bhagat Singh leaned against the cold stone wall, his gaze distant but resolute. Sukhdev paced restlessly, his mind seemingly racing with thoughts of what was to come. Rajguru sat in stillness, his head bowed in quiet contemplation, his thoughts lost in the silence of the moment.

"Is it wrong to ask for freedom?" Sukhdev's voice cracked with raw emotion.

Rajguru sighed, a deep ache in his chest. "Did we do the right thing? Will it matter? Will they remember us?"

Bhagat Singh's voice broke through the uncertainty, calm and unwavering. "They may forget us. But what we fought for, what we believed in—that will remain, regardless of whether anyone remembers our names."

Sukhdev's hand tightened around the cold iron bars of his cell, his fingers trembling. "It's okay to be afraid, isn't it? I miss home... my family. Is it cowardice to feel this way?"

Bhagat Singh placed a steady hand on his shoulder, offering comfort and strength. "Fear is natural, Sukhdev. What matters is that we don't let it break us. We are not dying, we are becoming part of something far greater."

Rajguru's voice came softly, as if he was still testing his own thoughts. "Is this sacrifice? Or is it just... a surrender?"

Bhagat Singh's lips curved into a faint, yet knowing smile. "Neither. It is a step toward the future—a free future."

That morning, a British officer approached Bhagat Singh's cell. There was something in his eyes that day—a deep sadness that hadn't been there before.

"Please, Bhagat," the officer urged, his voice almost pleading. "Plead for mercy. Your life could be spared. You could still change the world. If you had been born in England, you would have been a great leader. I admire you, truly."

Bhagat Singh met his gaze, unwavering. "If you truly understood my cause, you would be standing with me, not against me."

The officer's expression softened, his voice faltering. "Why? Why this sacrifice? What will change? Will your people even remember you? I wish I could have done more for you."

Bhagat Singh's voice was firm, yet filled with quiet conviction. "A cause greater than oneself is worth any price. If my death sparks even a single soul to rise against tyranny, then it will not have been in vain. Revolution is built upon sacrifice, not pleas for mercy."

He then recited softly, his words carrying the weight of his belief:

"बस कि दुश्वार है हर काम का आसाँ होना,
आदमी को भी मयस्सर नहीं इंसां होना।"

(It's hard for any task to be easy,
Even a man struggles to become truly human.)

The officer stood frozen, his words failing him. Bhagat Singh, his resolve unshaken, turned away, his voice a quiet command: "Abandon weakness. Rise with courage. A warrior's duty is to uphold righteousness—not to be paralyzed by doubt."

Their final request was granted. They asked for one last moment together, unchained, to embrace one another. As they walked to the gallows, they did so with the dignity of men who had already transcended fear. Their heads were held high, their eyes steady with purpose. They smiled, their voices rising in unison:

"मेरा रंग दे बसंती चोला, माय रंग दे बसंती चोला..."

(Make my clothes the color of basanti, O Mother, make my clothes the color of basanti...)

The British officers, who had once viewed them as criminals, now stood silent, burdened with the realization that they had not executed rebels—but had extinguished the lives of three fearless, radiant souls whose only crime was dreaming of a free land.

They had asked for nothing more than to breathe freely, to walk upon the land that was their birthright, to live without chains. And though they were gone, their legacy remained, burning bright.

Though they were made an example of, the truth endured: those who fight for what is right never truly perish. They live on in history, in the hearts of those who dare to stand for justice. Doubt and weakness were never options. They stood for duty. They stood for a cause greater than themselves.

In those final moments, Bhagat Singh, Sukhdev, and Rajguru demonstrated what true courage is—a refusal to bow to fear, doubt, or weakness. They embodied the essence of a warrior's duty: to rise above the paralyzing grip of uncertainty and stand firm in the pursuit of righteousness.

Their sacrifice was not just an act of defiance but a testament to the power of unwavering belief in the cause for justice.

As we reflect on their bravery, we are reminded that courage is not the absence of fear, but the strength to rise in spite of it. In our own lives, we are often faced with moments where doubt clouds our path and fear holds us back. But just as they did, we must learn to abandon weakness and rise with courage. The true test of our character lies not in how we stand in the face of comfort, but how we rise when the world expects us to fall.

So, let's think—what is your duty in those 30 seconds of your life when the weight of doubt threatens to paralyze you? Will you cower in fear, or will you rise to uphold what is right, even when the odds seem insurmountable? Will you find the strength to choose righteousness over ease? The choice, as always, lies within you.

Julius Caesar: The Price of Ambition

Julius Caesar, born into the esteemed Julius family, had always known that his destiny was greater than the life of an ordinary Roman noble. His childhood had been spent amid the grandeur of Rome, where political power and influence reigned supreme. Yet despite his noble lineage, Caesar's family was not rich in power. He was a man who, from an early age, had dreamt of greatness, of surpassing the humble limits of his birth. And over the years, he had done just that—rising from the streets of Rome to become a brilliant general, earning victories in Gaul and solidifying his name as a master of warfare.

However, his rise to power came at a great cost. Rome, the republic he had fought for, was crumbling under the weight of its own corruption. The Senate, a body that was supposed to represent the will of the people, had become a tool of the elite, using its power to suppress the common citizens and uphold the interests of the few. Caesar had seen first hand how the Senate had betrayed its duty to the people, how it had failed to protect Rome's heart and soul, how it had placed its own wealth and power above the wellbeing of the citizens who fought and died for Rome's glory.

This made Caesar form his army, an army with an aligned vision, an army of brave hearts, an army ready to make history. His military success had made him not only a hero in the eyes of the common people but also a threat to the political elite. The Senate, once his ally, had grown increasingly wary of his influence, with Pompey, his former friend and comrade, leading the charge to strip Caesar of his power. By 49 BCE, tensions had reached a boiling point. The Senate had ordered Caesar to disband his army and return to Rome, a decree that was tantamount to stripping him of his status as a leader. Caesar knew that compliance would mean losing everything: his army, his authority, his future.

His only option was to defy the Senate. The Rubicon River, a small but symbolically significant boundary, stood between him and Rome. To cross it with his army would mean committing treason. It would mean war with Rome itself. The consequences were staggering.

Caesar stood at the banks of the Rubicon, his mind a battlefield of its own. Behind him, his army, a seasoned and loyal force, waited for his decision. But Caesar's heart was heavy with doubt. He had always been a man of action, but this decision was unlike any other.

"What if I back down?" he thought. His chest tightened at the prospect. "If I back down, my soldiers will see me as weak. My enemies will call me a coward, a man who couldn't fulfill his promises. What would the people of Rome think of me? Would they forget me? Would they turn their backs on me? A man who couldn't even lead his own men into battle?"

In the stillness of the moment, the soft, familiar voice of Cornelia, his lover, broke through the fog of his thoughts. She approached him, her steps slow and measured. Her eyes, filled with concern, met his.

"Julius," Cornelia said softly, her hand gently resting on his arm, "You've already achieved everything you set out to do. Why throw it all away for more power? You've fought for Rome, you've conquered Gaul. What more do you need? What more could Rome ask of you?"

Caesar turned to her, his heart heavy with the weight of his inner conflict. "What if I am nothing without it?" he whispered. "What will become of me if I turn back? What will the people think of me? A man who failed to change Rome... A man who couldn't fulfill his own destiny. I cannot afford to be weak, Cornelia. I must act, or I will lose everything."

Cornelia's eyes filled with sorrow, but she didn't pull away. "Julius, I love you. But I don't want to see you lose yourself in your ambition. Power is fleeting. It comes at a cost. What if you gain the empire, but lose your soul? What will be left of you then?"

Caesar's heart tightened. He had always been driven by ambition—by the belief that he was destined for greatness. But what if that greatness came at too high a cost? What if this ambition was a trap, leading him to a fate he couldn't escape?

Just as his mind swirled with doubt, a voice, deep and commanding, echoed through his thoughts. His father's voice. Gaius Julius Caesar, the man who had never realized the full potential of his name, appeared before him, as if summoned by the very weight of the decision he faced.

"Julius, my son," the ghostly voice resonated in Caesar's mind. His father's image, a figure of faded grandeur, stood before him. His presence was not physical, but palpable. "I sought glory, but I never achieved what I desired. I dreamed of power, of ruling Rome, but I never took the necessary steps to make it mine. You, my son, are different. You have the opportunity to do what I could not. But know this—power comes with a price."

Caesar looked at the image of his father, his throat tightening. "Father, I have spent my entire life chasing what you never had. I will not be remembered like you—obscure and forgotten. I will be the one who changes Rome. I will leave a legacy, something greater than you could ever imagine."

"At what cost?" his father's voice asked, his tone softer now. "I wanted power, but I lost my soul in the pursuit of it. You, my son, have the chance to do things differently. But remember this: Rome is a republic, not a kingdom. If you act out of ambition alone, you may find yourself as its master, but at what cost to Rome? And to yourself?"

Caesar turned away, feeling his father's words gnaw at him. The vision of his father faded, but the doubt lingered. His eyes drifted back to Cornelia, whose face reflected the same concern his father's words had stirred.

"I can't let fear hold me back," Caesar muttered to himself, his voice filled with frustration. "If I turn back now, I will lose everything. I will be forgotten. But if I move forward… I risk war. I risk everything."

Cornelia stepped closer, her voice soft but firm. "Julius, I know you. I know your heart. But you cannot ignore the price of your ambition. What will Rome think of you if you cross that river? Will they see you as a savior? Or will they see you as a tyrant?"

Caesar closed his eyes, wrestling with the thought of his army, his legacy, and his future. He had always prided himself on being a man of destiny, a man who would change Rome forever. But now, as he stood at the edge of the Rubicon, he realized that his decision would define him forever.

"What if I fail?" Caesar asked aloud, his voice raw. "What if I lead my men into war, only to watch Rome burn? What will the world say of me then?"

Cornelia looked at him, her expression full of love and sadness. "Julius, if you act from a place of fear, you will never know peace. But if you act from courage, from the belief that you are doing what is right, you will have my support. You will have the support of the people, too. But you must choose your path."

For a long moment, there was only silence. Caesar stood there, torn between his desire for greatness and the heavy cost of that ambition. The Rubicon lay before him, a river that separated him from his future.

He felt his father's presence again, the last echo of his words ringing in his mind. "Remember, my son, greatness is not measured by power alone, but by how you wield it."

Finally, Caesar looked up, his expression hardening. He turned to his army, his generals, his loyal soldiers who had followed him through thick and thin. They waited for his command, their eyes filled with anticipation.

He took a deep breath, his heart steadying. "We march forward," he declared, his voice steady, his gaze unwavering. "We cross the Rubicon. This is my destiny. This is the moment that will define us."

His generals and soldiers roared in agreement, their loyalty to him unwavering. Caesar mounted his horse, and with a single, resolute command, the march began.

The world would change. Rome would change. Caesar's destiny had been sealed, and there would be no turning back. But as the Rubicon was crossed, Caesar could not help but wonder—what would the world say of him? Would he be remembered as a liberator, or a tyrant? The question would haunt him for the rest of his life.

As Caesar's army began to march across the Rubicon, the weight of the decision pressed down on him like the weight of an entire empire. The once peaceful river now symbolized the point of no return, a silent witness to the end of one chapter and the beginning of another. The sound of boots marching in unison filled the air, echoing off the surrounding hills like the heartbeat of Rome itself.

Caesar's gaze lingered on the rippling waters of the river. He could still hear the whispers of his father's voice, fading with the winds, and Cornelia's sorrowful words that lingered in his heart. But now, as he looked forward, there was only the path ahead—a path that promised glory, but at the cost of peace, at the cost of everything he had once held dear.

He looked to his soldiers, their eyes filled with resolve and loyalty, their faces shadowed in the light of the setting sun. Each man carried a part of Caesar within him now—a piece of his ambition, his dream, his soul. There would be no turning back.

"I have crossed the Rubicon," Caesar thought, his heart steady with the knowledge that this moment would define the rest of his life. "Whatever comes next, I will face it. For Rome, for my destiny, for myself."

As the sun dipped below the horizon, casting long shadows across the land, Caesar's voice rose above the clamor of his men, clear and commanding. "Forward!" His command rang out, firm and unshakable.

In those final moments, as the world seemed to hold its breath, Caesar understood something deeply profound—power, ambition, and legacy were not measured in the victories alone, but in the courage to face the unknown, to rise above doubt and embrace what lay ahead.

The river behind him now felt like a distant memory, as the future surged forward with all the force of an unstoppable tide. And as the last rays of sunlight disappeared, Caesar, the man who had crossed the Rubicon, was no longer a mere mortal. He was a legend in the making, bound to be remembered for eternity, for his choice was not simply to march into Rome—it was to define the fate of an empire, and his own.

But in those 30 seconds—those brief moments of hesitation—Caesar had made his choice. He had risen above doubt and embraced the future.

Reflection: The Strength to Choose

Life constantly presents us with choices—some simple, some life-altering. But the most difficult choices are often the ones where doubt clouds judgment, where the weight of emotions and responsibilities collide with the necessity of action. In these moments, hesitation is natural, but it is in overcoming that hesitation that true strength is found.

Arjuna stood on the battlefield of Kurukshetra, paralyzed by doubt. His heart wavered as he faced his own kin, his mentors, and the ghosts of relationships that had once defined him. In that moment, the warrior in him faltered, questioning the righteousness of his duty. Yet, Krishna's wisdom revealed that dharma is not dictated by personal attachment—it is the unwavering pursuit of righteousness, even when the heart protests. The choice before Arjuna was not just about war; it was about whether he had the strength to fulfill his purpose despite the turmoil within. In the end, his clarity was found not in abandoning his role, but in embracing it completely. His strength did not come from his bow, but from his ability to rise above doubt and step forward into destiny.

Like Arjuna, Bhagat Singh, Sukhdev, and Rajguru faced a defining moment of choice. The colonial rulers sought to silence them, to suppress the voices of those who dared to demand justice. But rather than surrender to fear, they chose to act—not through blind violence, but through a revolution of thought and sacrifice. They understood that the path they walked would lead to martyrdom, but they did not waver. Their strength lay in their conviction, in the belief that their sacrifice would ignite the fire of freedom in the hearts of millions. And so, they did not fear death; they welcomed it as the price of change.

Julius Caesar, too, stood at the precipice of an irreversible decision. The Rubicon was not just a river—it was the boundary between caution and conquest, between retreat and history. The weight of ambition, of power, of the unknown loomed over him. Would he be seen as a liberator or a tyrant? Would history remember him as Rome's savior or its downfall? Yet, in the end, the fear of regret outweighed the fear of failure. Caesar understood that hesitation was the true enemy of greatness. With unwavering resolve, he stepped forward, sealing his fate and forever altering the course of history.

Each of these stories reminds us that strength is not the absence of fear or uncertainty—it is the ability to act despite them. It is in these critical moments that one's character is forged. Do we let doubt consume us, or do we rise above it? Do we surrender to fear, or do we walk forward, even when the path is uncertain?

Because in the end, the strength to choose is what defines us. And the choices we make—not just in battle, not just in revolution, but in the quiet moments of hesitation—shape the legacy we leave behind.

Rising Above Doubt: An Introspection

Doubt is a universal experience. It creeps into our minds before major decisions, in moments of uncertainty, and when the weight of responsibility feels unbearable. Sometimes, it masquerades as caution, convincing us to wait a little longer, to seek more reassurance. Other times, it paralyzes us, keeping us from moving forward when action is needed the most.

But hesitation has a cost. The moments we spend trapped in doubt are moments we never get back. Every great leader, warrior, or visionary has faced this inner conflict. Yet, what separates them is their ability to rise above it. To act, even when fear and uncertainty threaten to hold them back.

As you reflect on your own journey, ask yourself:

- Have you ever stood at a crossroads, unable to decide? What held you back—the fear of failure, or the fear of what others might think?

- When faced with doubt, do you seek clarity through reflection, or do you allow hesitation to control your actions?

- Do you trust yourself enough to make decisions, or do you often wait for external validation before taking a step forward?

- How many opportunities have you lost because doubt whispered that you were not ready, not good enough, not capable?

- When making difficult choices, do you focus only on the immediate consequences, or do you consider the long-term impact of inaction?

- If today was a defining moment in your life—like Arjuna on the battlefield, Bhagat Singh in court, or Caesar at the Rubicon—would you choose action, or would you let hesitation decide for you?

- What would your life look like if, in your moments of doubt, you had chosen courage over fear?

The truth is, doubt will always be present. But rising above it is a choice—one that only you can make. The next time hesitation grips you, take a moment to ask yourself: *Am I delaying because I truly need more time, or because I am afraid to move forward?*

In the end, history is not shaped by those who waited for the perfect moment. It is written by those who chose to act, despite the uncertainty.

Perspective Shifts That Transform Reality

Bhagavad Gita, Chapter 2, Verse 69:

या निशा सर्वभूतानां तस्यां जागर्ति संयमी।
यस्यां जाग्रति भूतानि सा निशा पश्यतो मुनेः।।

(What is night for all beings is the time of awakening
for the self-controlled; and the time of awakening for
all beings is night for the introspective sage.)

Beyond the Surface, Beneath the Obvious

Life often presents us with fragmented pieces of truth, much like a puzzle. Each piece holds meaning, yet it takes time, patience, and reflection to see the whole picture. Without pause, we risk clinging to incomplete truths, leading to misunderstandings, conflict, or even irreversible decisions. What one perceives as reality may be entirely hidden to another, and in that divergence of perspectives lies the need for self-awareness and clarity.

This chapter explores the transformative power of those 30 Seconds—how a fleeting moment of reflection, listening, or reconsideration can reveal hidden truths, mend relationships, and foster deeper connections. Through timeless parables and relatable stories, it reminds us that perspective is not just about seeing, but truly understanding—and that the willingness to pause, even briefly, can change everything.

173

The Elephant and the Blind Men: A Timeless Allegory

In a quiet, dusty village nestled at the foot of a great mountain, life moved at an unhurried pace. The villagers knew each other's names, their lives intertwined through shared traditions, stories, and the comforting rhythm of daily life. Children played by the river, the scent of cooking fires drifted through the air, and the grand banyan tree stood tall in the village square, offering shade to those who gathered beneath its sprawling branches.

Among the villagers were six blind men, well-respected for their wisdom and deep conversations. Though they could not see the world, they had learned to navigate it through touch, sound, and intuition. They trusted their senses implicitly, piecing together reality in ways the sighted could not comprehend. Their debates, often philosophical, fascinated the villagers—sometimes mundane, sometimes profound. Yet, for all their wisdom, there was one fundamental limitation they did not recognize: the incompleteness of their own perspectives.

One day, an unexpected event challenged their understanding of the world. A wandering merchant arrived in the village with a majestic elephant—a creature none of the blind men had ever encountered before. The villagers, amazed by the animal's size and strength, spoke of it in hushed awe. But for the blind men, the descriptions meant little. What did it truly mean for something to be "enormous" or "mighty" if they had never touched or heard anything like it before?

Curiosity sparked within them. For days, they discussed what the elephant might be like. Some imagined it as a powerful beast, others thought it must resemble familiar animals like oxen or horses. But words alone could not satisfy them. They needed to experience it for themselves.

The merchant, amused by their curiosity, graciously agreed to let them examine the elephant. One by one, the blind men stepped forward, their hands outstretched, eager to uncover the truth.

The first man, reaching for the tusk, felt its smooth, curved surface and ran his fingers along its sharp edge. "The elephant is like a spear," he declared. "Strong, pointed, and unyielding." To him, the creature was a weapon of power.

The second man, grasping the trunk, shook his head. "No, the elephant is like a snake—long, flexible, and alive with movement." The way it curled, twisted, and responded to his touch convinced him that the elephant was something agile and fluid.

The third man, placing his hands on one of the massive legs, scoffed at their descriptions. "You are both mistaken. The elephant is like a pillar—solid and unshakable." He felt the thick, sturdy structure and imagined the creature as something immovable, like the foundation of a temple.

The fourth man, exploring the large, flapping ears, disagreed entirely. "The elephant is nothing like that! It is like a fan, with wide surfaces that move air around." The gentle breeze created by the elephant's ears gave him an entirely different impression—not of strength, but of lightness and grace.

The fifth man, pressing his hands against the elephant's vast belly, laughed. "You are all wrong. The elephant is like a wall, massive and unyielding." To him, the creature felt like a great, impenetrable barrier.

The sixth man, grasping the tail, confidently stated, "None of you see the truth. The elephant is like a rope—thin, coarse, and flexible." To him, the elephant was nothing more than a long, twisting cord.

Each man, convinced of his own experience, refused to believe the others.

"You are wrong!" one shouted.

"No, it is you who does not understand!" another argued.

Their voices clashed, each one defending his own truth, unable to accept that the others might be right in their own way. They had all touched the same elephant, yet each had only grasped a part of it. In their certainty, they mistook their limited understanding for the whole truth.

From a distance, the villagers exchanged knowing smiles. Unlike the blind men, they could see the entire elephant standing before them—every tusk, ear, trunk, and leg forming a complete reality. But the blind men, caught in the boundaries of their own perceptions, remained unaware of what they were missing.

Had they paused for just 30 seconds, silenced their need to be right, and truly listened to one another, they might have woven their fragmented truths into a greater understanding. Instead, their unwillingness to consider another viewpoint kept them locked in their separate realities, unable to see the whole picture.

Because sometimes, the limits we perceive are not in our senses, but in our unwillingness to see beyond our own perspective.

Sibling Love: Lost in Conflict, Found in Reflection

Ritika sat in the sterile, quiet waiting room of the hospital, her hands folded tightly in her lap. The fluorescent lights above her buzzed softly, adding to the oppressive atmosphere. Her mind was racing as she reflected on the years of tension that had built up in her family. Her father had been the center of their world, a man of stern discipline, lofty expectations, and unwavering control. But age and illness had chipped away at that image. Now, he was gone.

Their father's passing had left them shattered, but instead of uniting them, it had deepened the emotional rift between her siblings Anuj and Rhea. For years, they had competed for their father's approval, each trying to prove their worth. The resentment had only festered as they took turns caring for him in his final days. Anuj had been the one physically present, managing hospital visits, medications, and daily needs, while Rhea had contributed financially and tried to make up for her absence in other ways. Both felt their sacrifices had gone unnoticed by the other.

"You always act like you did everything," Anuj said bitterly, his voice tinged with exhaustion. "But throwing money at the problem isn't the same as being there, Rhea. I was the one who sat with him when he could barely breathe. Where were you then?"

Rhea's eyes flashed with hurt, but she refused to back down. "And you think being physically there is the only thing that matters? Who do you think paid for his treatments, his hospital bills? Just because I wasn't here every second doesn't mean I did any less."

Their arguments had always taken this shape—each trying to outdo the other, proving they had loved their father more, done more, sacrificed more. Even as children, they had battled for his attention. Rhea had studied tirelessly, determined to outshine Anuj academically, while Anuj had pushed himself in sports, earning medals their father displayed proudly. Their father had unknowingly fuelled their rivalry, never openly favouring one, yet setting impossibly high standards that made them feel they had to fight for his recognition.

Anuj remembered the day he won the state-level football championship. His heart had swelled with pride as he waited for his father's words of appreciation. Instead, his father had merely nodded and said, "Good. But Rhea just got into IIT. That's real achievement." The sting of that moment had never left him.

Rhea, too, had her scars. She recalled coming home one day, her face glowing with excitement after winning a prestigious debate competition. But before she could even tell her father, he had brushed past her to ask Anuj about his upcoming match. She had stood there, trophy in hand, feeling invisible.

The pain of those childhood wounds had carried into adulthood, shaping their strained relationship. And now, even in their father's death, they were still fighting to prove their worth.

As the eldest, Ritika had always been the bridge between her siblings, the one who soothed tensions and tried to keep the family from unravelling. But now, even she felt the weight of exhaustion pressing down on her. Sitting in the waiting room, she realized that if they didn't find a way to move past their resentment now, they might never do so.

She took a deep breath, her voice steady yet resolute as she cut through the rising tension. "Enough," she said, her tone firm but not unkind. "What if we're all holding onto different pieces of the same struggle? Like the blind men and the elephant? Before we say anything else, let's just take 30 seconds to step back and truly consider where the other is coming from.

The analogy hit Rhea like a wave. She had heard of the parable before—the one about the blind men and the elephant—but never had it felt so relevant. The three of them had been blindly groping for solutions, each convinced that their approach was the right one. But they were missing the bigger picture. They had been fighting for their father, yet they had spent more time fighting each other.

For the first time in weeks, silence fell over the three siblings—not the heavy silence of anger, but the quiet of introspection. The seconds ticked by, stretching like an eternity. As the pause settled in, Anuj sat down beside Rhea, his face softening. "I... I guess I've been too harsh," he admitted, his voice thick with emotion. "I didn't realize how much you've been handling on your own. I was so caught up in my own frustrations that I didn't see how much you were doing."

Rhea's eyes filled with tears, her guard slowly coming down. "And I didn't think about how hard it must be for you to juggle everything else—work, your family, and still try to be here for him."

It was as if something clicked within them both. The walls of resentment and misunderstanding that had separated them for so long began to crumble. They began to talk, not to defend their actions, but to understand one another's experiences. They shared their fears—Anuj's fear of never being enough, Rhea's fear of being overlooked, and Ritika's fear of losing her ability to hold the family together. For the first time in years, they listened without judgment, without the need to be right.

And then, Ritika posed a question that sent a chill down their spines. "What if we hadn't taken that pause? What if we had let our anger consume us?"

Anuj and Rhea both knew the answer. Their fights had nearly torn them apart before—what if this had been the final straw? What if their father's passing had become just another reason to stay bitter, to cut ties, to never speak again? The mere thought of it sent a shudder through them. The weight of all their unresolved resentment could have crushed whatever love remained between them.

By the time the doctor entered the room to finalize the paperwork for their father's passing, the siblings had found a new sense of unity. The grief was still raw, but even in the face of this loss, something had shifted between them. Together, they were ready to face the challenges ahead—not as adversaries, but as partners, bound by their shared love for their father.

In the days that followed, their relationship continued to evolve. The bitterness that had once defined their interactions gave way to more honest, vulnerable conversations. Ritika no longer had to bear the weight of being the mediator; Anuj and Rhea began to mediate their own conflicts, acknowledging the strengths and limitations in each other's approaches. They learned that honouring their father's memory wasn't about proving who had done more—it was about standing together, despite their differences.

Sitting in the hospital cafeteria a few days later, sharing a quiet meal, Ritika looked at her siblings and felt a sense of peace. Their father was gone, but his lessons remained. And in that moment, she knew that their fractured bond had been restored—not through grand gestures, but through the simple act of pausing, reflecting, and seeing each other for who they truly were.

Socrates' Final Stand: A Legacy Beyond Life

The year was 399 BCE, and Athens, once the shining city of intellect and democracy, now found itself at the crossroads of a turbulent moment. Socrates, the philosopher who had spent his life questioning the very fabric of society, stood accused before the Athenian court. The charges were severe: corrupting the youth and impiety, the very beliefs that had earned him admiration from some, but disdain from others. On this fateful day, Socrates was not merely standing in defense of his life; he was defending his life's work—the pursuit of truth and wisdom. Yet, as the charges against him filled the courtroom, a deep sense of conflict stirred within his soul. Socrates had always believed that truth could never be bound by the constraints of popular opinion or conventional belief. But now, he stood before the law, accused of challenging the very foundations upon which Athens had built its identity.

As the trial unfolded, Socrates' mind drifted not to his accusers but to the questions that had always plagued him—questions that had led him here. He had never feared death, yet, in this moment, he was overcome by a deeper sorrow. His entire life had been devoted to the pursuit of wisdom, to understanding the world and encouraging others to do the same. But now, he wondered if he had gone too far. Had his constant questioning, his refusal to conform, led him to this place of judgment? Would the city that had once revered him now condemn him for the very beliefs that made him who he was?

He could hear the voice of his loyal friend Crito in his mind. Crito, who had always stood by him, had visited him in his cell after the trial and pleaded for him to escape. "Socrates, you cannot let them do this," he had urged. "You can flee. We can help you. Think of your family, your disciples. Think of all the good you can still do. Don't let them take you from us." But Socrates had remained calm, his face steady. He knew that his friend's words were spoken out of love, but in his heart, Socrates knew what he had to do. To escape would be to abandon his own principles, to live in fear rather than in truth. His life had been one of defiance, not against people, but against complacency and ignorance. To flee now would be to betray everything he had ever believed in.

That night, as he sat alone in his cell, Socrates pondered his choices. The execution date loomed, and Crito had visited once more, his eyes filled with urgency. Crito's voice trembled as he spoke, his desperation now mixed with sorrow. "But Socrates, you've always said that wisdom must be shared. If you die today, won't your teachings die with you? How can your words guide others if you are no longer here to speak them?"

Socrates met his friend's gaze, his expression unwavering, his voice steady. "Crito, you see my life as the vessel for my teachings, but I see my death as their ultimate lesson." He exhaled softly, as if surrendering not to fate, but to the truth he had always lived by. "If I flee, I contradict everything I have ever stood for. I have spent my life teaching that one must act with integrity, no matter the cost. What kind of message would I send if, when faced with the test of my own philosophy, I abandoned it for the sake of survival?"

Crito's breath hitched. He had spent so long trying to save his friend that he had failed to see that Socrates was saving something far greater—his ideals.

Socrates continued, his voice calm yet resolute. "You fear that my work will end with me, but true wisdom does not die with the body. It lives in those who listen, those who question, those who seek truth beyond their own fears. My death is not the loss of my teachings; it is the fulfillment of them. If I embrace this moment, I show the world that death is not to be feared, and that the soul, and the truth it carries, is eternal."

Crito lowered his head, his chest tight with grief but also with understanding. For the first time, he truly saw the depth of Socrates' conviction. They both wanted the same thing—to ensure that Socrates' teachings would endure. Crito had believed that preserving Socrates' life was the only way to achieve that. But Socrates saw a greater truth—that his acceptance of death would immortalize his message far beyond his physical existence.

As the final day arrived, Socrates found himself at peace. He had spent his last hours speaking with his students, imparting his final teachings. He spoke of virtue, justice, and the nature of the soul. He spoke of living a life driven by purpose, not by fear of death. And through all of it, he remained calm. In his final moments, he had no fear, no regrets. He had lived a life according to his principles, and in that, he found peace. The idea of death no longer seemed like an enemy; it was simply another step on the journey of the soul.

He had embraced it, knowing that his life—his search for truth—had been worth living.

When the executioner arrived to carry out the sentence, Socrates did not resist. With a quiet dignity, he drank the hemlock that would take his life. As the poison began to work its way through his body, he turned to his friend Crito, who was standing at his side, and spoke his final words. "Crito, we owe a cock to Asclepius. Please, don't forget to pay the debt."

To most, these words seemed strange, even cryptic. But to Socrates, they were simple. Asclepius, the god of healing, had always been associated with the idea of healing the soul. In these final words, Socrates was acknowledging that his journey had come to an end, but that it was not an end of the soul. His work was complete, and his peace was found in the acceptance of death—not as something to fear, but as a natural part of the cycle of life.

As the poison took hold and his body grew still, Socrates' spirit was at peace. His death marked the end of his life, but not the end of his mission. The questions he had asked, the truths he had uncovered, would live on in the hearts and minds of those who had listened to him. His death would not silence his voice, for it was the voice of truth. In that final moment, as his thoughts drifted away and his breath slowed, it wasn't the poison that claimed him—it was his choice to embrace death, not in fear, but with the clarity of a mind that had seen beyond the immediate.

For Socrates, those 30 seconds before his final breath were not merely the passing of time—they were the culmination of a life devoted to introspection, to questioning, and to seeing beyond the immediate. In that brief moment, his choice and Crito's plea stood side by side, not in contradiction, but as two perspectives of the same truth. Crito believed that preserving Socrates' life was the way to keep his teachings alive, while Socrates saw that embracing his death would immortalize them beyond his physical existence.

Had Crito paused long enough to step beyond his own fears, he would have seen that they were not opposing forces, but seekers of the same outcome—to ensure that wisdom endures. In those final 30 seconds, Socrates had not only accepted his fate but had also affirmed his life's purpose. And in that pause, in that moment of stillness before the end, he had achieved what so many struggle to grasp in their lifetime: that truth, when seen from different perspectives, does not divide us—it connects us.

His peace was not merely in accepting death, but in understanding that by standing firm in his truth, his work would live on, shaping generations to come. His final breath was not an ending, but a continuation—a testament to the power of a pause, the clarity of introspection, and the ability to see beyond one's own perspective to embrace the greater whole.

Reflection: From Conflict to Clarity - The Space Between Reaction and Understanding

In each of these stories—the blind men and the elephant, Ritika's family, and Socrates' final moments—we see how perspective, when left unchallenged, can limit understanding, create conflict, or even obscure the truth. Yet, in each case, a pause—whether taken or missed—had the power to reshape reality, not by changing the facts, but by altering the way they were perceived.

The blind men argued because they believed their individual experiences of the elephant were absolute. Had they paused to listen instead of insisting on being right, they might have seen that their truths were incomplete, not incorrect. Similarly, Anuj and Rhea, though deeply hurt, were not divided by hatred but by their need for validation. In stepping back, they realized their pain came from the same source—love—and that their battle had always been with the past, not with each other. Socrates and Crito, too, sought the same outcome: for wisdom to live on. But where Crito saw survival as the answer, Socrates saw integrity as the means to immortality. His acceptance of death was not a resignation but a conscious choice to ensure that his teachings transcended his existence.

In all these moments, the facts did not change—the elephant remained an elephant, grief remained grief, and death remained inevitable. But the way these realities were understood changed everything. The 30-second pause was the bridge between conflict and clarity, between isolation and connection, between short-sightedness and wisdom. It is not the events themselves, but how we choose to perceive them, that transforms our reality.

In our fast-paced lives, where decisions are often made in the heat of the moment, we forget that taking a step back—breathing, reflecting, and understanding—can lead to life-changing outcomes. In these 30 seconds, we find the space to realign with our deeper truths, to consider other perspectives, and to choose a path that is more thoughtful, more compassionate, and more aligned with who we truly are.

Introspection: The Space Between Perception and Truth

As you reflect on the stories in this chapter, consider the moments in your own life where a shift in perspective could have changed everything.

- Have you ever been so certain of your own viewpoint that you dismissed others, only to realize later that you had only seen part of the picture?

- Have you ever found yourself in conflict, believing you were right, only to later understand that the other person was not wrong—just seeing things differently?

- Have you ever been so focused on proving a point that you missed the deeper truth beneath the argument?

- Have you ever judged someone's actions without understanding their reasoning, only to later realize their intentions were not what you assumed?

- Have you ever felt trapped by your circumstances, only to realize later that shifting the way you saw the situation could have changed everything?

- Have you ever experienced a moment where a simple pause—just 30 seconds—allowed you to see beyond your initial emotions and recognize a bigger truth?

Because sometimes, all it takes is 30 seconds to step beyond your own perspective and into a reality far greater than the one you thought you knew.

The Strength to Let Go, The Courage to Begin

Bhagavad Gita, Chapter 2, Verse 22 (BG 2.22)

वासांसि जीर्णानि यथा विहाय

(As a person sheds worn-out garments and wears new ones, so does the soul shed a worn-out body and enter a new one.)

The Art of Letting Go: Shedding the Old, Embracing the New

Life is a continuous process of change—of shedding the past to make space for what lies ahead. Just as a soul discards an old body to take on a new one, we, too, must release worn-out identities, relationships, and burdens that no longer serve us. But letting go is rarely easy. The weight of memories, attachments, and fears can make us resist the inevitable, clinging to what is familiar even when it holds us back.

Yet, transformation is not found in holding on—it is found in release. The Bhagavad Gita reminds us that change is not an end, but a passage—a necessary step in our journey toward growth. When we learn to embrace this truth, we find that what seems like loss is often a rebirth in disguise.

In the moments before stepping into the unknown, we face hesitation, uncertainty, and sometimes even grief. But it is in these moments that our future is shaped—not by what we leave behind, but by our willingness to walk forward.

Let's explore three stories of individuals who stood at the crossroads of change—facing the pull of the past and the promise of the future. Through their journeys, we witness the strength it takes to let go and the courage required to embrace what comes next.

Kurukshetra: From War to Wisdom

The great Kurukshetra war had ended, but the battlefield still haunted Yudhishthir. This was no ordinary war—it was a battle between the Pandavas and the Kauravas, cousins torn apart by greed, ambition, and destiny. The struggle for dharma had claimed thousands of lives, including revered warriors and beloved kin. The echoes of clashing steel, the cries of the fallen, and the final, anguished wails of those left behind lived within him. He had won, yet victory felt like a hollow whisper against the weight of loss.

Tonight, the great hall of Indraprastha was empty. The golden throne of Hastinapur stood before him, bathed in the flickering glow of torches. It was no longer just a seat of power—it was a monument to the cost of war.

The Kurukshetra war had been the final reckoning between dharma and adharma, a battle fought between the Pandavas and the Kauravas for righteousness, justice, and the rightful claim to the throne of Hastinapur. The war had lasted eighteen brutal days, leaving the battlefield littered with the bodies of warriors who had once been revered legends. The great Bhishma, the noble Karna, the wise Drona, and the fearless Abhimanyu had all perished. The land that had once been fertile was now soaked in the blood of brothers and kin, and the air still carried the weight of unspeakable sorrow.

His feet felt heavy as he stepped closer, as if the weight of countless souls clung to him, refusing to let go. Every life lost—Abhimanyu, Drona, Karna, Bhishma—was not just a memory but a wound carved deep into his being. He saw their faces in the polished gold of the throne, their eyes staring back at him, questioning, accusing, longing. The echoes of their voices rang in his mind—Karna's silent acceptance of fate, Bhishma's sorrowful blessing, Abhimanyu's fearless charge into death. Could he sit upon this throne when it was built upon their ashes? Could he wear a crown that once belonged to the very men he had been forced to destroy?

The silence of the chamber was suffocating. Then, a familiar voice broke through.

"Yudhishthir."

Krishna stood at the entrance, his presence as calm as the still waters of a deep ocean. His eyes held neither judgment nor expectation, only knowing.

Yudhishthir turned slowly, his heart full of conflict. "I have earned this throne, Krishna. But do I deserve it?" His voice wavered under the weight of his doubt. "At what cost have I gained it? The land is ours, but the soil is soaked with the blood of our own kin."

His voice grew more anguished. "I see their faces, Krishna. Every time I close my eyes, I see Bhishma lying on that bed of arrows, his wisdom lost to time. I see Karna, a warrior denied dignity until his last breath. I see Abhimanyu, a boy who never lived to see his father's embrace again. What right do I have to sit upon this throne when I could not save them?"

His hands trembled as he gestured toward the seat of power. "This throne is not mine—it belongs to those who fell. It belongs to every mother who weeps for her son, to every widow left behind. How can I rule when my very presence in this palace is a reminder of what was lost?"

Krishna walked forward, placing a gentle hand on Yudhishthir's shoulder. "Tell me, Yudhishthir, what do you see before you?"

Yudhishthir looked at the throne, his throat tightening. "I see a seat of power that has devoured generations in its hunger. I see a prize that demanded too great a sacrifice. I see a war that should have never been fought."

Krishna sighed, his voice carrying both the weight of the cosmos and the tenderness of a friend. "Then you still carry the battlefield within you, Yudhishthir. But tell me, how long will you let the ghosts of war chain you to the past?"

He stepped closer, his eyes piercing yet compassionate. "You grieve for those who are gone, but do you grieve for those who remain? The widowed mothers, the orphaned children, the broken land—do they not deserve a king who chooses to heal instead of mourn?"

Krishna's voice grew firmer, almost challenging. "You call this throne a monument of war, but what if you make it a beacon of peace? You lament the cost of victory, but if you refuse to rule, then every sacrifice becomes meaningless. Abhimanyu gave his life believing in a future you were meant to lead. Ghatotkacha embraced death so you could stand here today. Draupadi endured humiliation and loss with faith in dharma. Kunti bore the pain of separation, yet never faltered in her belief in righteousness. Gandhari, despite her grief, accepted the will of destiny. And Parikshit, the only heir of this generation, needs a kingdom that is just, not haunted by regret. Will you let the past consume you, or will you rise and fulfill the dharma you were born for?"

Yudhishthir clenched his fists. "How, Krishna? The war may be over, but my heart remains on that battlefield. I still see Duryodhana's last breath, Karna's sorrowful smile as he fell, Bhishma's body resting on a bed of arrows. How do I rule when my soul is still trapped in those moments?"

Krishna's voice was gentle but firm. "Just as a man discards old garments and wears new ones, so too must the soul shed the past and embrace what is to come. You mourn the old, but do you not see? This is not the end—this is a new beginning. You are not meant to rule for ambition, nor for vengeance, but for dharma. Do not see the throne as a burden of war; see it as a responsibility of peace."

Yudhishthir's breath caught in his throat. He closed his eyes, but the darkness offered no escape. It only brought forth the images that haunted him—the dying gasps of warriors, the lifeless bodies of his brothers-in-arms, the anguished cries of mothers who had lost their sons. His chest tightened as if the weight of an entire kingdom was pressing upon him, crushing him beneath the burden of sorrow and regret.

"Krishna, tell me... is this the fate of a righteous man? To walk the path of dharma, only to be left with nothing but ashes? If this is justice, why does it feel so cruel?"

And in that moment—those moments of silence—he stood at the crossroads of his soul. The war would never truly leave him, nor would the echoes of the cries that once filled the battlefield. Yet, he had to choose: remain shackled to the past, or rise beyond it.

He took a deep breath, feeling the weight of every soul lost in the war pressing upon him. "I cannot bring them back," he whispered, his voice raw. "But if I drown in their memories, I will betray their sacrifice."

Yudhishthir clenched his fists, his body trembling with the war between grief and duty. "I have spent nights wishing I had fallen in their place. I have cursed the fate that spared me while it took them. But Krishna, if I continue to grieve, am I not dishonouring them? Was their sacrifice meant to create a broken king?"

Tears welled in his eyes as he exhaled. And then, with a will forged in the fires of suffering, he let the war fade. He let go—not to forget, but to free himself. Not that he would erase the past, but that he would not let it define him.

Slowly, he reached for his crown and removed it. He placed it on the throne before him—not as a symbol of power, but as a symbol of service.

When he turned back to Krishna, his voice was steady. "I will rule, Krishna. But I will rule for the people, not for myself."

Krishna smiled, his eyes gleaming with both wisdom and warmth. "Then, my friend, you have truly won. But remember, the path of a king is long, and the burdens of the past will try to weigh you down. Every morning, you must remind yourself—your duty is not to grieve but to serve. Rule with justice, lead with compassion, and let dharma be your guiding light."

He placed a reassuring hand on Yudhishthir's shoulder. "The past is unchangeable, but the future is yours to shape. Rise above sorrow, not by forgetting, but by honouring those who fell through your deeds. Make this kingdom a place where no mother fears losing her child, where no brother raises arms against his kin, where peace is not a fleeting dream but a lasting truth."

Yudhishthir sat upon the throne—not as a conqueror, not as a victor, but as a king reborn. The ghosts of war would always whisper, but they would no longer chain him. His reign would not be defined by the battles fought but by the peace he would bring. His people needed more than a ruler—they needed a healer, a guardian of dharma, and a leader who understood the weight of sacrifice.

As he sat, the echoes of the past softened, replaced by the distant laughter of children, the rustling of the wind through the trees, and the quiet hope of a kingdom waiting to heal. And in that moment, Yudhishthir finally understood—true victory was not in conquest, but in the courage to rebuild from the ashes.

Meera: An Eternal Love, Bound Beyond Time

Born as Jashoda, later known as Meera Bai, Meera had been raised in the royal family of Mewar, the daughter of Ratan Singh and Veer Kumari, a princess surrounded by the grandeur of palaces, silk-draped halls, and the unyielding traditions of Rajput honor. It was her deep, unshakable love for Krishna that transformed her identity, and people began calling her Meera, a name that resonated with her devotion rather than her royal lineage. Over time, her unwavering devotion to Krishna became her very identity, and people began calling her Meera, a name that resonated with her deep spiritual love rather than her royal lineage. From the time she could walk, she had been taught that duty to family and kingdom came above all else. But from the moment she had first heard the tales of Krishna, something within her had stirred—an unshakable love that only grew stronger with time.

Her love for Krishna had begun in childhood, sparked by an unexpected moment of destiny. One day, a wandering Brahmin had arrived at the palace, seeking shelter. Meera's grandmother, a devout woman, welcomed him with reverence. As he rested, he placed a small, beautifully carved idol of Krishna on the floor beside him. Young Meera, curious and drawn by an unseen force, approached the idol. The moment her eyes met His, something within her shifted. She felt as if she had known Him forever.

The next morning, as the Brahmin prepared to leave, Meera clung to his robes, her eyes filled with desperate longing. "Please, let me keep Him!" she pleaded, pointing to the idol. Her grandmother frowned, attempting to pull her away. "Meera, you cannot demand such things from holy men! Let the Brahmin take his Krishna with him."

But Meera would not let go. Tears welled in her eyes as she insisted, "He belongs with me! Please, I cannot be without Him!" Seeing the depth of her devotion, the Brahmin knelt before her and placed the idol gently in her small hands. "Then never leave Him behind, child," he said with a knowing smile. "Wherever you go, take Him with you—in your heart, in your soul. Never let this love fade."

That night, unable to sleep, she tiptoed to where the idol had been placed, her tiny fingers trembling as she traced Krishna's serene face. A deep, inexplicable love bloomed in her heart, as though she had found the one she had always been searching for. From that day on, Krishna became her closest companion. She danced before His idol, whispering secrets into His ears as if He were her dearest friend. She would wake before dawn to offer flowers at His feet, her heart filled with an unbreakable longing. Even when she was married into another kingdom, expected to serve as a dutiful wife and queen, Krishna's name remained on her lips, His presence her only solace in the lonely corridors of the palace.

Meera was married at a young age to Bhoj Raj Singh Sisodia, the crown prince of Mewar, as was customary for Rajput princesses of her time. She was expected to uphold the honor of her new family, the Sisodias of Mewar, and embrace her role as a dutiful wife and future queen. At first, her husband, whom she addressed as Rana, tolerated her devotion to Krishna, dismissing it as the harmless fantasies of a young girl. He even admired her unwavering faith, believing it to be a passing phase. However, as time passed, whispers turned into taunts, and admiration transformed into frustration. His family members ridiculed him, questioning his authority and mocking him for having a wife who sang to an unseen god rather than fulfilling her expected duties as a queen.

The court murmured behind his back, and the weight of his lineage pressed heavily upon him. Rana Sangha, his father and the mighty King of Mewar, had built an empire on valor and sacrifice, and Bhoj Raj found himself struggling between upholding that legacy and defending a wife whose love for Krishna defied all social norms. At first, he tried to reason with her, gently asking her to limit her devotion to private moments, away from the eyes of the court.

"Meera," he said one evening, his voice filled with both affection and frustration. "I understand your love for Krishna, but must it be so public? The court whispers, the nobles mock... You put me in a difficult position."

Meera looked at him, her eyes filled with a divine glow. "Rana, how can I hide the very essence of my soul? Krishna is not just my God—He is my breath, my being. How can you ask me to live without breath?"

She stepped closer, her voice soft yet unwavering. "You are my Swami, Rana, and I am your wife. I have and will never betray your trust, Rana. But if you think that my devotion to Krishna is being unfaithful to you, then you are wrong. I cannot compare both of you. You are my husband, my honor, my pride. My Krishna is my soul, the reason for my being, the purpose of my life. Now you tell me, how can anyone live without a soul?"

Slowly and gradually, Bhoj's frustration increased and amounted to a level of non-tolerance. He clenched his fists, frustration simmering beneath his noble demeanour. What he had once accepted now became a source of deep embarrassment. The man who had once watched her devotion with indulgence now viewed it as defiance, an act of rebellion that no king or family could comprehend. His patience wore thin, and his tolerance turned to resentment, as he struggled between his duty as a prince and the growing storm of disapproval that surrounded them both.

But deep down, Bhoj Raj truly loved Meera. He was sympathetic towards her and never wanted her to suffer the relentless judgment of his family and the world. His heart ached every time he saw her standing alone, ostracized by the very people she once called her own. He struggled between his love for her and the burden of his duty, between protecting her and upholding the expectations of his lineage.

"Why must you test my patience, Meera?" he muttered one evening, his voice thick with unspoken turmoil. He paced the chamber, torn between love and duty, between his heart and the weight of his lineage. "You have turned our love into a battlefield where I stand alone, fighting against a force I cannot see nor defeat. Tell me, how can I compete with a god?"

He clenched his fists, looking away as pain flickered in his eyes. "I have fought wars, Meera, but this... this is a battle I cannot win. Do you not see what you are doing to me? To us? The court laughs at me, my own blood mocks me, and yet, you stand unshaken—unmoved by the storm you have brought upon this palace. Tell me, do I mean so little to you?"

His voice faltered, and for a moment, vulnerability broke through his anger. "I love you, Meera. But I cannot bear this torment any longer."

Her words both pained and infuriated him. He turned away, fists clenched, as the weight of his family's taunts and the court's ridicule crushed him.

Rana always loved Meera with the bottom of his heart, but he could not bear the insult and laughter he had to face for Meera and for himself. The whispers in the court turned into sharp-edged taunts, and the judgmental eyes of his family weighed down on him. Every step he took, every decision he made, was overshadowed by the scorn of those around him. He fought within himself, torn between his devotion to Meera and his duty to his people. The conflict burned him from within until he could take it no longer. He finally decided to take a step—a step that would free them both from this torment, a step that pained him more than any battle he had ever fought.

One night, with a heavy heart, he prepared a bowl of milk, its surface calm, hiding the deadly poison mixed within. His hands trembled as he offered it to her, his voice hollow. "Meera, this is Krishna's prasad. Drink it."

Meera, trusting her Rana, took the bowl with devotion. Without hesitation, she drank the entire offering, her lips parting into a serene smile. Bhoj Raj held his breath, waiting for the poison to take effect. But nothing happened. Meera looked up at him, her eyes filled with unwavering faith. "Rana, if you wanted me to drink poison, you should have simply said so.

But when you say this is a prasad for my Krishna, do you think my Krishna would let me die? My Krishna will never let me die in His name."

Bhoj Raj's face turned pale. The weight of his actions crushed him as he realized that he could never sever Meera's bond with Krishna. Overcome with shame and helplessness, he left her, unable to face her divine love anymore. The palace doors closed behind her, and Meera found herself alone in the vast world. But she did not waver.

Meera reached her father's home, hoping for solace, but instead, she was met with cold eyes and harsh words. Her father, Ratan Singh, stood with his arms crossed, his face dark with anger. "You have disgraced our name, Meera!" he thundered. "Do you realize what shame you have brought upon this family? Do you know what people say about us? That we raised a woman who abandoned her husband, who sings and dances in devotion like a common fakir!"

Her brother stepped forward, his voice laced with contempt. "Sister, have you no sense of dignity? You were born into a royal family, yet you roam like a beggar in the streets, lost in your madness for Krishna. How can you not see what you have done? You have turned your back on us, and for what? An idol? A dream?"

Meera's eyes filled with tears, but she held her ground. "Father, Brother, I have not abandoned my family. I have simply followed my heart. My Krishna is my world, my universe. How can I turn away from Him?"

Ratan Singh's face hardened. "Then you are no daughter of mine! Leave, Meera. We disown you. You are dead to us."

The words cut through her like a blade, but Meera did not protest. With one last look at the home she had once known, she turned away. She had lost everything, but she still had Krishna.

As she walked away, the weight of rejection, of love unreturned, of a world that could not understand her, fell from her shoulders like an old, tattered garment. She did not turn back. The palace, the family, the name—everything she had once been—had dissolved into the past. And in that moment, of stillness between despair and surrender, she was reborn.

The Meera they had known was gone. What remained was pure devotion, unshaken, untamed. The road ahead was unknown, but she walked with the certainty that Krishna was beside her, within her, carrying her forward. The world had cast her away, but she had embraced something far greater.

The burden of expectations had perished, and in its place, a soul free of fear emerged, clothed in nothing but faith.

She was no longer just Meera. She was reborn. She was Krishna's Meera—eternal, untouched by time, untethered by the world. And as she stepped into the vast unknown, a smile touched her lips, for she knew: she had finally come home.

Beethoven: The Music Beyond Sound

It was Vienna, 1824. The grand chandeliers of the Theater am Kärntnertor cast a golden glow over the audience—nobles, scholars, musicians, and critics. The hall was packed beyond capacity. The people of Vienna knew this was no ordinary concert. That night, they would witness something impossible.

At the center of it all stood a lone figure, commanding the space with an air of defiant intensity. His wild gray hair flared like a tempest, his coat hung loosely over his gaunt frame, the fabric worn from years of toil. His face—etched with deep lines, a map of battles fought not with swords but with silence—told the story of his suffering. And yet, there was something unbreakable in his eyes, something that burned like an eternal flame.

Ludwig van Beethoven. The world's greatest composer. A man who had challenged fate itself and refused to bow.

And he was completely deaf.

Not partially. Not momentarily. Not a fleeting affliction that time might heal. He was lost in a world of silence, cut off from the very thing that had once defined him. The rustling of the audience's clothes, the murmurs of anticipation, the subtle coughs, the scraping of chairs—he heard none of it. Even the music that was about to erupt under his command would be nothing but a ghost in his mind, a memory of a sound he would never truly experience again.

And yet, he stood. Ready. Unshaken. Defiant.

For the past six years, he had been trapped in an abyss of silence—not the distant chatter of the streets, not the murmured comforts of friends, not even the music that had once coursed through his veins like lifeblood. The world had faded into quiet oblivion, yet there he was, on the precipice of history, about to conduct the premiere of his greatest masterpiece—Symphony No. 9.

A symphony he had never heard. A creation born of defiance, of agony, of an indomitable spirit that refused to die.

The air was electric, the weight of expectation thick, and still, he remained—a titan unshaken, daring fate to do its worst.

The audience watched in reverence. Some with admiration. Others with doubt. Murmurs rippled through the hall like a restless tide.

"How will he do it?" someone whispered.

"He cannot even hear his own music," another muttered, shaking his head.

A noblewoman clutched her fan, eyes wide with curiosity. "A deaf composer conducting his own symphony… It's madness. Or genius."

A skeptic in the back scoffed. "This is a disaster waiting to happen."

Another voice, sharper, laced with disdain. "This is nothing but a bluff! He just wants our sympathy. How can he compose what he cannot hear?"

A man in the corner sneered. "They say he feels the vibrations. Hah! More likely, his assistants wrote half of it, and he's here to take the glory."

But then, silence. The hush before a storm. All eyes fixed on the lone figure at the podium. Whatever their doubts, they could not look away. The moment had arrived.

Beethoven could not hear the whispers, but he could feel them—like a storm gathering on the horizon. The weight of doubt, the electric crackle of curiosity, the silent accusations woven into every glance. He knew what they said. That he was a fraud. That this was a spectacle. That a deaf man could not command an orchestra. But they did not know him. They did not know the fire that burned within him, the symphony that lived in his very bones.

Let them doubt. Let them whisper. Soon, the music would answer for him.

The Making of a Titan

To understand that moment, one had to go back.

Germany, 1770. Ludwig van Beethoven was born into a world of music. His father, an alcoholic court singer, dreamed of turning him into the next Mozart—the child prodigy who, only a few years earlier, had astonished Europe with his genius. Wolfgang Amadeus Mozart, the darling of Vienna, had composed music before he could even write, performed for kings and emperors, and become a legend in his own time.

Beethoven's father, desperate to mold his son into the same phenomenon, did not ask—it was demanded. From the age of four, Beethoven was forced to practice endlessly. The piano was not an instrument of joy, but of suffering. His small fingers ached, his body trembled from exhaustion. If he faltered, punishment followed swiftly—a slap, a shouted curse, the looming threat of being locked away in a room with nothing but the cold keys before him. He sobbed in the dim candlelight, his tiny hands trembling over the keyboard, the notes blurring through his tears.

There was no warmth in his childhood, no gentle encouragement—only the relentless expectation that he must be great, that he must surpass Mozart. But perfection came at a price, and Beethoven paid it in suffering.

By his twenties, he was in Vienna, a force of nature that no one could ignore. He did not just play the piano—he attacked it, his fingers crashing against the keys like thunder, his body swaying as if possessed by the music itself. Audiences were left breathless, awed by the raw intensity of his performances. He did not merely compose; he conjured storms, weaving melodies that shook the soul. Vienna had never seen a musician like him. And it never would again.

But then, fate struck its cruelest blow.

In his late twenties, Beethoven noticed something strange. The music he once commanded with godlike precision was slipping away. The high notes of the violin seemed distant, the resonance of the piano felt muted. Conversations became a blur, muffled like voices speaking through water.

Terror gripped him. He sat at his piano, pressing the keys harder and harder, desperate to make the notes ring clear. But the sound grew fainter. A horrifying realization crept in—he was losing his hearing.

By his thirties, the deafness worsened. He tried everything—consulted doctors who shook their heads in helplessness, soaked his head in herbal concoctions that burned his skin but did nothing to restore sound, even clutched metal rods between his teeth, hoping to feel the music through vibrations alone.

Nothing worked. The silence was unrelenting, a prison tightening around him.

For a musician, to lose one's hearing was worse than death. And for Beethoven, who lived through music, it was an unimaginable curse.

But even as despair coiled around him, another voice rose—one that did not belong to fate, nor to God, but to himself.

No. He would not be defeated.

In 1802, he retreated to the countryside and wrote the Heiligenstadt Testament—a letter not just of despair, but of torment, of a man clawing at the walls of his own prison.

"I was on the verge of ending my life," he confessed. "Every day, I ask why I should go on when fate has rendered me useless in the very thing I was born to do."

But then, the words changed.

"My art, my purpose, holds me back. If I must suffer, then let my suffering be transformed into music. Let the world hear what I no longer can."

It was in that moment, in that letter, that Beethoven made his choice. He would not surrender. He would compose—not for fame, not for approval, but because music lived within him. Even if he never heard another note, he would create music for the world to hear.

And now, there he stood—two decades later—before an orchestra, about to conduct a symphony he had never heard.

The first note erupted like thunder.

Beethoven could not hear the violins. He could not hear the cellos. But he did not need to. The music was inside him.

The choir rose, voices thundering:

"Freude, schöner Götterfunken!" (Joy, beautiful spark of the gods!)

The final note resounded through the hall.

And in that moment, Beethoven knew.

He had won.

Not over the critics. Not over society.

Over fate itself.

Reflection: The Courage to Let Go and Begin Again

Through the ebb and flow of life, we all face moments where we must shed the past—whether it be grief, attachments, or expectations—to step into a new beginning. This chapter explores the journeys of three individuals who confronted profound loss, endured the weight of expectations, and ultimately chose transformation over stagnation.

In Yudhishthir's story, victory came at an unbearable cost. The Kurukshetra war had been fought and won, but the echoes of fallen warriors haunted him. Faced with the burden of ruling a kingdom built on sacrifice, he questioned whether he even deserved the throne. But Krishna's wisdom reminded him that true leadership is not about mourning the past—it is about serving the future. Letting go of guilt did not mean forgetting; it meant honoring those who had fallen by creating a kingdom of peace.

Meera too was asked to let go—but not of grief, rather of societal expectations. Her love for Krishna was unwavering, yet the world demanded that she conform. Rejected by her family, abandoned by those who could not understand her devotion, she could have been broken. But instead, she embraced her truth. She cast aside the chains of worldly identity and walked forward, not as a princess, not as a wife, but as Krishna's Meera. In surrendering to her faith, she was not lost—she was found.

And then, there was Beethoven—a man who had lived through music, only to have it stolen from him by fate. Deafness was meant to be his undoing. The world doubted him, mocked him, even pitied him. But he refused to surrender. He let go of the musician who had relied on sound, and in his place, he became something greater—a composer who could hear with his soul. As he conducted the premiere of Symphony No. 9, the world saw not a broken man, but a defiant spirit who had conquered silence itself.

Each of these stories reveals a profound truth—letting go is not about forgetting or giving up, but about transforming. It is about shedding what no longer serves us so we may step into who we are meant to be. Yudhishthir, Meera, and Beethoven all found the courage to move beyond what they had lost, embracing the path that lay ahead. And in doing so, they did not merely survive—they became legends.

Shedding the Past: An Introspection

Life is a journey of continuous change, yet we often cling to the past—old identities, painful memories, or attachments that no longer serve us. We resist letting go, fearing the unknown, even when holding on weighs us down.

But just as the soul discards a worn-out body to embrace a new one, growth requires release. Transformation begins when we accept that not everything is meant to stay forever.

Take a moment to reflect:

- What parts of your past are you still carrying, even though they no longer define you?

- Do you struggle to let go of past failures, heartbreaks, or regrets? Why?

- Are you afraid of moving forward because you are too familiar with what you must leave behind?

- When change comes, do you resist it, or do you trust that something greater lies ahead?

- Are you holding onto relationships, ambitions, or beliefs that once served you but now limit your growth?

- If you could free yourself from one burden of the past today, what would it be?

Letting go is not about forgetting—it is about freeing yourself to step into something new. It is about understanding that every ending carries within it the seed of a new beginning.

So, what are you ready to release in order to become who you are meant to be?

The Mind's Dilemma: Friend or Foe?

Bhagavad Gita, Chapter 6, Verse 5 (6.5)

उद्धरेदात्मनाऽऽत्मानं नात्मानमवसादयेत्।
आत्मैव ह्यात्मनो बन्धुरात्मैव रिपुरात्मनः॥

(Lift yourself with your own mind; do not degrade yourself.
The mind can be your best friend or worst enemy.)

Taming the Inner Storm

Our mind is both the architect of our success and the root of our struggles. It has the power to uplift us to greatness or pull us into despair. In every moment, in every thought, the mind is shaping our reality—either as a friend that empowers us or an enemy that sabotages us. But which role it plays is not determined by fate; it is determined by us.

When we master our mind, we gain clarity, resilience, and a sense of direction that propels us forward. A disciplined mind becomes our greatest ally, helping us overcome challenges, silence self-doubt, and harness our full potential. But when the mind is left unchecked, when it is consumed by negativity, fear, or distractions, it becomes our worst adversary—keeping us trapped in cycles of self-sabotage, insecurity, and hesitation.

This chapter explores the power of the mind through real-life stories of individuals who faced internal battles—some who conquered their minds to achieve greatness, and others who succumbed to their own thoughts and emotions, leading to their downfall. It delves into the ways in which our thoughts shape our decisions, our emotions influence our actions, and our mindset determines our destiny.

The mind, when disciplined, becomes a source of wisdom, confidence, and inner strength. But if left untamed, it can become a prison of anxiety, fear, and stagnation. The choice is ours.

This chapter is not just about understanding the mind—it is about learning how to master it, so that we can rise above limitations and create a life of clarity, purpose, and fulfilment.

J. Robert Oppenheimer: The Cost of Creation

July 16, 1945 – The New Mexico Desert, Trinity Test Site

The night had been swallowed by artificial daylight, an unholy dawn tearing through the heavens like a celestial wound. A massive fireball, hotter than the sun, roared into the sky, its core a seething, pulsating heart of destruction, an eye of judgment gazing upon the earth. The mountains trembled, as if recoiling from a force not meant for mortals, their ancient silence shattered by an apocalyptic hymn. A shockwave ripped through the air, an invisible hand flattening everything in its path, bending steel as though it were mere straw, igniting the dry desert brush into ghostly flames that danced like lost souls. The desert sand melted into glass, an obsidian mirror reflecting the face of a new god—one born not of divinity, but of mankind's own reckless ambition. The first atomic bomb had just been born, and with it, a terrible prophecy fulfilled. The world would never be the same again.

J. Robert Oppenheimer stood at the edge of history, his breath shallow, his hands clenched into fists. Around him, the other scientists erupted in an almost delirious joy, their exultant voices filling the air like the rising crescendo of a triumphant symphony. Some threw their arms around each other, laughing, crying, shaking with the sheer weight of what they had accomplished. A few dropped to their knees, overcome with awe, staring at the mushroom cloud as if it were a divine revelation.

"We did it!" one scientist shouted, his voice cracking with emotion. "My God, we actually did it!"

Another grabbed Oppenheimer by the shoulders, his eyes gleaming with triumph. "Robert, can you believe it? We split the heavens! We have rewritten history!"

Ernest Lawrence, grinning like a madman, clapped him on the back. "This will end the war, Robert! We are heroes!"

"Heroes..." Oppenheimer murmured, his voice barely above a whisper. The word felt foreign on his tongue.

Fermi turned to him, eyes filled with both pride and calculation. "This is what we worked for, Robert. Science has triumphed."

"Science?" Oppenheimer's gaze was still locked on the rising inferno. "Or have we unleashed something beyond our control?"

The group of scientists, drunk on victory, paid little mind to his hesitation. They laughed, exchanged handshakes, and embraced each other like soldiers after a long and bloody battle.

"Let's drink to this!" one of them cheered, wiping the sweat and dust from his brow. "We deserve it!"

Oppenheimer forced a smile as someone handed him a flask. The cheers swelled around him, hands reached for him, pats on the back, jubilant cries.

Yet, in the center of it all, he felt utterly alone.

A few days earlier—The Conversation with General Groves

The dimly lit office smelled of stale coffee and old paper, the air thick with tension. General Leslie Groves sat across from Oppenheimer, his gaze unyielding.

"Robert," Groves said, voice firm, "this war is unlike any other. If we don't end it, millions more will die. The Germans, the Japanese—they're relentless. If they develop this weapon first, do you understand what that would mean?"

Oppenheimer rubbed his temple, his mind already exhausted from sleepless nights. "And if we use it first? What will that make us?"

"It will make us the victors," Groves shot back. "The world isn't ruled by ideals, Robert. It's ruled by power. The sooner we accept that, the sooner we can bring this war to an end."

Oppenheimer leaned forward, his voice low but edged with frustration. "And what if we open a door that can never be closed? What if we create something so terrible that we condemn the future to an endless cycle of destruction?"

Groves exhaled sharply. "Damn it, Robert. You're the most brilliant mind we have. You know as well as I do that this is inevitable. Someone will do it—if not us, then the Soviets, the Germans. The world is moving forward, and we have to decide whether we lead or follow."

Oppenheimer shook his head. "But at what cost? My entire life has been devoted to understanding the universe, to unraveling its mysteries. And now, I am being asked to forge its greatest weapon?"

Groves leaned in, his eyes steely. "This isn't just about science, Robert. It's about survival. Do you want to see another Normandy? Another Pearl Harbor? This bomb will end that. No more young men dying in trenches. No more cities burned to the ground. One strike, one decisive act, and we can force them to surrender. We can end this war."

Oppenheimer looked away, his jaw clenched, his breath shallow with frustration. "And if we do this, if we succeed... what happens next? Do we become the gods of war? The architects of annihilation? Do we crown ourselves as masters of destruction?"

His voice wavered, a mix of anger and sorrow. "We tell ourselves it's for peace, but what if this is just the beginning of something far worse? Are we so arrogant to believe we can control what we've set loose? That we can contain the fire we've ignited?"

Groves didn't hesitate. He leaned forward, his voice low and persuasive. "We become the ones who saved millions of lives, Robert. You—you—will be the man who changed history. This is the moment, the moment where science and power intersect, where a mind like yours isn't just theorizing about the universe—it's shaping it."

He let the words settle before continuing, his tone almost reverent. "Think of all the soldiers who will get to go home because of what you build. Think of the wars that won't happen because the world will know—America holds the key to ultimate power. Would you rather stand aside and let someone else wield it first? Or will you be the one history remembers as the man who ended war as we know it?"

Oppenheimer exhaled, closing his eyes for a brief moment. "And what if I'm building the end of the world? What if this isn't a victory, but a curse we've unleashed? The burden of knowledge, the burden of creation—have I used my mind as my friend, or has it betrayed me?"

He let out a bitter laugh, shaking his head. "I spent my life chasing understanding, unweaving the universe's mysteries, and now—now I have rewritten the rules of destruction instead. Tell me, General, do you still sleep soundly at night? Because I can already feel the ghosts forming. I can already hear the echoes of what we have done."

Groves stood, his expression unyielding. "Then let's pray that when that day comes, we're the ones holding the reins.

Back at the test site, the sky still burned. Oppenheimer's fingers trembled as he clasped them together. His breathing was ragged, his heart pounding against his ribs. Sweat clung to his skin, cold despite the desert heat.

"I was meant to lift humanity, to understand the universe, not to unleash this... this nightmare. Have I become a creator or a destroyer?"

The words of the Bhagavad Gita pulsed in his mind, heavier now than ever before. 'Now I am become Death, the destroyer of worlds.' He had recited them before, but now they felt as though they had been written for him alone.

"Three years... three relentless years. Equations on chalkboards, frantic calculations, sleepless nights. We split the atom, pried open the secrets of the universe. But at what cost?"

His hands shook violently, as though his very body recoiled from the knowledge of what he had done. Had his mind been his greatest ally, guiding him toward enlightenment, or had it deceived him, leading him down the path of ruin? He wiped his brow, but his fingers came away damp, trembling, unmoored. Had he wielded his intellect for creation or devastation? Was this brilliance or blasphemy? His breath hitched in his throat, a shallow gasp escaping as the weight of his actions crashed over him.

I have spent years unravelling the universe's deepest mysteries, only to weave them into a tapestry of destruction. My mind—the very thing that was to illuminate humanity's path—has cast a shadow that may never be lifted.

What have I done? The words barely formed in his mind, lost amidst the deafening roar of celebration around him. His stomach twisted. He felt the ground beneath him sway—not from the blast, but from the unbearable gravity of realization. The distant cheers, the triumphant laughter, all sounded warped, distorted, as if carried by the wind from some other world, some other reality where he had not crossed this line.

Was this the moment I became my own enemy? Have I wielded my mind as a force of progress, or have I twisted its power into something monstrous? I devoted my life to the pursuit of truth, yet here I stand, drowning in the consequences of my own brilliance. Did I truly seek enlightenment, or have I simply built a machine of annihilation? Has my intellect served me, or have I become enslaved by it?

The laughter and cheers around him felt distant, muffled, as if he were submerged in water. Scientists embraced, toasting their triumph, their faces alive with exhilaration. But Oppenheimer stood frozen, watching the mushroom cloud rise like an omen, its towering form stretching beyond the heavens.

"The celebration hall was filled with an intoxicating energy—glasses clinking, laughter ringing out, voices merging into an unrelenting chorus of victory. Scientists, generals, officials—they all stood together, basking in their triumph. A hush fell over the room as Oppenheimer was called to the front. A speech, they demanded. A few words on the miracle they had just achieved.

He stepped forward, the spotlight unnervingly bright, illuminating the storm within him. His throat was dry, his hands cold despite the oppressive heat in the room. He cleared his throat, gripping the edges of the podium, his voice steady yet laced with something unspoken.

"We have done something today that no mankind has ever imagined possible. We have cracked open the very fabric of the universe and rewritten the laws of power. This—" he gestured vaguely, "—is a moment that will be remembered long after we are gone."

A roar of applause erupted, but Oppenheimer did not smile. His fingers tightened, knuckles white.

"We are scientists. We are thinkers, dreamers. And yet, we are now something else entirely. We are makers of history, but also its prisoners. For history will not judge us on what we have achieved—it will judge us on how we choose to wield it."

The cheers softened. Faces leaned in, eager, waiting. He let out a slow breath.

"The mind... is a strange thing. It is our greatest ally, our closest friend. But left unchecked, it can become our greatest foe. What we have built here is not just a machine—it is a choice. A test. And how we use it will determine what kind of men we truly are."

A deep silence settled over the room, and for a moment, Oppenheimer wondered if he had said too much. He forced a small smile, nodding slightly before stepping away from the podium.

The applause resumed, hesitant at first, then louder, but he barely heard it. He had spoken, but not completely. He had warned them, but not fully. He had planted a seed, but whether it would grow into wisdom or blind ambition—only time would tell.

The world had changed forever, and he was its architect. But as he stood amidst the echoes of triumph and the weight of his own mind, he questioned whether he had built a monument to progress or carved the first tombstone of humanity's undoing.

But he was no longer sure if he had built a new future or set the world on an irreversible path toward oblivion. Had he truly forged a path to peace, or had he merely unlocked a door to endless destruction? The weight of that question pressed upon him, heavier than the force of the explosion itself.

The Unkillable Monk and the Fate of Russia

The cold air of Petrograd seeped through the cracks of the Moika Palace, a grand estate belonging to Prince Felix Yusupov, heir to one of the wealthiest families in Russia. A descendant of noble lineage, Yusupov had lived a life of indulgence, but now, his opulent home had become the setting for a murder that would echo through history. Gilded chandeliers cast trembling shadows across the silk-draped walls, their golden glow failing to soften the tension thickening in the air. The scent of candle wax and aged wood mingled with something more insidious—fear, betrayal, the final death rattle of an empire on the brink of collapse.

At the center of it all sat Grigori Rasputin, his piercing eyes scanning the room, his lips curling into an amused smirk. He lifted his goblet, swirling the wine before taking a slow sip. "You think you hold power over life and death?" he mused, his voice thick with amusement. "Fools. Death has tried to take me before and failed. Why should tonight be any different?"

Prince Felix Yusupov tensed, watching the man before him with a mix of revulsion and unease. "You have poisoned this empire long enough," he said, his voice steady but laced with anger. "You have controlled the Tsarina, whispered in the ears of rulers, and dragged Russia into ruin. It ends tonight."

Rasputin chuckled, the sound low and guttural. "You think you understand fate, young prince? I have seen things you would not dare dream of. The empire is already doomed—not by me, but by the blindness of its rulers. You can kill me, but it will not save them. The Romanovs are marked. Russia will drown in its own blood."

The room fell into a heavy silence, the weight of his words pressing down on those gathered. The air thickened with something beyond fear—an eerie sense of inevitability.

Outside the palace, Russia itself teetered on the edge of revolution. The rule of Tsar Nicholas II had grown fragile, weighed down by the catastrophic failures of World War I, economic collapse, and the growing unrest of the people who had lost faith in their ruler. Once believed to be divinely appointed, Nicholas struggled to maintain control over his crumbling empire. His reclusive nature, his resistance to reform, and his unwavering belief in autocracy only alienated him further from the suffering masses.

Inside the palace, a more intimate battle raged. "You do not understand what you have done, Alexandra!" Nicholas slammed his fist onto the polished table, his voice trembling with frustration. "Our people despise us. They whisper that I am weak, that I have surrendered my empire to a charlatan. All because of him! Do you know what they are saying about you? Have you seen the vulgar posters—filthy caricatures of you and Rasputin? I cannot even bear to describe them. And you... you cannot deny how it looks!"

His piercing blue eyes burned with desperation and pain as he looked at his wife. "I love you, Alexandra. But I cannot keep fighting my own people! I am the Tsar, yet I am becoming a prisoner in my own empire!"

Tsarina Alexandra's face, pale and worn with sleepless nights, hardened with defiance. She did not deny Nicholas' words, nor did she flinch at the accusations. Instead, she leaned forward, her hands trembling as she clutched the arms of her chair.

"And what of Alexei?" she shot back, her voice laced with anguish. "He is the heir to the throne, the future of Russia! What if something happens to him? What will happen to Russia then? Without him, the dynasty crumbles!" Her breath was ragged, her eyes wild, as if she were caught in some trance. "Rasputin is the only one who can save him, Nicholas. He is a God-send—not just for our son, but for me and for Russia itself!"

Nicholas ran a hand through his thinning hair, exhaling sharply. His voice rose, thick with frustration. "At what cost, Alexandra? Just last week, a mob outside the Winter Palace burned effigies of us—of you and him! The ministers say he meddles in affairs he does not understand. The generals loathe him, the people see his debauchery, his drinking, his obscene influence over you! They blame him for our failures—and they blame you!"

His fists clenched as his breath hitched. "Do you think I do not see what they see? Do you think I do not hear the whispers? They call me a puppet, Alexandra! My own soldiers hesitate before obeying my commands. They call you..." His voice faltered, pain flashing across his face. "They call you his whore. And I cannot even fight back, because I cannot deny how it looks!"

Alexandra's eyes glistened with unshed tears, but her resolve did not waver. "Let them say what they will, Nicholas. Let them whisper, let them curse my name—I do not care! As long as Alexei breathes, I will do anything and everything, with anyone, for any reason—do you hear me? If it takes my soul, if it takes my dignity, if it takes my very life—I will not abandon the man who has saved him. Rasputin is our only hope. Without him, our son is lost. And if Alexei dies... Russia dies with him."

A heavy silence stretched between them, the weight of an empire pressing down on their shoulders. Nicholas turned away, staring out the frost-covered window at the restless city beyond. "God help us, Alexandra," he whispered. "Because soon, not even Rasputin will be able to."

His wife, Tsarina Alexandra, had become even more reviled. A German-born empress in the midst of a war against Germany, she was accused of undue influence over the tsar and the empire. But in truth, her deepest concern lay within the walls of the palace—her desperate prayers for the survival of her son, Tsarevich Alexei. The long-awaited heir to the Romanov dynasty had been born with hemophilia, the "royal disease" that plagued European monarchies. His frequent bouts of illness left Alexandra in constant despair, her faith shaken, her nights sleepless.

Then came Rasputin—a wandering holy man from Siberia, a self-proclaimed mystic with piercing eyes and an uncanny ability to soothe Alexei's suffering. Born into a peasant family in the remote village of Pokrovskoye, he spent his early years as a drifter, gaining a reputation as a healer and spiritual guide. Some saw him as a prophet; others whispered of dark powers and debauchery.

His arrival at the Russian court was almost accidental—a series of chance encounters with influential aristocrats led him to the Tsarina's ear. To her, he was nothing short of a miracle, a man sent by God to protect her son and, by extension, the dynasty. His apparent ability to ease Alexei's pain, whether through prayer, hypnosis, or sheer force of will, convinced her of his divine nature. She clung to his every word, trusting his visions over the advice of noblemen, priests, and even her own husband.

But who was Rasputin, truly? A holy man or a cunning manipulator? His rise to power had been swift, and with it came rumors—of drunken orgies, of political meddling, of a man who wielded influence over the empire itself. To the devout, he was a saint. To the aristocracy, he was a dangerous fraud. And yet, no one could deny his hold over Alexandra, nor his uncanny ability to survive every attempt to remove him.

Rasputin's influence over the Tsarina grew stronger with each passing year, and with it, his hold over the empire.

To the Russian aristocracy, Rasputin was not a savior but a symptom of decay—a charlatan whose unchecked power threatened the stability of the throne. They blamed him for the empire's misfortunes, whispering of his debauchery, his excesses, and his manipulation of the royal family. He had to be eliminated.

Grigori Rasputin sat at the heavy oak table, his wild eyes flickering with amusement as he surveyed his surroundings. This palace, a monument to aristocratic excess, now served as the stage for his reckoning. He swirled the wine in his goblet, its ruby surface reflecting the flickering candlelight. His lips curved into a knowing smirk—there was no place more fitting for the supposed end of the Mad Monk, the man who had slithered from the Siberian wilderness into the very heart of Russia's imperial court.

"I am no mere man; I am chosen," Rasputin thought, a slow smile creeping across his lips. "A divine vessel. God Himself has sent me to Russia, not just to guide the Tsarina, not just to heal the boy, but to shape history itself." He let his fingers trail along the rim of his goblet, savoring the weight of his own power. "The nobles—blind, feeble, envious—call me a peasant, a fraud, a corrupter. But what do they know of true power? True power is not gold, nor a throne; it is the mind—the ability to bend others, to make them see what I wish them to see, to believe what I wish them to believe.

I do not merely influence fate; I am fate." He chuckled under his breath, eyes flickering with a dangerous light. "They fear me because they do not understand me. They despise me because they cannot control me. I am Rasputin—the holy man, the prophet, the savior. The mind is the greatest gift, and I use mine better than any emperor, any general, any priest. They whisper that I am a demon, that I am drowning Russia in sin. But I ask you, my God—if I wield such power, is it not because You willed it? Have You not chosen me to stand above them all?" His grip on the goblet tightened as a shadow of doubt flickered in his mind. But am I truly righteous? He scoffed at the thought, shaking his head. "It does not matter. Righteousness is for the weak. I am beyond their judgment. I am Russia's fate, and whether I stand in light or darkness, the empire will not exist without me."

And yet, deep within he thought that His mind, his greatest weapon, could be a beacon of divine wisdom—or a shadowed abyss of self-deception. Had he wielded his gift for the will of God, or for his own hunger for control?

His fingers tightened around the goblet. It did not matter. He was Russia's fate, and whether he stood in light or darkness, the empire would not exist without him.

"They think they can kill me," he murmured to himself, lifting the drink to his lips. The sweet taste of Madeira filled his mouth, but something bitter lingered underneath. His throat burned, his stomach twisted. He gasped, gripping the table as his vision wavered. "Poison? Hah! Fools, they think poison can kill Rasputin?" He let out a hoarse chuckle, his breath ragged. "I have danced with death before and walked away. Do they not know? I am beyond their reach… beyond mortal suffering."

His fingers trembled as he clutched his chest. A strange numbness spread through his limbs, but he forced himself to stand, his wild eyes locking onto his murderers. "Is this all you have? Pathetic," he spat, his voice thick with defiance. "You strike at me like cowards in the shadows, but Rasputin does not die so easily!" His breath hitched, a bead of sweat rolling down his forehead. He swayed but clenched his fists. "I am Russia! I am its fate!" He staggered forward, his grin twisted with both madness and unyielding will. "And even in death, I will not leave you. I will haunt your dreams. I will crawl into your minds. You will never be free of me!"

The faces of his assassins surrounded him—Prince Felix Yusupov, Grand Duke Dmitri, others lurking in the shadows. He could see the unease in their eyes, the tremor in their hands. They feared him, as they should. He had survived too much to fall to mere mortals. The Tsarina's protector, the Romanovs' holy man—he was untouchable.

It was a clever trick, he thought. But he had foreseen this. They had fed him enough cyanide to kill ten men, yet he still sat there, still breathed, still smiled. His mind soared with certainty—I am chosen, I am beyond death.

And yet… was he?

A flicker of doubt, like a shadow in the corner of his vision. He blinked. His limbs felt heavy. His body, his temple of invincibility, betrayed him with a shudder. The world wavered, his mind oscillating between power and paranoia. Had his visions been real, or had he only convinced himself of them? Had he truly healed the Tsarevich, or had it all been luck? Had he steered the empire with divine guidance, or had he merely been a puppet dancing in the candlelight of illusion?

No. No! He would not fall. He would rise, like he always did.

With a grunt, he pushed himself up, staggering toward his assassins. Gasps filled the air. Their fear bolstered him—he was still Rasputin, still the man they could not kill.

A gunshot cracked through the night.

A sharp pain exploded in his chest. He stumbled back, hands clawing at his ribs, feeling the wet warmth seep through his tunic. The room spun, but he refused to fall. Another shot, and another. Darkness edged his vision, but his mind fought against it.

I cannot die. I am beyond them. I have seen the future. I have seen the fall of the Romanovs. My prophecy must come true.

But what if he was wrong?

As the blood pooled around him, a strange sense of detachment settled over his mind. Was he watching himself from above? He could almost hear the echoes of fate—his own voice, whispering through time.

"If I die, the empire dies with me."

A final shot. Silence.

The last thing he heard was laughter—his own, hoarse and rasping, yet triumphant. His assassins would never forget it. His mind, his greatest ally and his most fearsome enemy, had carried him to the end.

But in that last breath, in those last thirty seconds, did he truly believe in his own prophecy? Or had he simply been swallowed by the delusion he had woven for himself? Had his mind, the gift he had always believed was from God, been his greatest friend—or his ultimate foe? Had he used it for righteousness, or had it led him astray into the abyss of self-deception? Even as the darkness closed in, the question clawed at him, unanswered, lingering like a specter over his fading consciousness.

History would decide.

And Rasputin, the mad monk, would live forever in its pages.

Meghnath: Bound by Duty, Torn by Truth

The battlefield of Lanka was thick with the stench of death—blood soaked the very earth, turning the once-golden sands into a macabre swamp of gore. Severed limbs lay scattered like broken branches after a storm, and the air was filled with the agonized screams of dying warriors, their bodies impaled upon jagged spears. The sky, once a vast expanse of serenity, was now a choking mass of ash and smoke, blotting out the sun. The carrion birds had begun their grim feast, pecking at the flesh of the fallen even as the battle raged on. Meghnath, the son of the mighty Ravana, stood in the midst of the chaos, his golden armor splattered with blood—some his own, much of it belonging to those who had perished by his hand. Around him, dying soldiers clutched at his feet, their fingers twitching in their final throes, their lips forming prayers that would never be answered.

Meghnath, son of the mighty Ravana and Queen Mandodari, was not just any warrior—he was Indrajit, the conqueror of Indra himself. From a young age, he had been forged in the fires of war, trained by the greatest of asuras and blessed by the gods he had defeated. His prowess was unmatched; his devotion to his father unwavering. He had once taken great pride in being the undefeated warrior, the only one who had ever vanquished Indra, earning him the name Indrajit. Gifted with powerful boons, he had mastered the art of becoming invisible in battle, wielded celestial weapons bestowed upon him by Lord Brahma, and was nearly invincible after performing the sacred yagna. And yet, as he stood atop his chariot, bow in hand, he found himself at war not just with Lord Rama's army, but with his own conscience.

His eyes, sharp as an eagle's, fell upon Rama, who stood at the heart of the battlefield—a beacon of calm in the storm of war. There was no malice in his gaze, no arrogance in his stance. Meghnath had fought countless warriors, but never one like Rama. His stillness amidst the chaos was almost unnatural, his presence exuding a quiet authority that shook Meghnath to his core. Was this truly his enemy? Was this the man he was meant to destroy? Rama's unwavering composure made Meghnath question everything. Why did he not seem threatened? Why did he not exude hatred? Meghnath's mind spun with doubt. Are we right in keeping Sita in Lanka? Is this war even just? Have I become a mere instrument of my father's pride, blind to the truth? The warrior in him urged him to strike, but something deeper held him back, forcing him to confront the unrelenting storm of his conscience.

A voice in his head whispered: Is this my war?

Meghnath had always been the perfect son, the warrior Ravana relied upon. But now, for the first time, his father's words felt like chains, binding him to a path he was no longer sure of.

Meghnath was called to the court of Ravana. He had been expecting this summons—he knew his father's stubbornness, his ruthlessness, his arrogance. Ravana would sacrifice anything for his pride—his children, his brother, even his marriage. Meghnath entered the grand hall, its pillars towering above him like silent sentinels, their shadows stretching across the cold stone floor. The air was thick with the scent of burning incense, a stark contrast to the blood-soaked battlefield he had just left behind.

"Meghnath!" Ravana's commanding voice rang in his ears, as though his father could hear the doubts creeping into his mind. "You must fight! You must not waver! Our honor, our kingdom, our legacy—everything depends on you! Do you hear me? You are Indrajit, the conqueror of Indra! The gods themselves have trembled before you. Do not disgrace the name I have given you. You were born for war, for victory! The blood of the asuras runs through your veins—show no weakness! Strike them down without hesitation, for hesitation is defeat! You will not return unless you bring me Rama's head, do you understand?"

After hearing and taking command from his father, Meghnath came in his royal suit where his wife, Savitri, was waiting for him. She could clearly see what was going on in Meghnath's mind. She stepped forward, her eyes filled with concern.

"What happened, my love? Please tell me," she pleaded, her voice barely above a whisper. "I know you do not want to fight this war. I understand that. But why must you be the one to bear the weight of your father's pride? Why must you sacrifice your soul for his vengeance?

Look into my eyes, Meghnath. I see the battle within you. I see the questions you do not speak aloud. Does honor come from blind obedience, or from choosing what is right? Is this war truly yours to fight, or are you merely a weapon forged by your father's will?

I fear for you, my love. Not for your body, but for your soul. If you go into this war with doubt in your heart, you may never return—not as the man I love. Tell me, Meghnath, is this truly the path you wish to walk?"

Meghnath turned away, his fists clenched. "I have no choice, Savitri. My father has commanded it. Our honor, our legacy—it all rests upon my shoulders."

Savitri placed a gentle hand on his arm. "Honor? Legacy? Or is it just his pride? Have you ever stopped to ask yourself if this war is just? If what we are doing is right? If keeping Sita in Lanka is right?"

Meghnath exhaled sharply, his turmoil growing. "I cannot defy my father. You know what he is. He would rather see his own blood spilled than accept defeat."

Savitri's eyes welled with tears. "But at what cost, Meghnath? At the cost of your soul? I see the war raging within you, and it terrifies me more than the war outside these walls."

Meghnath turned to Savitri, his voice trembling with an emotion he could no longer contain. "You are right, Savitri. Maybe I do not want this war. Maybe I do not want to fight. I see the truth—I know what is right and what is wrong. And I want to tell my father that..."

His breath hitched as he continued, his anguish spilling out. "How can he keep someone else's wife in Lanka? How can he justify this? How can he abandon his own marriage, let go of my mother so easily? My mother—an obedient, loving wife—has always understood him, tolerated his every action, every flaw. How can he not see the pain he has inflicted upon her? How can he be so blind? If I fight this battle, I am not just betraying my conscience—I am betraying my mother."

He turned away, his fingers pressing against his temples, as if trying to suppress the storm raging within. "She always taught me that a true warrior is not the one who wields the most powerful weapons or knows the deadliest skills. A true warrior is the one who sees the difference between right and wrong and always chooses what is right. And yet, here I am, about to let go of everything she has ever taught me."

His voice dropped to a whisper, but it carried the weight of his breaking spirit. "He is not right, Savitri. He is not fair. My father is being unreasonable, and he expects me to support him blindly. Do I really want to be remembered like this? As a warrior who stood by injustice? Is this the legacy I want to leave behind? This... this is not me, Savitri."

Savitri stepped closer, her voice steady yet brimming with emotion. "Swami, you are so learned, a master of wisdom. You have studied the Vedas, absorbed the teachings of the greatest gurus, and carry the knowledge of the gods themselves. I know I may not need to remind you of dharma, but as your wife, I must speak my heart. When I chose to marry you, it was not just your strength or valor that drew me to you—it was your unwavering sense of righteousness. You have always known what is just, and above all, you have believed in Kartavya—duty, responsibility, and doing what is right, not just for yourself but for those who depend on you.

But Swami, our minds are strange things. They offer us choices—one path of virtue and another of destruction. They can be our closest allies or our worst enemies. The choice is always ours. Now, it is your moment to choose. Will you let your mind guide you toward truth, or will you allow it to be clouded by the weight of expectation? Please, my love, listen to your heart, to the teachings that shaped you. Choose the path that is right—not just for your father, not just for your kingdom, but for your soul."

Was his mind his friend, guiding him toward righteousness? Or was it his enemy, filling him with doubt and cowardice?

In that moment, a thirty-second silence fell over him—a pause in the chaos. Time itself seemed to stretch, forcing him to confront the storm within.

If I refuse to fight, I betray my father, my lineage.

If I continue to fight, I betray my own soul.

His breath hitched. The burden of his choice weighed heavily upon him, crushing his spirit. He looked up at the heavens, as if seeking an answer. But the gods remained silent. This was his battle to fight—within himself, not just on the field.

Meghnath chose Kartavya—his duty—over his will to do what was righteous. This was the moment of his choice. He was willing to betray his mother for the sake of his father. He convinced himself that he was still standing for her, that his presence in this war was, in some way, for her as well. But deep down, he knew the truth—if he did not obey and support his father, he would fail in his karma as a Yodha—a warrior. This was the moment of his truth, and he knew that his choice would define how he was remembered forever.

His fingers trembled on the string of his bow. He looked upon the soldiers he was about to strike down. These were not his enemies. They had done him no personal wrong. And yet, here he was, commanded to kill in the name of his father's pride. The weight of his conscience pressed upon him like a suffocating shroud. Each face he saw bore the same fear, the same desperation, the same question in their eyes—why must we die for another man's arrogance? His grip tightened, but his heart wavered. The screams of the dying, the stench of burning flesh, the rivers of blood pooling beneath him—all of it blurred into one suffocating reality. He was no longer a warrior; he was an executioner, a pawn in a war that gnawed at his soul. And in that moment, for the first time, he feared not death, but what he was becoming.

A shout from his father's ranks broke his trance. The enemy was advancing. He had no more time to hesitate. Meghnath clenched his jaw, forced his hands to steady, and released the arrow. It cut through the air like a streak of lightning.

But even as it flew toward its target, Meghnath knew—no victory on this battlefield could ever quell the war within him.

Reflection: The Crossroads of Genius and Delusion

The human mind is a powerful force—it can unlock the secrets of the universe, bend reality to its will, and push the boundaries of what was once thought impossible. Yet, it is also the greatest source of destruction, capable of justifying the unthinkable and leading even the most brilliant individuals astray.

J. Robert Oppenheimer stood at the precipice of history, his intellect having forged the greatest weapon of war mankind had ever known. He had spent years unraveling the deepest mysteries of the cosmos, only to find himself shackled by the consequences of his own brilliance. Had he truly created a path to peace, or had he simply opened the door to an era of unending destruction? The weight of his actions pressed upon him, forcing him to question whether he was a creator or a destroyer, a savior or the harbinger of annihilation.

Grigori Rasputin, the self-proclaimed mystic, wielded his mind as a weapon—an instrument of influence over Russia's imperial court. To some, he was a divine healer; to others, a manipulative charlatan who steered the Romanovs toward their doom. Even as death loomed over him, he refused to believe he was merely a man. Was he truly the chosen one, or had he fallen victim to his own illusions of grandeur? The answer died with him, leaving behind a legacy that blurred the line between prophecy and paranoia.

Meghnath, the formidable warrior of Lanka, found himself standing on a battlefield not just against Rama, but against his own conscience. He had been raised to serve his father, to fight without question, to uphold the honor of the asuras. But what if honor was just another name for blind obedience? Torn between his duty and his sense of righteousness, he had to make a choice—one that would determine not only the course of the war but also how history would remember him. Did he fight for justice, or did he surrender to the expectations placed upon him?

Each of these men—Oppenheimer, Rasputin, and Meghnath—stood at a crossroads where intellect, conviction, and self-deception collided. Their minds were both their greatest allies and their most formidable enemies. In the end, the choices they made shaped not only their own fates but the destiny of entire civilizations.

Mastering the Mind: An Introspection

The human mind is a battlefield. It has the power to create, to destroy, to justify, and to deceive. It can be our greatest friend—guiding us toward truth, enlightenment, and progress—or our most formidable enemy, leading us down the path of ruin.

Consider Oppenheimer, a man who devoted his life to knowledge, only to stand at the edge of history, questioning whether his genius had birthed salvation or destruction. Rasputin, who believed so deeply in his own destiny that he refused to acknowledge the walls of delusion closing in around him. And Meghnath, torn between the duty instilled in him since birth and the uncomfortable realization that he was fighting a war that was not his own.

Each of them had immense power—of intellect, of influence, of strength. Yet, their struggles were not external battles alone. Their greatest war was within themselves. And isn't that true for all of us?

Pause for a moment and ask yourself:

- Have you ever been so convinced of your own choices that you ignored the warning signs around you?

- Have you ever justified an action, not because it was right, but because it was expected of you?

- When faced with a moment of doubt, did you listen to your inner voice, or did you silence it out of fear?

- How often do you let external forces—expectations, ambition, ego—drive your decisions, rather than your own sense of what is right?

- Have you ever achieved something you thought you wanted, only to later wonder if the cost was too high?

The mind is a powerful force, but unchecked, it can lead even the greatest among us into darkness. The true test is not just in intelligence or strength, but in the ability to pause, reflect, and choose wisely.

So the next time you stand at a crossroads, when your mind whispers conflicting truths, take a moment. **Are you in control of your mind, or has it begun to control you?**

For in the end, history remembers not just what we accomplish, but who we become in the process.